Ramón María
del Valle-Inclán:
Questions of Gender

Ramón María del Valle-Inclán: Questions of Gender

Edited by
Carol Maier and Roberta L. Salper

Lewisburg
Bucknell University Press
London and Toronto: Associated University Presses

Associated University Presses
440 Forsgate Drive
Cranbury, NJ 08512

Associated University Presses
25 Sicilian Avenue
London WC1A 2QH, England

Associated University Presses
P.O. Box 338, Port Credit
Mississauga, Ontario
Canada L5G 4L8

The paper used in this publication meets the requirements
of the American National Standard for Permanence of Paper
for Printed Library Materials Z39.48-1984.

Library of Congress Cataloging-in-Publication Data

Ramón María del Valle-Inclán : questions of gender / edited by Carol
  Maier and Roberta L. Salper.
    p.   cm.
  Includes bibliographical references.
  ISBN 0-8387-5261-6 (alk. paper)
    1. Valle-Inclán, Ramón del, 1866–1936—Criticism and
interpretation.   2. Women in literature.   3. Sex role in literature.
I. Maier, Carol, 1943– .   II. Salper, Roberta L.
PQ6641.A47Z782   1994
868'.509—dc20   93-42561
                                                            CIP

PRINTED IN THE UNITED STATES OF AMERICA

Contents

Acknowledgments

Our sincere thanks go to Kimberly Talentino and Carmen Gómez for their translation of Biruté Ciplijauskaité's essay, as well as to Kent State University's Institute for Applied Linguistics and to Point Park College for enabling us to commission their work. We also want to express our appreciation to Lisa Holstrom for her help in preparing the final manuscript, and to Penn State/Erie and the Research Council of Kent State University for their support.

Permission to reprint the following articles is also noted with appreciation:

Hispania, for Catherine Nickel's "Valle-Inclán's 'La Generala': Woman as Birdbrain."

MLN, for Noël Valis's "Novel as Feminine Entrapment: Valle-Inclán's *Sonata de otoño.*"

Editorial Orígenes (Madrid), for Biruté Ciplijauskaité's "Role of Language in the Creation of Valle-Inclán's Female Characters" ["La Función del lenguaje en la configuración del personaje femenino valleinclanesco"]

Finally, many thanks to Xosé Conde Corbal for his generosity in permitting us to use his print from the *Luces de Bohemia* series.

Ramón María
del Valle-Inclán:
Questions of Gender

Part 1
Introduction

Points of Departure

CAROL MAIER, with ROBERTA L. SALPER

As a writer who verbalized his aesthetics primarily through words spoken in the animated discussion of bars and cafés, Ramón del Valle-Inclán (1866–1936) might well be pleased by the fact that the present collection of essays originated not in a special session dedicated to his work at an academic conference but in Madrid's Café Gijón. There, in the summer of 1989 I met Roberta Salper, and we soon found ourselves talking about the Valle-Inclán criticism that has appeared during the last twenty-five years. Those years have born witness to a rich proliferation of critiques since an outpouring of centennial studies initiated the reevaluation of a writer the eminent Spanish novelist Gonzalo Torrente Ballester has declared "el máximo escritor español de nuestro siglo" ["the greatest Spanish writer of our century"].[1] Much of the critical emphasis since the 1970s has focused on Valle-Inclán's historical commitment and on his relentless exposure of a decadent, corrupt Spanish national reality.[2] Although biographical and archival information is still relatively sketchy, important documents and bibliographical information have been recently published.[3] Moreover, Valle-Inclán's aesthetic thought, especially *La lámpara maravillosa* [*The Lamp of Marvels*], has begun to receive serious attention,[4] and new anthologies[5] and monographs[6] testify to continued critical enthusiasm for his literary production. With a few exceptions,[7] however, the application of feminist theory and scholarship to Valle-Inclán's texts are virtually absent from the numerous books and articles prompted by the fiftieth anniversary of his death. This dearth is magnified if one situates Valle-Inclán with respect to turn-of-the-century Spain and searches for interpretations of his generation that take gender relations into account,[8] since feminist analysis has also been largely ignored even in recent criticism about Modernist Spain.[9]

In the last twenty-five years, however, as Valle-Inclán's critics pursued other areas of investigation, an understanding of the complexities of gender as a cultural phenomenon has emerged from scholarly work carried out in many different fields. It is now generally recognized (in the same way that Hispanists have begun to recognize as a historical construction the Generation of '98 in which Valle-Incláns's membership has long been hotly debated),[10] that gender boundaries, like those of class, are drawn to serve a variety of political, economic, and social functions. In other words, mediated by the layered interactions of a broad range of economic, political, and religious institutions, the production of gender stereotypes creates gender boundaries that not only operate in the material base of a culture, but also in the imagined world of the writer of fiction. Thus, although the norms of gender are more often communicated implicitly than stated explicitly, literary texts reveal the specific categories assigned to women and men in a myriad of ways: through gender-specific language, archetypal narrative forms that assume a male protagonist, and so on. They also reveal the extent to which categories of gender vary over time, and how socially condoned behavior is culturally and historically specific and widely disparate. In this way, for example, a study of Valle-Inclán's *Femeninas* [Feminine portraits] (1895) can indicate the contingent or arbitrary nature of masculine and feminine roles at turn-of-the-century Spain.

To approach Valle-Inclán from this perspective of gender is to read in a focused way but not necessarily a reductive one. Rather, to read Valle-Inclán with an eye to gender, is to explore a highly contradictory impulse, present throughout his work, to strive for totality and, simultaneously, to question any and all experiences and phenomena that might be "totalizing." This impulse, evident as early as the incidents in "Babel" (1888) or "Psiquismo" ["Psychism"] (1892), for example (and as late as *El ruedo ibérico* [The Iberian ring], which was left unfinished at the time of his death), is also manifest to a surprising degree in complex conflicts concomitant with the markedly binary nature of gender definitions. Although Valle-Inclán certainly did not speak of either those conflicts or those definitions in terms of what would currently be referred to as "gender," he did identify repeatedly both a constant tension between the sexes, and also a continual abrasion between biologically determined roles and roles assigned by gender conventions. Thus, to cite an example from the most theoretical of Valle-Inclán's works, at the "heart" of *La lámpara maravillosa,* in the central chapter of this collection of "spiritual exercises" that he designated the first volume of his *Opera omnia* [Complete works], is found "la interpretación hermética" ["the hermetic interpretation"] of the world that keeps it spinning: "la lucha entre el hombre y la mujer" ["the struggle between man and woman"], in which "la mujer debe resistir al hombre y el hombre debe fascinarla, para someterla" ["woman must resist man and man must captivate her so as to subdue her"].[11]

With respect to gender issues, however, what is no doubt most pertinent is not Valle-Inclán's evocation of an age-old principle of *acción* ["action"] and *negación* ["negation"] dramatized as a battle between the sexes. What is most intriguing is the creation of a poet "Redeemer" who not only offers "salvation" by assuming the multiple dichotomies enumerated in *La lámpara maravillosa*, but also realizes that "assumption" by turning himself into an explicitly androgynous figure. In this capacity, as *cifra* ["cipher" or "symbol"], the poet who narrates *La lámpara maravillosa* makes it clear that his will to encompass the feminine as well as the maculine aspects of verbal creation exceeds a "mere" play on words and a reference to the Alchemical Christ.[12] He explicitly considers himself the mother as well as the father of his creations, and he has felt "el estremecimiento natal" ["the birth tremor"] of each word. Moreover, although the "masters" with whom the poet identifies in his apprenticeship are uniformly male, his *madrina* ["godmother"] was the one who initiated him into the experience of literary intuition ("Quietismo estético" ["Aesthetic Quietism"] 8). A woman also provides him with a model for the timeless stories he would most like to tell; she is the blind old seamstress he remembers from his childhood ("Quietismo estético" 10). And the figure of a woman hovers between the lines of his description of the poet-Christ in *La lámpara maravillosa* ("Exégesis trina" ["Three-part Exegesis"] 5).[13]

At this point, it is important to stress the poet's description of himself as a *cifra*, because it is far more as figure than as individual that he presents himself in *La lámpara maravillosa*. To become a poet, he suggests, is to become a work of art and thus—and only thus—to become an agent for change, one capable of breaking the constraints and fickleness of language and literary convention. That both language and the regendering of his poet have significance beyond the incidents in *La lámpara maravillosa* is evident in Valle-Inclán's comment, made shortly after the book's publication, that "toda obra de arte es un andrógeno" ["every work of art is an androgyne"].[14] When he made that remark, Valle-Inclán apparently did not elaborate on its implications either for his work or for art in general. He did refer, however, to the "actions" ["acciones"] produced by creative work, and—given his thorough familiarity with alchemy, theosophy, and mysticism, he was undoubtedly aware of the subversive potential of his poet-Redeemer (Christ)-androgyne. Specifically, he would certainly have been cognizant of the androgyne as the vehicle of "osmosis" described recently by Loretta Frattale, which bridged the opposing turn-of-the-century paths of materialism and idealism.[15]

One must of course be hesitant about applying to earlier works the "insights" of current critical theory. The frequent discrepancies, however, between the affirmation of the androgyne in *La lámpara maravillosa* and disparaging comments made by Valle-Inclán and his characters, not to mention some of the highly unappealing and weak female characters he created, suggest that Valle-Inclán also recognized and experienced the extent to which an androgynous poet, whether metaphorical or "real," could threaten both an individual identity and an entire "spectrum of social roles."[16] This is linked, at least in part, to the ambivalence or even aversion with respect to "the feminine" in the description offered by the poet of *La lámpara maravillosa* of "la tierra madre, paridora y devoradora de carne humana" ["mother earth, who both gives birth to and devours human flesh"]. Or Valle-Inclán's own remarks about women, made in response to questions asked about new (Republican) Spain during an interview in 1931. "En la presente civilización" ["In the present civilization"], he is quoted as saying, "no tienen nada que hacer las mujeres" [there is no role for women].[17]

Like Valle-Inclán's classification, in the same interview, of feminism as one of "tres tópicos horribles" ["three sorry old stories"],[18] his comment about women's uselessness suggests a possible discrepancy between, on the one hand, some of his strong, autonomous female characters or his efforts to dramatize the poet as a figure simultaneously feminine and masculine and, on the other, the derogatory statements he made about women in everyday life. At the same time, however, that discrepancy also indicates, perhaps, the enormity of the task Valle-Inclán saw awaiting any "pilgrim" who sets out to resolve an "eternal antagonism" without falling into the sterility of an eternal circling. After all, as the poet-narrator explains in *La lámpara maravillosa,* "La mujer *debe* resistir al hombre y el hombre *debe* fascinarla. . . ." ["Woman *must* resist man and man *must* captivate her. . . ."] ("Exégesis trina" 5; emphasisis added). The repetition of "must" [*debe*] evokes continual conflict, even eternal conflict, whose resolution may well lie outside the bounds of human possibility. What is more, that repetition itself evokes a tormented, impossible "union" linked not only with a struggle between genders but also with the complex social and historical contexts in which that struggle is inscribed and with the difficulties inherent in the poet's struggle for expression.[19]

Given the precariousness of the androgyne postulated in *La lámpara maravillosa* and the ambivalence toward the "feminine" elements of creativity manifest in Valle-Inclán's writing, at first glance it may seem that any redemptive "power" that might be attained by a poet simultaneously masculine and feminine is virtually subverted, or even negated, in his work.[20] On the other hand, and it is this "hand" that guided the planning of the present collection, the very contradictions in Valle-Inclán's androgynous poet and in his seemingly inconsistent stance with respect to (what are now referred to as) gender-related issues promise richer and more complex readings of his texts. If to uproot those texts so as to consider them in terms of gender is to prompt an anachronism, it is also to prompt an anachronism similar to the somewhat extravagant but carefully calculated gestures of uprooting and relocation for which Valle-Inclán was known himself. Those gestures occur both within his work and "without," arising, for example, in his spoken remarks about contemporary events, or when his plays were staged and their "historical commentary" was refracted in a new context. Dru Dougherty has discussed this "retórica distanciadora" ["distancing rhetoric"] at length, explaining its effect on a reader who at first finds that the analogies suggested are implausible but on reflection is given a new perspective on an immediate situation.[21] What starts as the distancing that accompanies anachronism, then, becomes an altered approach, which is to say, a closeness. In a similar way, current considerations of gender can inform and be informed by works written several decades before those considerations would have been articulated in "gendered" terms.

Because of the relative "novelty" of addressing Valle-Inclán's work in terms of gender, the present collection of essays has been conceived as *introductory* in the truest sense of the word. From the outset, its purpose has been to initiate and to question, and it therefore includes works by both seasoned "Valleinclanistas" and other scholars willing to take on the task of reading Valle-Inclán's texts for gender. Since the intent of the editors was to encourage risks, contributors were neither provided with a definition of gender nor asked to work from a given point of departure. Similarly, there was no attempt made to analyze all of Valle-Inclán's texts nor provide a panoramic view of his writing. On the contrary, contributors were asked to establish their own parameters as they read for gender and to choose the texts appropriate to their discussions. As editors, we did make it clear, however, that we equated the study of gender not with an effort limited to the "feminine," but with the need identified by Joan Wallach Scott for "a refusal of the fixed and permanent quality of the binary opposition, a genuine historicization and deconstruction of the terms of sexual difference."[22] Contributors were asked to explore the hint of Scott's "refusal," "historicization and deconstruction" that we saw in Valle-Inclán's writing. In this way, we believed, they would be encouraged to address issues of gender in his work but not restricted to focus their inquiry from a predetermined perspective.

In order to create a context in which the essays might be situated with respect to Hispanic literary criticism, the book is not composed solely of new pieces. The scant attention Valle-Inclán scholars have traditionally paid to gender-related topics means that any pieces one might choose to reprint will not date back very far. Several published essays, however, addressed precisely the issues engaged in *Ramón María del Valle-Inclán: Questions of Gender,* and three of them open the book. Of those essays, Catherine Nickel's article on "La Generala" is placed first. Published in 1988,[23] it deals with one of Valle-Inclán's earliest stories and offers an analysis of how his work at once exemplifies and undermines some of the prevalent cultural and literary clichés of late nineteenth-century Spain. The same could be said of Noël Valis's piece, which follows. When *Ramón María del Valle-Inclán* was planned, Valis had just published her essay; the original version, however, had been written several years before.[24] It raises provocative questions about possible (gender-related) limits to Valle-Inclán's imagination, and suggests that Valle-Inclán—as well as Bradomín—was trapped in the myth of the (patriarchal) author. This is an entrapment closely linked to another implicit in the third "historical" piece. In that essay, written in 1986 for a symposium about Valle-Inclán held at Purdue University,[25] Biruté Ciplijauskaité questions the limits of Valle-Inclán's "subversive" language by comparing it to the work of French feminist writers, especially that of Luce Irigaray. Although Ciplijauskaité notes some striking similarities between Valle-Inclán's goals for language and the goals of certain feminists, she also indicates crucial points of divergence. In particular, she emphasizes Valle-Inclán's position within the patriarchy, showing that, ironically, any "feminist" discourse that might be attributed to him is not found in the speeches of his female characters, but in the words of his (male) narrators.

These first three essays are followed by two pieces that address

Valle-Inclán's work as a whole. Iris M. Zavala's essay provides an excellent point of departure because it articulates a position that embodies Valle-Inclán's entire oeuvre. Using Bakhtinian "dialogics," Zavala considers what she refers to as Valle-Inclán's deconstruction of contemporary ideology. Such a deconstruction, she argues, inevitably includes women (an argument that leads her to affirm that questions of gender "are a part of Valle-Inclán's national project and social imaginary"). She finds that "Valle-Inclán avoids implicit gendering situations," and that his negative representations of women are therefore to be read ironically.[26] Zavala does not speak for all of the contributors to *Ramón María del Valle-Inclán*, but many of her comments are confirmed or refracted in the other essays. This is certainly true in the case of the essay by Mary K. Addis and Roberta L. Salper who, like Zavala, stress the importance of studying gender as a phenomenon integrally related to historical and political factors. In their reading of "Octavia Santino," *El yermo de las almas* [The wasteland of souls], and *La hija del capitán* [The captain's daughter], Addis and Salper look at one of Valle-Inclán's latest pieces in light of his earliest work. Not only do they chart a pronounced alteration in Valle-Inclán's female characters, but they initiate a discussion of his representation of the family as a malfunctioning, deformed, and disintegrating social institution. In particular, by examining the relationship between la Sini and her father in *La hija del capitán*, they show how the "detached daughter" is linked to Valle-Inclán's understanding of the political chaos he found in early twentieth-century Spain and to his hopes for the Second Republic.

Of the new essays, two are focused on Valle-Inclán's early fiction. The critical methods employed by their authors are different, but both of the contributors address concerns that are strikingly complementary with regard to an ambivalence they encounter in Valle-Inclán's representation of women. Working with *Femeninas* and *Epitalamio* [Epithalamion], Catherine Davies uncovers what she terms a "problematic centering of narrative,"[27] in which a male writing subject directs a work that appears, and perhaps in some respects *is*, "woman-centered."[28] As discussed by Davies, this occurrence—of fiction that at first glance might look "radical" or "feminist"[29]—occasions a "double view" not unlike the "dual positionality" or "double pleasure" studied by Maryellen Bieder in "Rosarito."[30] However, Bieder,—using recent film criticism and taking as a point of departure one of her own earlier essays—[31] works with two readers, male and female, to show that the ambivalence provoked by Valle-Inclán's "aesthetic quietism"[32] will satisfy only a male reader. A female reader, she contends, will remain unsatisfied because she will be excluded from a gaze that is ultimately male, despite its apparently inclusive polarity.[33]

These suggestions of a highly problematized ambivalence are followed by Michael P. Predmore's study of *Aguila de blasón* [*Heraldic Eagle*], the thesis of which challenges Davies and Bieder implicitly through its affirmation that several of Valle-Inclán's female characters indicate a "dramatic movement" in his work "toward a more liberated world."[34] Predmore's primary example is Sabelita, whom he considers the "dynamic center" of *Aguila*,[35] but he also discusses the strong female voices he finds in the *esperpentos,* particularly *La hija del capitán.* This development of increasingly strong female characters in Valle-Inclán's later work— a phenomenon noted as well by Ciplijauskaité and Addis and Salper in their essays—is also central in the essays by Carol Maier and C. Christopher Soufas, Jr. Maier, however, simultaneously affirms and interrogates that centrality in her study of Mari-Gaila and *Divinas palabras* [*Divine Words*]. She argues that Mari-Gaila, who is clearly identified with the poetic word, has a principle role in both the incident of the play and Valle-Inclán's meditation on language, but she questions the extent to which Mari-Gaila is truly a female subject, as opposed to a self-reflection, a portrait of Valle-Inclán's own consciousness. Soufas, of course, does not answer her directly, but his essay indicates that he might well attribute any ambivalence that arises from Valle-Inclán's female characters to the "infelicitous gender dynamics" he finds at the crux of *Tirano Banderas* [*The Tyrant. A Novel of Warm Lands*].[36] This "unhappy wedding" would be linked to a subversive "feminine" element manifest in the "double identity" of Lupita.[37] Capable of untying the perverse interactions that bind men and women—and hence an entire society—this force, or a recognition of it, would also be capable of allowing the novel's reader to imagine a way of breaking the vicious circle that keeps the genders revolving in continual conflict.

The final essay in the collection also involves a revolution, although of a different sort. In this instance, the revolution belongs to the critic Roberta Johnson, who turns the tables and reverses the "direction" of most studies about intertexuality and Valle-Inclán's work. Rather than discuss the presence in Valle-Inclán's texts of works by other writers, she examines the presence of *Sonata de otoño* [*Sonata of Autumn*] in Marina Mayoral's *Cándida otra vez* [Cándida, once more] (1979), which she finds to be a "retroactive reading" of Valle-Inclán's novel. Mayoral, she explains, foregrounds gender and class,[38] simultaneously incorporating and critiquing their role in Valle-Inclán's work.[39] Because Johnson addresses Valle-Inclán's early fiction, her essay could well have been placed toward the beginning of this collection instead of the end. It is placed last, however, as an acknowledgment of the rereading and rewriting by critics, novelists, poets, and playwrights to which Valle-Inclán's representations of gender have begun—and will continue—to give rise.

The Janus-like glance elicited by Johnson's article offers an appropriately open closure for another reason as well, since it could be said to suggest the way in which an introduction precedes the work it presents but is, of necessity, written after that work has been completed. As such, although an introduction must look back, it must also look forward, anticipating future discussions. In the case of *Ramón María del Valle-Inclán,* the essays that follow offer an affirmative answer to the original questions that occasioned the volume. At the same time, however, they pose new questions, which, hopefully, will encourage further study. If those questions are expressed here only in outline form, it is to let the essays seek their own readers and readings without the burden of excessive editorializing.

First, what might account for the fact that much of the criticism that does exist about women and their role in Valle-Inclán's work focuses on the *Sonatas* and on his other early fiction? This work has always received a great deal of critical attention, but is it truly more accessible than later work like the "esperpentos"? Or might gender constructions be "nearer the surface" in collections like *Femeninas* and *Corte de amor* [Court of love]?

Second, how will gender-related criticism alter the context of other recent works about Valle-Inclán, his contemporaries, and turn-of-the-century Spain? What, for example, is the relation between gender as the "center" for Valle-Inclán's work, as discussed in several of the essays in this collection, and sex—which, according to Dougherty, "frequently figures as a motivating force in the dramatic world [of Valle-Inclán]"—,[40] or between gender and the erotic, studied at length by Lily Litvak[41] and others and cited by Martha LaFollette Miller as "the locus of the rivalry and undifferentiation that constitutes a crisis of order"?[42] To what extent are considerations of gender linked to other areas of Valle-Inclán studies still in need of extensive work—the publication and scrutiny of early versions,[43] for instance, or the preparation of critical editions and translations? Will a more thorough understanding of gender issues in Valle-Inclán's work affect current perceptions of his writing as "misogynist,"[44] or "reductive and essentialist" with respect to gendering?[45] Or will that understanding confirm Roberta Johnson's suggestion that Valle-Inclán's thinking must be considered somewhat "apart" from that of his contemporaries vis-à-vis what Johnson has termed the "idea(l) women of the Generation of '98"?[46]

Third, given the insight that gender criticism provides into social and cultural systems, how will reading for gender realign Valle-Inclán's work with respect to his own aesthetics and also to the history of Spanish literature?

Finally, it is time to offer a brief explanation of *Ramón María del Valle-Inclán: Questions of Gender,* the title of this collection. The poet of *La lámpara maravillosa* was not the only aesthetic *cifra* that Valle-Inclán created. Another was his own pen name, in which he apparently combined his given name, which was also that of his father, with the given name of his mother.[47] Although the incorporation of "María" in the names given to Spanish males is not uncommon, by adding it deliberately himself, as an adult, Valle-Inclán added a feminine component to his identity as a writer. As Rubén Darío indicated in his "Balada laudatoria a Don Ramón María del Valle-Inclán" ["Laudatory Ballad to Don Ramón María del Valle-Inclán"], Valle-Inclán also insured that his entire name, don Ramón María del Valle-Inclán, formed a perfect Alexandrine. It is impossible to ascertain Valle-Inclán's thinking as he created Ramón María, and it would be foolish to argue that the decision was motivated by a desire either to have his poetic persona comprise both of his parents, or to allude to the fusion, hinted at by Darío in the "envío" ["envoi"] of his poem, of masculine (Apollo) and feminine (Moon). The fact is, however, that it does, and that in his name Valle-Inclán also managed to allude to the complex interrelation of opposites he considered to be the crux of his aesthetics. Since that interrelation formed the beginning of *Ramón María del Valle-Inclán* when the project originated in the Café Gijón,[48] it seems fitting that it be the first thing a reader encounters: Valle-Inclán's signature and ours.

Notes

    1. Cited in José Carlos Mainer, "Libros sobre Valle-Inclán," *Revista de Occidente* 59 (April 1986): 79.
    2. See, to name a few frequently cited studies: Rodolfo Cardona and Anthony N. Zahareas, *Visión del esperpento: Teoría y práctica en los esperpentos de Valle-Inclán* (Madrid: Castalia, 1970) and "The Historical Function of Specta-

cle," in *Selected Proceedings of the "Singularidad y Trascendencia" Conference,* ed. Nora Marval-McNair (Boulder, Colo.: Society of Spanish and Spanish-American Studies, 1990), 131–48; Dru Dougherty, *Valle-Inclán y la Segunda República* (Valentia: Pre-Textos, 1986); Juan Antonio Hormigón, *Ramón del Valle-Inclán: La política, la cultura, el realismo y el pueblo* (Madrid: Alberto Corazón, 1972); José Antonio Maravall, "La imagen de la sociedad arcaica en Valle-Inclán," *Revista de Occidente* 4, nos. 44–45 (1969): 225–56; Leda Schiavo, *Historia y novela en Valle-Inclán: Para leer "El ruedo ibérico"* (Madrid: Castalia, 1980); and Anthony N. Zaharaes, "The Esperpento and the Aesthetics of Commitment," *Modern Language Notes* 81 (1966): 159–73.

3. Most notably by Dougherty, *Valle-Inclán y la Segunda República;* Juan Antonio Hormigón, *Valle-Inclán: Cronología, escritos dispersos, epistolario* (Madrid: Fundación Banco Exterior, 1987); Elaine Lavaud, *Valle-Inclán du journal au roman (1888–1915)* (Paris: Klincksieck, 1979); and Javier Serrano Alonso, *Ramón del Valle-Inclán: Artículos completos y páginas olvidadas* (Madrid: Istmo, 1987).

4. For a recent review of critical work on *La lámpara maravillosa,* see Virginia Garlitz, "*La lámpara maravillosa:* Humo y luz," *Insula* 531 (March 1991): 11–12.

5. These anthologies include Clara Barbeito, ed., *Valle-Inclán: Nueva valoración de su obra (Estudios críticos en el cincuentenario de su muerte* (Barcelona: PPU, 1988); John P. Gabriele, ed., *Genio y virtuosismo en Valle-Inclán* (Madrid: Orígenes, 1987) and *Suma Valleinclaniana: Homenaje a Emma Susana Speratti-Piñero* (Barcelona: Anthropos, 1992); Juan Antonio Hormigón, ed., *Quimera, Cántico: Busca y rebusca de Valle-Inclán* (Madrid: Ministerio de Cultura, 1989); Angel Loureiro, coord., *Estelas, laberintos, nuevas sendas: Unamuno. Valle-Inclán. García Lorca. La Guerra Civil* (Barcelona: Anthropos, 1988); Nora de Marval-McNair, ed., *Selected Proceedings;* and J. M. García de la Torre, ed., *Valle-Inclán (1866–1936): Creación y lenguaje* (Amsterdam: Rodopi, 1988).

6. For example, Luis T. González del Valle, *La ficción breve de Valle-Inclán: Hermenéutica y estrategias narrativas* (Barcelona: Anthropos, 1990); and Iris Zavala, *La musa funambulesca: Poética de la carnavalización en Valle-Inclán* (Madrid: Orígenes, 1990).

7. Among them, the essays by Biruté Ciplijauskaité, Catherine Nickel, and Noël Valis, reprinted in this volume, and Lily Litvak, *Erotismo fin de siglo* (Barcelona: Antoni Bosch, 1979); Carol Maier, "Toward a Definition of Woman as Reader in Valle-Inclán's Aesthetics," *Boletín del Museo de Pontevedra* (Spain) 40 (1986): 121–30; Martha LaFollette Miller, "The Feminization and Emasculation of Galicia in Valle-Inclán's *Jardín umbrío, Romance Quarterly* 30, no. 1 (1992): 87–92; Nickel, "Recasting the Image of the Fallen Woman in Valle-Inclán's 'Eulalia,'" *Studies in Short Fiction* 24 (1987): 289–94; "The Relationship of Gender to Discourse in Valle-Inclán's 'Augusta,'" *Romance Notes* 30, no. 2 (1989): 141–47, and "Representations and Gender in Valle-Inclán's 'Rosita,'" *Revista de Estudios Hispánicos* 25, no. 3 (1991); Claire Paolini, "Valle-Inclán's Modernistic Women: The Devout Virgin and the Devout Adultress," *Hispanófila* 88 (1986): 27–41; and Roberta L. Salper, "Las dos Micaelas de Valle-Inclán: Un arquetipo de mujer," in *Divergencias y unidad: Perspectivas sobre la Generación del 98 y Antonio Machado,* ed. John P. Gabriele (Madrid: Orígenes, 1990), 141–59. Jean Andrews's essay, "Saints and Strumpets: Female Stereotypes in Valle-Inclán," which became available to us only after this Introduction was completed, should also be noted here (*Feminist Readings on Spanish and Latin-American Literature,* eds. L. P. Condé and S. M. Hart [Lewiston, N.Y.: The Edwin Mellen Press, 1991], 27–35).

8. "Generation" is deliberately not capitalized here, in keeping with recent ap-

praisals of the "Generation of '98." See, for example, the essays by E. Inman Fox, "'La Generación de 1898' como concepto historiográfico," in *Divergencias y unidad,* 23–38; and José-Carlos Mainer, "1900–1910: New Literature, New Publics" and Antonio Ramos-Gascón, "Spanish Literature as a Historiographic Invention: The Case of the Generation of 1898," in *The Crisis of Instutitionalized Literature in Spain,* trans. Carrie Legus, with the assistance of Gwendolyn Barnes, et al., eds. Wlad Godzich and Nicholas Spadaccini (Minneapolis: The Prisma Institute, 1988), 195–227 and 167–93, respectively.

9. For example, there is no mention of gender or gender-related issues in the essays cited in n. 8. That critics are beginning to address gender in late nineteenth- and early twentieth-century Spanish male writers is evidenced by studies such as the pieces about Unamuno by Nancy Newton ("Sexuality and Narrativity: The Example of Unamuno," paper delivered at the MMLA Convention, 1989), and Harriet S. Turner ("Distorciones teresianas de *La tia Tula,*" in *Los hallazgos de la lectura: Estudio dedicado a Miguel Enguídanos,* eds. John Crispin, Enrique Pupo-Walker, and Luis Lorenzo-Rivero (Madrid: Porrúa, 1989), 131–51. Other examples would be Noël M. Valis's comments about Clarín in "La crisis de la autoridad en el 'fin de siglo' español: 'Cuesta abajo,' de Clarín," in *Realismo y naturalismo en España en la segunda mitad del siglo XIX,* ed. Yvan Lissourges (Barcelona: Anthropos, 1988), 400–420; Lou Charnon-Deutsch's *Gender and Representation: Women in Spanish Realist Fiction* (Amsterdam: John Benjamins, 1990); and the chapters on Galdós and García Lorca in Paul Julian Smith's *Body Hispanic: Gender and Sexuality in Spanish and Spanish American Literature* (Oxford: Clarendon Press, 1989).

10. See, for example, E. Inman Fox," "'La Generación de 1989' como concepto historiográfico" in *Divergencias y unidad* and Antonio Ramos-Gascón, "Spanish Literature as a Historiographic Invention" in *The Crisis of Institutionalized Literature in Spain.*

11. "Quietismo estético" ["Aesthetic Quietism"] 5, in *La lámpara maravillosa* (1916; 2d ed., Madrid: Artes de la Ilustración, 1922). All references to *La lámpara maravillosa* are to chapters in this edition. Translations are our own. An English translation of *La lámpara maravillosa* was published by Robert Lima in 1986, (*The Lamp of Marvels* [West Stockbridge, Mass.: Lindesfarne Press]).

12. For a discussion of "the occult" and related phenomena in *La lámpara maravillosa,* see Virginia M. Garlitz, "Fuentes del ocultismo modernista en *La lámpara maravillosa,*" in *Genio y virtuosismo en Valle-Inclán,* 101–13 and "El concepto de karma en dos magos españoles: Don Ramón del Valle-Inclán y don Mario Roso de Luna," in *Estelas, laberintos, nuevas sendas,* 151–70.

13. For further discussion of the narrator of *La lámpara maravillosa* as a feminine figure see Carol Maier, "De cifras, desciframiento, y una lectura literal de *La lámpara maravillosa,*" in *Suma Valleinclaniana* 223–49. Jean Andrews also discusses androgyny with respect to *La lámpara maravillosa,* although she finds that "woman as inspiration is absent" (30) there. It is regrettable that Andrews's essay was not available as this Introduction was written, because her comment about the absence of woman made possible a rethinking of the fact (I previously perceived as contradictory) that one could feel excluded as a woman from the "brotherhood" of poets in *La lámpara maravillosa* but nevertheless detect and proceed to document a feminine presence ("¿Palabras de armonía?: Reflexiones sobre la lectura, los limites y la estética de Valle-Inclán," in *Estelas, laberintos, nuevas sendas,* 151–70. This disjunction or "slippage" deserves further study, and it is addressed, albeit in somewhat different terms, in Maier's "From Words to Divinity?" Question of Language and Gender in *Divinas palabras,*" included in this volume.

14. Cited by Alfonso Reyes in 1917 ("Apuntes sobre Valle-Inclán"). Reprinted in José Esteban, *Valle-Inclán visto por . . .* (Madrid: Colección Espejo, 1973), 84.

15. Loretta Frattale, Introduction (trans. Vicente Martín Pindado) to José Antich, *Andrógino,* ed. Loretta Frattale (Madrid: Tecnos, 1989), 41.

16. Francette Pacteau, "The Impossible Referent: Representations of the Androgyne," in *Formations of Fantasy,* eds. Victor Burgin, James Donald, and Cora Kaplan (New York: Methuen, 1986), 43.

17. Francisco Lucientes, "¿Cómo será España bajo la futura constitución? La nueva República, entre veras y burlas." *El Sol* (Madrid), 20 November 1931. Reprinted in Dougherty, *Un Valle-Inclán olvidado: Entrevistas y conferencias* (Madrid: Fundamentos, 1982), 223.

18. Ibid., 221.

19. The extent to which the elusiveness of the androgeny in *La lámpara maravillosa* might arise from a reticence on Valle-Inclán's part to risk a brush with (charges of) homosexuality is a topic that merits further consideration. Certainly the poet of *La lámpara maravillosa* takes pains to point out his own weakness for women ("La piedra del sabio" ["The Philosopher's Stone" 5]) and the "lujuria estéril" ["sterile lust"] of sexual relationships that do not lead to pregnancy: "El Incubo, Sodoma y Onan" ("The Incubus, Sodom, and Onan"] ("Exégesis trina" ["Three-Part Exegesis"] 9). A similar insistence on heterosexuality appears in other works as well. Bradomín's self-proclaimed "inability" to indulge in this "bello pecado" ["beautiful sin"] is only one example (*Sonata de estío* [*Sonata of Summer*], (1903; reprint, 7th ed. Madrid: Espasa-Calpe, 1969), 135–36 and *Sonata de invierno* [*Sonata of Winter*], 1905; reprint, 5th ed. Madrid: Espasa-Calpe, 1966), 152–53. No doubt Sylvia Molloy's recent comments on Latin American turn-of-the-century (herero)sexuality have relevance for Spain as well: "Too Wilde for Comfort: Desire and Ideology in Fin-de-Siècle Spanish America," *Social Text 31/32* 10, nos. 2–3 (1992): 182–201. See also Jean Andrews's discussion of Ortega's comments about the creation of a "phallocentric paradise" by an "apparently unmanly Valle" (28).

20. The masculine pronoun is used deliberately here because, despite the evidence of several feminine figures in *La lámpara maravillosa,* there is every reason to suspect that the poet-narrator's "brotherhood" of poets is exclusively male. See n. 13.

21. Dougherty, *Valle-Inclán y la Segunda República,* 34–38.

22. Joan Wallach Scott, "Gender: A Useful Category of Historical Analysis," in *Gender and the Politics of History* (New York: Columbia University Press, 1988), 40–41. Scott's article was originally published in 1985. It is noted here because Scott's work was influential in the conceptualization of this project. To cite all of the studies we found helpful as work progressed would require more space than that available in an endnote, but collections such as *Out of Bounds: Male Writers and Gender(ed) Criticism,* eds. Laura Claridge and Elizabeth Langland (Amherst: University of Massachusetts Press, 1990) were particularly useful.

23. Catherine Nickel, "Valle-Inclán's 'La Generala': Woman as Birdbrain," *Hispania* 71 (1988): 228–34.

24. An early version was delivered at an MLA special session on the *Sonatas.* Chicago, 1985.

25. Ironically, Biruté Ciplijauskaité's essay was the one piece written for a session about women that did not materialize for the conference; at the time the participants contacted were not interested in focusing their work in gendered terms.

26. Zavala herself recognizes this, as is evident in her note about Noël Valis's argument. (See n. 20, in Zavala's essay in this volume.)

27. Catherine Davies, "'Venus impera?'" Women and Power in *Femeninas* and *Epitalamio*," essay in this volume, 131.

28. Davies, "'Venus impera?'" 133.

29. Ibid., 144.

30. Maryellen Bieder, "Woman Transfixed: Plotting the Fe/male Gaze in 'Rosarito,'" essay in this volume.

31. Our original request to Bieder was for permission to translate her essay, "La narración como arte visual. Focalización en 'Rosarito,'" which appeared in *Genio y virtuosismo de Valle-Inclán*. As she explains in "Woman Transfixed," the return to that essay prompted a whole new piece.

32. Although Bieder does not use it, this term (coined in *La lámpara maravillosa* and in the earlier essays in which it was prefigured) is an appropriate way to refer to Valle-Inclán's aesthetics.

33. Bieder, "Woman Transfixed," 172–73.

34. Michael P. Predmore, "The Central Role of Sabelita in *Aguila de Blasón*: Toward the Emergence of a Radical Vision of Women in the Later Art of the '*Esperpento*,'" essay in this volume.

35. Ibid., 185.

36. C. Christopher Soufas, Jr., "With This Ring: Woman as 'Revolutionary Inseparable' in Goya's *Caprichos* and Valle-Inclán's *Tirano Banderas*," essay in this volume.

37. Soufas, "With This Ring," 227–35.

38. Roberta Johnson, "Marina Mayoral's *Cándida otra vez:* Invitation to a Retroactive Reading of *Sonata de ontoño*," essay in this volume.

39. Ibid., 248.

40. Dru Dougherty, "Theater and Eroticism: Valle-Inclán's *Farsa y licencia de la Reina castiza, Hispanic Review* 55, no. 1 (1987): 19.

41. See, for example, Litvak, *Erotismo fin de siglo*.

42. Martha LaFollette Miller, "Disorder and Sacrifice in *Sonata de otoño*," *Romance Quarterly* 36, no. 3 (1989): 332.

43. For just one example, see the confirmation of Predmore's argument about Sabelita to be found in the fragments published recently by Javier Serrano Alonso as early versions of *Aguila de blasón* ("La génesis de *Aguila de blasón*," *Boletín de la Fundación Federico García Lorca* 4. nos. 7–8 [1990]: 83–125).

44. Constance Sullivan, "On Spanish Literary History and the Politics of Gender," *The Journal of the Midwest Modern Language Association* 23, no. 2 (1990): 32.

45. Maryellen Bieder, "Woman and the Twentieth-Century Spanish Literary Canon: The Lady Vanishes," in *ALEC,* in a special issue on "Reviewing the Canon: Spanish Fiction from 1900–1936," ed. Robert Spires, 17 (1992): 301–24.

46. Roberta Johnson, "The Idea(l) Women of the Generation of '98" (Paper delivered at the MMLA convention, 1990).

47. The surname "Valle-Inclán" had already been used by his father. See "Los apellidos de don Ramón," *Indice de Artes y Letras* (Madrid) 9, nos. 74–75 (April–May 1954): 26.

48. The distinction between beginnings and origins suggested here owes to Edward W. Said, *Beginnings: Intention and Method* (Baltimore, Md.: Johns Hopkins University Press, 1975).

Toward an Understanding of History and Gender in Valle-Inclán's Spain

ROBERTA L. SALPER, with CAROL MAIER

At the turn of the century, literature offered a rich arena for the examination of Spanish national identity. In fact, the literary text became a primary site of ideological struggle as the different members of the so-called Generation of '98[1] engaged in a complex, often contradictory interrogation of hegemonic social values and reigning definitions of national history. In this respect, the thematics of Valle-Inclán and his contemporaries Azorín, Baroja, Unamuno, and Machado, are well known. What has not generally been observed, however, is that these dramas of national redefinition were expressed largely in gendered terms.[2] Indeed, gender pressures, in addition to class conflicts, figured critically in the literary creation of the Generation of '98. The episodic, multilayered drama of national redefinition unfolded in shifting social constructs of manhood and womanhood during the period in which Valle-Inclán was writing, that is, between 1888 and 1936.[3]

Moments of Crisis: 1890–1910, 1917–1920, "The Later Years"

The troubled emergence of a hegemonic bourgeois culture in Spain throughout the nineteenth century and the consequent insecurity of bourgeois cultural premises impeded the creation of a literary discourse that embodied the new mentality. At the turn of the century, when Valle-Inclán began to write, the irregularity and uneven development of Spain's cultural transformations converged in a historical conjuncture generally referred to as the "crisis de fin de siglo" ["turn-of-the-century crisis"] that took place roughly between 1890 and 1910.

This historical conjuncture—one of the historical "moments" embedded in Valle-Inclán's trajectory—was the plight of a European nation that did not solidify as a modern bourgeois state until late in the nineteenth century and remained caught in a contradictory web, unable to mesh an outmoded dominant ideology with a modernized *but* dependent economy. Unlike France and England, where the solidification of the liberal state and the formation of a hegemonic middle class occurred in the eighteenth century, Spain would not see the consolidation of the modern state and the formation of a hegemonic bourgeois ideology until the later decades of the nineteenth century. More than in most other European countries, the prevalent mentality during the formation of the bourgeois state in Spain looked backward to the landed aristocracy, and by the time the middle class was solidly constituted late in the nineteenth century, this ideology had become predominant in the Spanish middle class itself.[4]

The second historical conjuncture, 1917–20, is a time in which the premises of bourgeois epistemology appeared to be crumbling throughout the Western world. Unlike the uniquely peninsular "fin de siglo crisis," Spain shared the experiences of these three years with the rest of Europe. With the aftereffects of the European war and subsequently the Soviet Revolution, new social forces burst forth in Spain threatening the old order. On the Iberian peninsula, as well as throughout the rest of Western Europe, workers' organizations (Communists, Anarchists, and Socialists) newly empowered by the Bolshevik triumph, challenged entrenched institutions and social hierarchies. Traditional "have-nots" now projected a symbolic representation of a new world order.[5]

As the ambiguous personae of the Marqués de Bradomín and Don Juan Manuel reveal throughout the *Sonatas* and the *Comedias bárbaras* [*Barbaric Comedies*], respectively, historical development seemed to point not only toward the waning of the once powerful landed aristocracy, but also toward the disappearance of its corollary "patrician construct of manhood." For centuries this construct had been an accepted male code of conduct based on a link to the land, and a distrust and distaste of aggressive materialism.[6] However, even though much of a feudal past might be eradicated with the evolution of a Spanish middle class, the sedimentations and enduring remnants of the old order undermined and weakened the emergence of a coherent new code of conduct— a new social construct—for the Spanish bourgeoisie. This is strikingly evident, for example, in Valle-Inclán's fictional re-creation of the Marqués de Salamanca (1811–83), one of Spain's few nineteenth-century entrepreneurial success stories.[7] A "self-made" powerful financier in the mode of the nineteenth-century American "robber barons," José Salamanca is, in Valle-Inclán's opinion, a ridiculous caricature of a bourgeois entrepreneur. The Marqués of *Baza de espadas* [Military tricks] ("obeso, enlevitado, rubicundo" [12] ["obese, frock-coated, rubicund"]) is corrupt and despicable. Implicit in Valle-Inclán's texts is the realization that Spain did not produce a hegemonic bourgeois social construct of manhood, as did the United States with the evolution of the entrepreneurial model that accompanied the Protestant ethic based on hard work, thrift, and honesty. Due in part, no doubt, to the strongly entrenched presence of traditional Catholicism, a social construct of middle-class manhood rooted in competitive individualism did not displace the patrician concept of the self so dear to the Marqués de Bradomín.

Throughout the 1920s the reverberations of the "Bolshevik triennium" became part of a conjunction of forces that led in Spain to the dictatorship of Primo de Rivera (1923–30), and to an intensification of Valle-Inclán's social criticism and mordant satire. These are the years of many of his masterpieces: the three "esperpentos" of *Martes de carnaval* [Shrove Tuesday carnival], *Tirano Banderas* [*The Tyrant. A Novel of Warm Lands*], and the *El ruedo ibérico* [The Iberian Ring]. Although Valle-Inclán would not write any major works after the fall of the military dictatorship, the circumstances leading up to, and the advent of, the Second Republic (April 1931) represent, in the words of Dru Doughtery, a new phase in Valle-Inclán's life, one "cargada de esperanza en la redención posible de España. . . . Sin que desaparezca del todo la militancia que caracterizaba sus ataques contra 'la España oficial' durante los años veinte, surge, como contrapeso al nihilismo esperpéntico, la esperanza de que la Segunda República bien podría servir de instrumento para la renovación de España"[8] ["filled with hope about the possible salvation of Spain. . . . Although the militancy that characterized his attacks against the official Spain during the 1920 does not completely disappear, the hope that the Second Republic might serve as an instrument to reform Spain appears, as a counterbalance to his esperpentic nihilism"]. It is important to emphasize that the utopian "vision" evidenced in Valle-Inclán's hope for the Second Republic, which Juan Antonio Hormigón also notes,[9] did not suddenly appear, fully articulated, in 1931. On the contrary, it can be glimpsed in all his work, even its most scathingly critical moments. If it is more openly expressed and closer to the surface toward the end of his life, this is no doubt because he sees a possibility for the political redemption of Spain with the defeat of the dictatorship and the advent of the Second Republic.

Modernism/Modernismo/Avant-Garde

Valle-Inclán's familiarity with contemporary European politics and literature is well documented in his texts, journalistic pieces, and spoken comments.[10] In addition, probably more than any of his *fin de siglo* peninsular contemporaries, Valle-Inclán was a "Hispanic" writer in the sense that he encompassed the historical problematic of the New World as well as the Old. From his early work and long before the publication of *Tirano Banderas* (1926), and *La cabeza del Bautista* [*The Head of the Baptist*] (1924) (with Don Igi, La Pepona, and El Jándalo), Valle-Inclán introduced Spanish American settings and characters, often in interaction with Spanish ones, in short narratives like "Bajo los trópicos" ["Under Tropical Skies"] (1892), "La Niña Chole" ["Mistress Chole"] (1893), and "Tula Varona" (1893). In fact, from the 1890s on, the problematics of the New World were sporadically present throughout all of Valle-Inclán's work. In this way, by reaching beyond the confines of the Iberian peninsula and making his world Hispanic, not just Spanish, one could say that he registered his own Modernist moment. Living and writing at the turn of the century, a time in which European capitalism had evolved to the point that it operated in an international arena, Valle-Inclán textualized a view of Spain's past imperialist adventures from the vantage point of the ongoing Western European overseas expansion and imperialist ventures. Importantly, this Modernist period signaled a time in which Spain, unlike the majority of Europe, was *losing* most of its economic power in the New World.

A distinction has usually been made between Modernism, a cultural manifestation of Western bourgeois dissidence and *modernismo,* traditionally defined as a Spanish-American turn-of-the-century movement. In fact, however, the two phenomena are integrally related. *Modernismo* is that manifestation of "Modernism" that took place in the Hispanic world approximately between 1890 and 1910. "Modernism," on the other hand, as Raymond Williams has explained,[11] cannot be periodized by drawing upon its own internal ideologies. Nor can any national tradition provide a general theory of Modernism. The phenomenon must both be understood historically and related globally to the class (and other) conflicts at the turn of the century.

According to Williams, Modernism, which spanned the nineteenth and twentieth centuries, gradually became the avant-garde. As experimental Modernists shifted their efforts from the creation of radically innovative groupings that sought to provide their own facilities of production, distribution, and publicity, they began to mount an attack in the name of art, on a whole social and cultural order. In other words, the avant-garde, as distinct from Modernism and according to individual and national differences, set out to challenge not only specific art institutions, but the institution of Art or Literature itself. In a broad Continental framework, as well as in a Spanish context, Valle-Inclán's literary production is enmeshed in this historical conjuncture of early Modernism and the shift to the more openly confrontational avant-garde.

To speak of a peninsular avant-garde is a complicated matter for several reasons. First of all, no general agreement exists as to exactly what constitutes the Spanish avant-garde. Are we speaking about the "vanguardia literaria" ["literary vanguard"] and certain texts of Benjamín Jarnés, Rosa Chacel, and Pedro Salinas, or does the term refer to the canonical Generation of '27? What about the importance of long-ignored narratives (e.g., José Díaz Fernández's *Venus mecánica* [The Mechanical Venus] (1929) of the "vanguardia de compromiso" ["politically committed vanguard"].[12] To what extent can Valle-Inclán be considered avant-garde? Although traditionally classified as a member of the Generation of '98, his works coincide in many respects with the general European avant-garde and Spain's own "vanguardia de compromiso."[13] What is more, within Valle-Inclán's oeuvre itself, and even within some of his individual works, characteristics clearly associated with *modernismo* or with the avant-garde appear simultaneously, at times working in tandem, at times countering each other, clashing in parody or burlesque. Although this simultaneity has been well documented and discussed,[14] it has not been considered with respect to gender. Nor have the reasons that Valle-Inclán and some of his contemporaries (to the exclusion of others) have been grouped under a rubric—the Generation of '98—that blurred important political differences been fully examined.

Although the attempt to distinguish between Modernism and the avant-garde remains, at best, a complex, thorny issue, it is generally accepted that the avant-garde privileged the creative process and the sovereign individual and rejected cultural traditions. With respect to gender issues, it is important to note that, above all, the avant-garde vehemently denounced bourgeois values and social constructs, particularly the canonical middle-class family. Significantly, in Spain, as in the rest of Europe, a critique of the bourgeois family came simultaneously from the avant-garde *and* from burgeoning feminist movements.[15]

The avant-garde's attitude toward women, however, particularly in the texts of the politically committed vanguard, has yet to be studied. Susan Suleiman has clarified how the European, particularly French, avant-garde was antibourgeois but not antipatriarchal.[16] Her study shows how, in their desire to liberate male psyches, the avant-garde objectified and vilified women. Although there is no reason to suppose a more favorable situation for women in Spain, this is another area of scholarship where much work remains to be done.[17]

Feminism in Spain

The feminist movement started much later and produced fewer significant reforms in Spain than elsewhere in Europe.[18] While in Great Britain and the United States the movement got underway in the 1840s and the 1850s and made important gains by the turn of the century, no serious public debate of women's issues took place in Spain until the early decades of the twentieth century. The conservative character of Spanish feminism can be understood by considering the historical conditions that favored the rise of feminism elsewhere. The primary impulse to improve the legal and social status of women throughout Europe came from two sources: the doctrine and ideology of the French Revolution, and the economic changes produced by the Industrial Revolution. According to Geraldine M. Scanlon, the countries in which feminism flourished were industrialized and Protestant. Industrialization produced, on the one hand, a relatively strong and affluent middle class that saw the need to provide improved educational opportunities for middle-class women. On the other hand, industrialization significantly increased the number of working-class women in the labor force and hence drew attention to the issue of women in the work force and the need for protective legislation.

Since Spain's economy was primarily agricultural, women were only an insignificant part of the work force and the middle class was historically weak. In view of the intense reaction in Spain against any notion of equal rights emanating from the ideology of the French Revolution, feminism was seen as just one more of those attacks on Spanish tradition from the North, and stigmatized as "un monstruo híbrido desatado por los enemigos de la fe y de

España con el fin expreso de destruir la vida familiar . . . española." ["a monstrous hybrid let loose by the enemies of the Faith and of Spain, with the express desire of destroying Spanish family life."][19]

The principal sources of authority for antifeminism were religion and science. Religion was invoked to persuade women that their status was God's will. Those who defended women's rights, Scanlon explains, were dismissed either as heretics bent on destroying the Church, Spanish society, and the family, or as hypocrites whose real motive was to remove women from their pedestal in order to dominate them more completely by depriving them of masculine protection. If these arguments were not sufficient, "scientific evidence" was readily available to refute the feminist contention that the inferiority of women was not innate, but the product of education and culture. Nineteenth-century theses circulated widely in Spain, in such works as González Serrano's *Estudios psicológicos* [Psychological studies], González Posada's *Amistad y el sexo. Cartas acerca de la educación de la mujer* [Friendship and sex. Letters concerning the education of women], and the writing of German author P. J. Moebius about the mental inferiority of women, which was known in Spain thanks to the translation of Carmen de Burgos.[20] Women's intellectual inferiority was allegedly due to her deficient craneal construction and was therefore permanent and unchangeable.

Outside the parameters of the circle of a limited number of female writers, little questioning of traditional gender constructs took place in Spain until the Revolution of 1868. Susan Kirkpatrick documents how, in the 1840s, a small group of women, most notably Carolina Coronado and Gertrudis Gómez de Avellaneda, struggled to make a space in the Spanish literary world for the woman's voice. And, as Kirkpatrick explains, "All the . . . emotions that the ideology of the *ángel del hogar* ["angel of the hearth"] rejected as unnatural and inappropriate in women, were incorporated in one form or another in the poetic self created in Coronado's poetry."[21] However, for the majority of the population, it was the social upheaval of 1868 that brought a new sense of freedom and introduced—albeit momentarily—notions of equality. The feminist movement benefited from the new constitution, which guaranteed freedom of speech, association, education, and religion, thus reducing the power and influence of the Monarchy and the Church. It is in this context that Concepción Arenal (and others) called for very mild reforms in the education of women.[22] With the Restoration of 1875, the possibilities for enlightened bourgeois evolution in tune with Western Europe were reduced and the Church recovered most of its influence and power.[23]

The extreme polarization of politics in twentieth-century Spain further inhibited the development of a progressively oriented feminist movement similar to the movements in Great Britain and the United States. From the turn of the century, Spanish feminism was split between the extreme left and extreme right, with the far right being much more successful in recruiting women. The arch-conservatives calculated that the best way to undermine what they judged to be dangerously liberal feminism was to create a feminist movement imbued with its own traditional and conservative credo. Thus Spain witnessed the curious phenomenon of a strong, conservative "Catholic" feminism that overshadowed in importance anything done on the left. It must also be noted that, with some exceptions, the Anarchists and Socialists only halfheartedly supported feminism as a politically serious occurrence.[24] This somewhat paradoxical situation thus left the prevalent definition and control of feminism in Spain largely in the hands of upper-class conservative characters such as Doña Simplicia and her colleagues created in Valle-Inclán's *La hija del capitán* [The Captain's daughter].[25]

If Spanish feminism in the first decades of the century was primarily concerned with winning a "better" education for middle-class women so that they could more knowledgeably fortify traditional socially condoned values, it was irrelevant for the women of the underprivileged classes—the female protagonists of *Martes de carnaval*, or the mother in *Luces de bohemia* [*Bohemian Lights*] (11). For them, the feminist movement did nothing to relieve the drudgery of life in Spain in the 1920s. For many poor women, a depressed economy frequently entailed abrupt uprooting from rural habitudes and migration from the countryside to urban centers. This migration often meant fruitless searches for work and the consequent abyss of poverty or prostitution. In addition, as La Daifa laments in *Las galas del difunto* [The dead man's regalia], poor women were left to fend for themselves as male breadwinners were conscripted to fight in Spain's colonial wars. "Se fue dejándome embarazada de cinco meses. Pasado un poco más tiempo no pude tenerlo oculto, y al descubrirse, mi padre me echó al camino. Por donde también a mi me alcanza la guerra."[26] (17) ["He went off leaving me five months pregnant. After a little while I couldn't hide it anymore, and when I started to show, my father threw me out. That's how the war gets me too"].

La Daifa's poignant complaint is but one instance of the ways in which the complex gender issues at play in early twentieth-century Spanish feminism are inscribed in Valle-Inclán's texts. Although those texts do not often address such issues directly, they do engage them provocatively and continually. Valle-Inclán's constant determination not to consider aesthetics and history as distinct phenomena, his heightened sense of historical events as lived experience, and his conviction that even the most significant aspects of such experiences are embedded in individual relationships, all promise to offer important commentary on questions of gender. To read and discuss that commentary is to appreciate more fully, both the "original" context of his work, and the dialogue it can initiate with current concerns.

Notes

Thanks to Mary K. Addis for her collaboration in the early stages of this section of the Introduction, and to Noël Valis for suggestions that improved the manuscript in its final stages.

1. The use of *Generation of '98* is deliberate; this essay acknowledges the term but also seeks to break away from it and to participate in "the task of conceiving as a whole (at the expense of the old terms of the '98-modernist aporia) the beginning of contemporary Spanish literature," José-Carlos Mainer, "1900–1910: New Literature, New Politics," in *The Crisis of Institutionalized Literature in Spain*, eds. W. Gadzich and N. Spadaccini (Minneapolis: The Prisma Institute, 1988), 195. Important historiographical work on turn-of-the-century Spanish literature has been done recently by E. Inman Fox, "La generación de 1898 como concepto historiográfico," in *Divergencias y unidad: Perspectivas sobre la Generación de 98 y Antonio Machado*, ed. John P. Gabriele (Madrid: Orígenes, 1990), 23–38; Antonio Ramos-Gascón, "Spanish Literature as a Historiographic Invention: The Case of the Generation of 1898"; and José Carlos Mainer, "1900–1910: New Literature, New Politics," both in *Crisis of Institutionalized Literature in Spain*, 167–93 and 195–227, respectively.

2. For analyses that do take gender into account, see the studies of Constance Sullivan, "On Spanish Literary History and the Politics of Gender," *The Journal of the Midwest Modern Language Association* 23 (1990): 26–41; Maryellen Bieder, "The Lady Vanishes: Woman and the Canon of Twentieth-Century Spanish Literature," *ALEC* 17 (1992): 301–24; and Roberta Johnson, "The Idea(l) Women of the Generation of '98" (paper delivered at the Midwest Modern Language Association Convention, Kansas City, November 1990).

3. Valle-Inclán's first literary texts, "En Molinares" ["In Molinares"] and "Babel" appeared in 1888 in the Galician journal, *Café con gotas*. His first book, *Femeninas* [Feminine portraits], was published in 1895. See Elaine Lavaud, *Valle-Inclán: Du journal au roman (1888–1915)* (Braga: Klincksieck, 1980) for publication history of Valle-Inclán's early texts.

4. This late and reluctant ascent of the middle class in Spain, and the endurance of a feudal mentality in the Restoration, would leave an indelible mark on Spain's entrance into the twentieth century. (For elaboration of this concept see Pierre Vilar's *Crecimiento y desarrollo: Reflexiones sobre el caso español* [Barcelona, 1964]). For an additional analysis about how peninsular society was increas-

ingly polarized after the failure of the Revolution of 1868, and the relationship between economic dependency and *fin de siglo* literature, see Carlos Blanco Aguinaga, *La juventud del 98* (Madrid: Siglo Veintiuno de España, 1970), 3–38. See also the analysis of the historians working under Mañuel Tuñón de Lara on his multivolume *Historia de España* [History of Spain] who maintain that Spain entered in a serious crisis only in 1917. They posit, in volume 8, the interpretation of the 1898 "Disaster" as a national catastrophe that affected all Spaniards, to be a simplification of the oligarchy who identified the economic difficulties of certain sectors of society with the collapse of an ideology that justified their existence. See Gabriel Tortella Casares, ed. *Revolución, oligarquía y constitucionalismo (1824–1923)* (Madrid: Editorial Labor, 1986), passim.

5. For a subtle analysis of how global events registered culturally during this period, see José B. Monleón, *A Specter Is Haunting Europe: A Sociohistorical Approach to the Fantastic* (Princeton: Princeton University Press, 1990), chap. 4, "The Eclipse of Reason." For further details on what has been called the "trienio bolchevique" in Spain, see Raymond Carr, *Spain 1808–1974* (London: Oxford University Press, 1979), 479–563; M. Tuñon de Lara, *Medio siglo de cultura española* (Madrid: Editorial Tecnos, 1970), 185–221; and Manuel Durán, "Valle-Inclán, la política española en 1917 y la superación del modernismo," *La Torre* 2, no. 5 (1988): 205–10.

6. This phrase is from David Leverenz who uses it in relation to nineteenth-century American literature in *Manhood and the American Renaissance* (Ithaca and London: Cornell University Press, 1989), 1–8. For an analysis of Bradomín that elaborates the point being made here, see Michael P. Predmore, "The Dominant Mode of the *Sonatas* of Valle-Inclán: Aestheticism, Ambiguity or Satire," *Ideologies and Literature* 2, no. 1 (1987): 63–83.

7. José Salamanca, born in Málaga in 1811, was politically progressive as a young man, and participated in the Torrijos uprising in 1831. He subsequently made a fortune as a banker politician, and built railroads, palaces, and the section of Madrid that bears his name today ("Barrio de Salamanca"). More and more conservative, he was secretary of the treasury in 1847, and by the time the Revolution of 1868 took place, was conspiring against it. Valle-Inclán has the Marqués de Salamanca meeting with the "sesudos carcamales de la disidencia moderada" ["prudent decrepit old men belonging to the moderate opposition"] in the opening paragraphs of *Baza de Espadas*. (He also appears in *Viva mi dueño* [Hurrah for my master]).

8. Dru Dougherty, *Valle-Inclán y la Segunda República* (Valencia: Pre-Textos, 1986), 13. Doughtery's book is an excellent reading and documentation of Valle-Inclán's last years.

9. See Juan Antonio Hormigón, *Ramón del Valle-Inclán: La política, la cultura, el realismo y el pueblo* (Madrid: Comunicación, 1972), 273.

10. See Javier Serrano Alonso, *Ramón del Valle-Inclán, Artículos completos y otras páginas olvidadas* (Madrid: Istmo, 1987); Juan Antonio Hormigón, *Valle-Inclán: Cronologia, escritos dispersos, epistolaria* (Madrid: Fundación Banco Exterior, 1987); and Dougherty, *Un Valle-Inclán olvidado: Entrevistas y conferencias* (Madrid: Fundamentos, 1983).

11. Raymond Williams, *The Politics of Modernism—Against the New Conformists* (London and New York: Verso, 1989), 49–64, passim. Fox, Mainer and Ramos-Gascón (arts. cits.) give state-of-the-art analyses of modernism with specific relation to Spain. For the purposes of this essay, they complement and complete much of what Williams posits.

12. For a study of the politically committed vanguard, see Anthony Geist, *La poética de la Generación de 27: De la vanguardia al compromiso: 1918–1936* (Barcelona: Labor, 1989). Also valuable are Jaime Brihuega, *La Vanguardia y la República* (Madrid: Cátedra, 1989); Laurent Boetsch, *José Diaz Fernández y la otra Generación del 27* (Madrid: Pliegos, 1985); Gustavo Pérez Firmat, *Idle Fictions. The Hispanic Vanguard Novel, 1926–1934* (Durham, N.C.: Duke University Press, 1982); and the sections of *Transparent Simulacra: Spanish Fiction, 1902–1926* (Columbia: University of Missouri Press, 1988) Robert Spires devotes to the vanguard novel. None of these studies, however, deals with gender and the avant-garde.

13. That by 1920 Valle-Inclán laughed at certain tendencies in the avant-garde to exoticize the non-European female is seen in his satirical poem, "Estética de la mujer de color" ["Aesthetics of the Woman of Color"] published in August 1920 in *Grecia,* one of the most successful of the "ultraismo" (manifestation of the Spanish avant-garde) journals. (Reproduced in J. Serrano Alonso, *Ramón de Valle-Inclán, Artículos completos,* 415–16.) We quote here only four lines. "En el círculo máximo del Ecuador, / me tomó un oriental sueño de amor, / y alcancé la estética de la mujer de color. / / ¡Yo soy un doctor!" ["In the Equator's consummate circle / an Oriental dream of love possessed me / and I created the aesthetics of the woman of color / I am such an expert!"]

14. See, for example, Spires's discussions of *Sonata de otoño [Sonata of Autumn]* and *Tirano Banderas* in *Transparent Simulacra;* Serrano Alonso's introduction to "Estética de la mujer de color," *Artículos completos,* 415; Humberto Antonio Maldonado Macías, *Valle-Inclán, agnóstico y vanguardista (La lámpara maravillosa)* (Mexico: UNAM, 1980); and Iris M. Zavala, *La musa funambulesca. Poética de la carnavalización en Valle-Inclán* (Madrid: Orígenes, 1990).

15. For Williams the denunciation of "the 'bourgeois family' with all its known characteristics of property and control, is often in effect a covering phrase for those rejections of women and children which take the form of rejection of 'domesticity.' The sovereign individual is confined by any such form. The genius is tamed by it. But since there is little option of celibacy, and only a limited option (though taken and newly valued, even directly associated with art) for homosexuality, the male campaign for liberation is often associated, as in the cases of Nietzsche and Strindberg, with great resentment and hatred of women. . . . Yet at the same time the claims for human liberation, against forms of property and other economic controls, are being much more widely made . . . by women," *Politics of Modernism,* 57.

16. Susan Suleiman, *Subversive Intent-Gender, Politics and the Avant-Garde* (Cambridge and London: Harvard University Press, 1990).

17. This is an issue that Noël Valis begins to undertake for turn-of-the-century Spain in "Two Ramóns: A View from the Margins of Modernist *Cursilería*," *ALEC* 17 (1992): 325–43.

18. Geraldine M. Scanlon's study, *La polémica feminista en la España contemporánea 1868–1974* (Madrid: Siglo Veintiuno de España, 1976; also reedited Madrid: Akal, 1986) is the principal source for the following recapitulation of feminism in Spain. We quote from the 1976 edition.

19. Ibid., 6. The irony is Scanlon's.

20. Ibid., 165.

21. Susan Kirkpatrick, *Las Románticas* (Berkeley: University of California Press, 1989), 242. For an excellent reading of Coronado, see chap. 6, "Waterflower, Carolina Coronado's Lyrical Self-Representation."

22. In *La mujer del porvenir* (Madrid: 1869) Arenal advocated improved education for women because "la ignorancia relativa no era una garantía de la virtud, domesticidad u obediencia" (quoted in Scanlon, 23) ["relative ignorance was not a guarantee of virtue, domesticity or obedience"].

23. For an elaboration of the Spanish bourgeoisie before and after the Revolution of 1868, see Miguel Artola, *La burguesía revolucionaria (1808–1860);* and Miguel Martínez Cuadrado, *La burguesía conservadora (1869–1931)* vols. 5 and 6 of *Historia de España Alfaguara* (Madrid: Ediciones Alfaguara, 1976).

24. For more information on the relationship of feminism with the left in Spain see Scanlon, chap. 5, and Temma Kaplan, "Spanish Anarchism and Women's Liberation," *Journal of Contemporary History* 7, no. 2 (1971): 101–10; and "Women and Spanish Anarchism," in *Becoming Visible. Women in European History,* eds. Renate Bridenthal and Claudia Koonz (Boston: Houghton Mifflin Co., 1977), 400–21.

25. In the short dramatic piece, *¿Para cuándo son las reclamaciones diplomáticas? [When Will There Be Diplomatic Reclamations?* (1922) Valle-Inclán shows he clearly understands (and scorns) the political thrust of Spanish feminism when he (Don Serenín) equates Concepción Arenal's politics with those of Vázquez de Mella, the Carlist leader. "Emplearé la manera profética del gran Vázquez de Mella; Doña Concepción Arenal, que hoy a no dudarlo hubiera militado con nosotros en las filas de la derecha" (241) ["I will use the prophetic manner of the great Vázquez de Mella; Doña Concepción Arenal without a doubt would have marched with us today in the ranks of the right"]. Elaine Lavaud briefly discusses Valle-Inclán's dislike of organized feminism as seen in his early texts, in *Valle-Inclán: Du Journal au Roman,* 218–22. Doughtery reproduces a "Valle invective" against women originally published in *El Sol* in 1931 in *Un Valle-Inclán olvidado: Entrevistas y conferencias* (Madrid: Fundamentos, 1983), 223. Valle-Inclán's attitude toward women, however, is more complicated than his sporadic outbursts indicate. The complexity of his regard/disregard for women is evident in the essays in the present collection.

26. It is illuminating to note that, in fact, La Daifa had no legal recourse for her destitute state; Scanlon (126) points out that the law is specifically intended to protect the man, and contains the clear inference that a woman who has an illegitimate child will be considered promiscuous and, therefore, undeserving of any legal compensation.

Valle-Inclán in English:
A Selected Bibliography

One of the major tasks currently facing Valle-Inclán scholars is that of translation. The titles that follow include the principal English-language translations of his work (not listed here are several short stories that have been translated individually and published in anthologies). It must be noted that many of them are either out of print or relatively inaccessible, or both.

With respect to *Ramón María del Valle-Inclán: Questions of Gender,* individual authors are responsible for the translation of passages cited in their essays, unless noted otherwise. Whenever possible, references are to published translations. For untranslated works, the translation of titles are most frequently those suggested by Anthony N. Zahareas and Gerald Gillespie in their translation of *Luces de Bohemia,* or Verity Smith in her *Ramón del Valle-Inclán* (New York: Twayne, 1973).

* * *

Barbaric Comedies: Silver Face, Heraldic Eagle, A Romance of Wolves [*Comedias bárbaras*]. Translated by Asa Zatz. New York: Marsilio, forthcoming.

Bohemian Lights [*Luces de Bohemia*]. Translated by Anthony N. Zahareas and Gerald Gillespie. Austin: University of Texas Press, 1976.

Divine Words. A Village Tragicomedy [*Divinas palabras*]. Translated by Edwin Williams. In *Modern Spanish Theatre*, edited by Michael Benedikt and George Wellwarth, 1–78. New York: Dutton, 1968.

Divine Words [*Divinas palabras*]. Trans. T. Faulkner. London: Heineman, 1977.

The Grotesque Farce of Mr. Punch the Cuckold [*Los cuernos de Don Friolera*]. Translated by Robin Warner and Dominic Keown. Warminster, England: Aris & Phillips Ltd., 1991.

The Lamp of Marvels [*La lámpara maravillosa*]. Translated by Robert Lima. West Stockbridge: Lindisfarne Press, 1986.

The Pleasant Memoirs of the Marquis de Bradomín: Four Sonatas [*Sonata de primavera, Sonata de estío, Sonata de otoño, Sonata de invierno*]. Translated by May Heywood Brown and Thomas Walsh. New York: Harcourt, Brace, 1924. Reprint. New York: H. Fertig, 1984.

Savage Acts. Four Plays. Translated by Robert Lima. Contains *Blood Pact* [*Ligaźon*], *The Paper Rose* [*La rosa de papel*], *The Head of the Baptist* [*La cabeza del Bautista*], and *Sacrilege* [*Sacrilegio*]. University Park, Pa.: Estreno, 1993.

The Tyrant. A Novel of Warm Lands [*Tirano Banderas*]. Translated by Margarita Pavitt. New York: Henry Holt & Co., 1929.

Wolves! Wolves! A Play of Savagery in Three Acts [*Romance de lobos*]. Translated by Cyril Bertram Lander. Birmingham: C. B. Lander, 1957.

Part 2
Essays on Gender in Valle-Inclán

Valle-Inclán's "La generala": Woman as Birdbrain

CATHERINE NICKEL

Throughout Europe, the late nineteenth century was a period in which the traditional views concerning women's role in society were subject to extensive debate. Permitting a woman to be educated outside the home was particularly controversial. In nineteenth-century Spain, very few women enjoyed an extensive formal education and there were even serious doubts about a woman's inherent capacity to think and learn. As María Laffitte has accurately observed, "Es creencia dominante en el siglo XIX que la falta de capacidad orgánica y funcional de su cerebro impide a la mujer enfrentarse con las grandes tareas mentales" ["The belief that the lack of organic and functional capacity of their brains prevented women from facing up to important mental tasks was prevalent in the nineteenth century"].[1] Though such beliefs were vigorously disputed by feminists of both genders, many people were equally convinced that the size and structure of women's brains made them inherently incapable of great intellectual achievement.[2]

This popular conception of a woman's intellectual limitations is exemplified by Currita, the female protagonist of Valle-Inclán's short story, "La Generala" ["The General's Wife"].[3] Though the preliminary description of Currita emphasizes positive aspects of her exuberant nature, the narrator casually dismisses her mental capacity by comparing her mind to that of a hummingbird. Specifically, her words are described as if coming from "una cabeza inquieta y parlanchina, donde apenas se asentaba un cerebro de colibrí, pintoresco y brillante . . ." ["a restless, talkative head, on which barely alighted the sparkling, picturesque brain of a hummingbird . . ."][4]

Despite this early characterization of the protagonist as a birdbrain, however, we cannot necessarily assume that the text as a

whole supports this misogynistic viewpoint. A careful reading of
the story indicates that in "La Generala," Valle-Inclán not only
provides a vivid depiction of the popular perception of women's
abilities and role in nineteenth-century Spain, but also subtly undermines a number of prevailing cultural and literary clichés.

The plot of "La Generala" is not at all elaborate. An irrepressibly
high-spirited teenager, Currita, marries a general in his sixties and
adopts the severely demure demeanor of her new position so thoroughly that she is nicknamed "La Generala." Her husband constantly invites young Lieutenant Sandoval to dinner to provide
himself with an excuse to be allowed to smoke, and the Lieutenant
eventually follows Currita everywhere. One day, as Sandoval reads
to her from a highly romantic French novel, Currita notices that
he has dyed his mustache in an attempt to appear more virile. She
brings water to wash off the mustache and the ensuing flirtation
evolves into kissing and embracing. The General arrives unexpect-
edly and pounds on the locked door demanding to be let in. Currita
calls out that the canary has escaped and that she will open the
door as soon as Sandoval returns it to its cage. The story ends as
the General enters and sees the Lieutenant standing on a chair
beneath the bird in its cage.

The ending is quite abrupt. The sudden interruption by the husband of a young woman kissing a man in her husband's house
represents an extremely dangerous situation. The resolution of this
sort of situation (even in nineteenth-century Spanish narrative and
drama) often involves physical violence or death since the code of
honor designates the death of the transgressors as appropriate in
such cases. Despite its strong potential for a violent or at least
dramatic resolution, the narrator at this point suspends the action
to concentrate on the image of the man standing beneath a bird
singing happily in its cage. The last sentence reads, "Cuando la
puerta fué abierta, el ayudante aun permancía en pie sobre una
silla, debajo de la jaula, mientras el pájaro cantaba alegremente,
balanceándose en la dorada anilla de su cárcel" ["When the door
was opened, the adjutant was still standing on a chair, underneath
the cage, while the bird sang happily, swinging in the gilded circle
of its jail"] (273). Although the situation appears to have been de-
fused by Currita's lie about the canary escaping, the action of the
story is frozen and the reader does not know how the General
reacted or what this amorous episode had on the future lives of
those involved. Instead of a definitive resolution to the action, the
narrator offers only the tableau of a young man standing on a chair
below a canary singing in its golden cage.

This image, of course, is highly significant since it symbolically portrays the position of the protagonist in society. Lourdes Ramos-Kuethe has pointed out that the last lines of the story "evocan a Currita en su situación de esposa joven de un viejo sesentón" ["recall Currita in her situation as the young wife of an aging sixty-year-old man"],[5] but the correspondence of the woman with the bird in the gilded cage has even more far-reaching implications. The caged canary is representative not only of a young woman confined by marriage to an old man, but of the restricted circumstances of Spanish women in general. Currita, like nearly all Spanish women of the middle or upper class, was controlled by her family until she married, and thereafter largely confined to her husband's house. Like the canary which sings happily in its prison, Currita likewise displays little awareness that the price of her comfortable surroundings includes a lack of freedom.

Currita's life in a cage did not begin with her marriage to the General. Her prisoner status prior to her marriage is clearly demonstrated in the only other episode besides her flirtation with Sandoval which the narrator delineates for the reader. Informing us that Currita was educated in a convent for nobility in an old Castilian city far away, the narrator overtly marks the convent's similarity to a prison by detailing its regimented daily routine and commenting that Currita lived there "entre rejas, sin sol y sin aire" ["behind bars, without sun and without air"] (249). The description of her family's arrival to take her from the convent when she was fifteen further underscores that institution's confining nature and its contrast with the free world outside. Thus we are told that "cuando sus padres fueron por ella, para sacarla definitivamente de aquel encierro y presentarla al mundo, la muchacha creyó volverse loca. . . ." ["when her parents went to get her, to take her out of that prison forever and present her to the world, the girl thought she would go crazy. . . ."] (249). As the distressed nuns look on, she tears off her veil and happily shouts her thanks to Santa Rita for answering her prayers for liberation.

Though the description of Currita's departure from the convent is not nearly as extensive as the later episode involving her flirtation with Sandoval, both scenes depict her as a person of limited mobility and independence, and both provide a specific connection between Currita and a bird. We are told that when she departed from the convent the nuns were left behind, "llorando la partida de su periquito" ["crying over the departure of their parakeet"] (250). This is the first instance of Currita being equated with a bird under the control of others. But while this scene describes her escape from one cage (the convent), she soon enters a different but still confining environment, her husband's home. Though it may be missing the bars and cells typical of the convent, the home in nineteenth-century Spain also served to limit a woman's contacts with the outside world. A married woman of the middle or upper class was expected to devote most of her attention and energy to the care of her husband and home.[6] Like other women of her station, Currita did not entirely lack interests outside of the home, but these were supposed to be secondary to domestic concerns.

Because of the narrator's previous associations between Currita and a parakeet, and between Currita and a hummingbird, her correlation with the canary in the last scene is difficult to ignore, and a comparison between the situation of the woman and that of the bird demonstrates strong similarities. Beyond their limited physical freedom, Currita and the canary share other salient characteristics. In nineteenth-century Spanish society women were highly valued, as were canaries, for their aesthetic qualities. As Laura Mulvey has pointed out, "In their traditional exhibitionist role women are simultaneously looked at and displayed, with their appearance coded for strong visual and erotic impact. . . ."[7] Like the canary, Currita is primarily valued because she is decorative and entertaining; her looks and her ability to chatter amusingly are esteemed by both the narrator and the other characters. For women, creating a good impression by looking and sounding pleasant took precedence over individual development or independence, and society offered very little opportunity for intellectual growth or self-expression. As Sara Delamont has noted: "Ladies were imprisoned in a showy, useless existence. . . . For the first fifty years of the nineteenth century all the daughters of the upper and middle classes, except for a few in exceptional nonconformist and intellectual families, received an education which was specifically designed to be *useless*. They were carefully brought up to be ornamental and not to have any vocation."[8] Currita's convent education clearly did not prepare her for a career outside the home and she does not demonstrate any particular intellectual inclination. The ideas that she does have, are attributed to other sources, with the clear implication what she has simply adopted certain concepts and opinions without reflecting upon them. Thus the comparison of her brain to that of a hummingbird's is followed immediately by the observation that "era desarregalda y genial como un bohemio; tenía supersticiones de gitana, e ideas de vieja miss sobre la emancipación femenina" ["she was unkempt and affable like a bohemian; she had the superstitions of a gypsy and ideas of an old 'miss' about women's emancipation"] (252). Despite her "ideas de vieja miss" ["ideas of an old 'miss'"], Currita clearly does not qualify as a dedicated or enlightened feminist.

She herself points out her lack of ability in certain intellectual endeavors. For example, she asks Sandoval to read the French novel to her, claiming, "Yo he sido siempre de lo más torpe para esto de lenguas" ["I've always been hopeless when it comes to languages"] (260). Her assertion that the French is too difficult for her might simply be a ruse, but there are other indications that intellectual acuity is not Currita's strong point.

When she and Sandoval discuss literature, it becomes very evident that she prefers novels for their emotional impact rather than for their literary quality. Daudet is her favorite author and she likes the novel *Jack* because it made her cry. She shocks Sandoval by comparing the novels of Zola with those of his Spanish imitator, Eduardo López Bago.[9] This comparison allows the narrator to use Currita's attitude as an example of something portrayed as a more general phenomenon, the female who treats literature like high fashion. The assertion that "Currita sonreía con el gracioso desenfado de las señoras que hablan de literatura como de modas" ["Currita smiled with the charming assurance of women who discuss literature the sam way they discuss current fashion"] (259) clearly implies that she was not unique in her simple-minded approach to literature. In addition, her irreflexive comparison of Zola and López Bago provides another opportunity to relate her to a caged bird since it makes her very similar to the young working-class women who love to read trashy fiction and are described as "criaturas risueñas y cantarinas, gentiles cabezas llenas de peines, pero horriblemente vacías, sin más meollo que los canarios y los jilgueros que alegraban sus buhardillas" ["smiling, singing creatures, lovely heads full of combs but horribly empty, with no more brains than the canaries and linnets that brightened their garrets"] (259–60). While this comparison of the empty-headed dressmakers with canaries and linnets may reflect the opinion of Sandoval rather than that of the narrator, the correspondence between Currita and the birdbrained *modistas* reinforces the narrator's earlier observation that Currita's demagogism came from a head hardly large enough for a hummingbird's brain.

The portrayal of Currita as a woman with typically limited mental abilities, however, must be considered in the context of the story as a whole, and particularly with respect to the difference between the opinions of the narrator and the standards of the implied author. Shlomith Rimmon-Kenan has pointed out how the implied author's worldview can contain norms quite distinct from those overtly espoused by the narrator.[10] In "La Generala," the narrator's assertions cannot always be taken at face value. In some cases the narrator's statements are clearly ironic while in others they implicitly contradict the governing consciousness of the story.

Thus, though the specific parallels between females and birds in the story tend to emphasize women's lack of intellectual prowess, the ultimate correspondence between Currita and the canary points more to the limitations imposed upon her by society than to any inherent deficiency she may have. Drawing attention to the caged bird in the last scene increases the reader's awareness that Currita too lives in an environment which is comfortable but confining and that, like the canary singing happily on its golden perch, she does not consciously recognize the severe limitations she suffers. At the end of the first chapter the narrator remarks that Currita maintained her intense love of freedom until she died, but we do not know what happened to her after the episode with Sandoval, and there is no indication within the story that her fate was different from that of the canary. Thus we are left with the possibility that she never enjoyed any more liberty than the songbird which supposedly escaped but never actually left its cage.

Lou Charnon-Deutsch has accurately observed that in nineteenth-century fiction "there are constant reminders to what society deems women's most and least appropriate roles, that is, to the roles she should and shouldn't play for moral reasons and to those she is either not capable of playing or plays best."[11] In "La Generala" the conflict between traditional and modern ideas of what a woman's proper role in life should be becomes very evident in the discussion of the Romantic French novel that Sandoval reads to Currita. In this novel the protagonist, la Condesa Iseult, goes against societal norms by sacrificing herself for the man she loves. The novel's ending is described in the following terms: "Era hondamente sugestivo aquel sacrificio de la heroína, aquella su compasión impúdica, pagana como diosa desnuda" ["That sacrifice made by the heroine was highly provocative, and her compassion shameless and pagan like a naked goddess"] (266). Sandoval finds the heroine's sacrifice an admirable and impressive gesture, and is surprised that Currita would not consider imitating such a noble example. Despite her highly emotional reaction to the novel, however, Currita insists that a woman must follow instead the traditional virtues of obedience to her husband, asserting that "la principal compasión en una mujer casada, debe ser para su marido" ["the principal compassion felt by a married woman should be directed toward her husband"] (268–69). In either case, the woman must subordinate her own self-interest to the requirements of her man. Neither Currita nor Sandoval appear willing to contemplate a situation in which the woman's concerns predominate.

This overt support for female roles involving self-sacrifice, however, is undercut by the implied author since the story shows that behavior considered appropriate for women in effect diminishes their physical and intellectual freedom. The reader gradually becomes aware of the contrast between what the characters and narrator believe about women, and their actual status in nineteenth-century Spanish society. Neither the narrator nor any of the characters, for example, suggest that Currita engage in intellectually stimulating activity outside of the home. Yet her complaint of utter boredom ("¡Si supiese usted cuánto me aburro. . . ." ["If you knew how bored I get. . . ."] [257]), is clearly the result of the confining life-style she and other women in her position were expected to lead.

The distinction between the norms of the implied author and those of the narrator and characters is evident as well in the reaction to Currita's betrayal of her husband. By kissing Sandoval she not only fails to follow the norms she has previously espoused, but violates the rules pertaining to the proper behavior of a married woman in such a way that one would expect a harsh condemnation of her behavior. The reader, however, does not react with shock and horror at Currita's serious infraction of the rules since her flirtation is presented as a playful assertion of her inherent spirit of independence. Because our attention has been drawn to her lack of freedom, her flirtation with Sandoval strikes us more as a rebellion against her restrictive environment than as a morally outrageous act. The reader is less likely to condemn her amorous encounter with Sandoval since, like the caged canary, Currita is in many ways a victim of circumstances beyond her control.

Before her marriage, Currita's lively disposition frequently led her to disregard social restrictions on her behavior. Even as a child she was a nonconformist, breaking fans and insulting those around her. When she marries, however, her rebelliousness and desire for emancipation seem to disappear, and she displays the same unrestrained enthusiasm for her role as General's wife that she previously devoted to her bohemian ways. It becomes clear, though, that this is merely another role she has chosen to play. Her propensity for role playing is emphasized in the last scene. Washing the dye off Sandoval's mustache, she first pretends to be the disapproving grandmother, calling him "hijo mío" ["my son"] and scolding him for his behavior. As the narrator observes, "Era muy divertida aquella comedia, en la cual él hacía de rapaz y ella de abuela regañona" ["It was a very amusing comedy, in which he played the young boy and she the scolding grandmother."] (271). Later she abandons this role to play the part of the coquet. But though Currita's roles may change, she consistently devotes herself to playing a part, and her dependence on such roles also contributes to her status as prisoner since they are essentially limiting.

Currita is not alone though in her reliance on role models. Sandoval depends heavily on gender-based generalizations. His efforts at impressing Currita, for example, are based on his perceptions of the typical female mentality and on his conception of appropriate masculine appearance and behavior. Thus we are informed that Sandoval "creía que para enamorar a una dama encopetada, lo primero que se necesitaba era un alarde varonil en forma de mostacho de mosquetero, o barba de capuchino. . . ." ["I believed that to win the heart of a grand lady, the first thing a man needed was to make a virile impression, with the mustache of a musketeer or the beard of a Capuchin friar. . . ."] (262). His belief that masculinity is manifested by abundant facial hair impels him to dye his incipient mustache. The image of Sandoval standing before the mirror twirling the ends of his imagined mustache before setting out to engage in "batallas de amor" ["battles of love"] gently pokes fun at the young man and demonstrates how ludicrous such stereotypes are.

Sandoval also differentiates between working-class and upper-class women, convinced that their nature and behavior are essentially dissimilar. While he feels confident of his ability to seduce the brainless seamstresses enamored of pulp fiction, he hasn't a clue about how to win the affection of a woman of higher social standing. "De las fragilidades de ciertas hembras algo se le alcanzaba; pero de las señoras, de las verdaderas señoras, estaba a obscuras completamente" ["He had some inkling of the fragilities of certain females, but when it came to ladies, real ladies, he was completely in the dark"] (262). Sandoval's propensity to categorize and judge people based on gender and class supports the observation that in the nineteenth century "the purity, virtue, spirituality, gentility and refinement of bourgeois femininity was constructed in gender in contrast to the definitions of masculinity, and against the impurity, animality and work of the working-class woman."[12] Sandoval is clearly as dependent upon popular concepts of masculinity and femininity as Currita, and no more inclined to examine them closely or question their validity.

The deliberate use of the bird motif to focus on the status of the female protagonist becomes very clear if the final version of "La Generala" is compared with the much shorter earlier version titled "El canario" ["The Canary"]. The names of the characters, their personalities, and the essential points of the plot are the same in both "El canario" and "La Generala." But though both stories relate the marriage of old General Rojas to the exuberant young Currita and her subsequent flirtation with young Sandoval, the focus of the stories is different.

The narrator's primary concern in "El canario" is the effect of this inappropriate marriage on the General. Like "La Generala," "El canario" begins with a description of old General Rojas but it ends with a very short chapter missing altogether from "La Generala." The fifth and last chapter in "El canario" is set a few days after the General pounds on the door demanding that Currita and Sandoval let him in, and it describes a superior officer's reaction to General Rojas's request that Lieutenant Sandoval be transferred. The narrator quotes for us the officer's malevolent remark, "¡Ah! sí el del canario!" ["Ah! Yes, the canary man!"] (162), thus indicating that the episode between Currita and Sandoval was by now common knowledge and that the old General has, as a consequence of this liaison between the young couple, become the object of ridicule, known by the derisive epithet of "el del canario." This version of the story begins and ends with direct reference to the General and invites us to contemplate (and perhaps even sympathize with) the foolish old man who brought about his own unhappy plight by marrying someone much younger than himself.

The emphasis changes from the fate of the old man in "El canario," to that of the young woman in "La Generala." In its later incarnation, Currita's dilemma preoccupies us far more than that of the General. Chapter 5 has been eliminated entirely from "La Generala," and the story now ends with the General's entrance into the room and the view of Sandoval standing beneath the bird singing in its cage. Rather than contemplating the General's public humiliation, we are left to wonder what happens next to Currita and to ponder the correlation between her fate and that of the canary. Currita quite clearly replaces the General as the primary focus of interest in "La Generala," and the new title which refers to her, rather than to the General, reflects this new emphasis.

We know much more about Currita in "La Generala," and her personality is not only better defined but more dominant in the later version of the story. The description of her life in the convent and of what she did when liberated from its confinement, for example, is completely absent from "El canario." Also missing from "El canario" are the discussion between Sandoval and Currita about literature, and the detailed account of her reaction to the French novel Sandoval has chosen to read to her. Her conversation with Sandoval while she is washing his mustache, is also expanded in "La Generala," and it becomes clear that she remains more emotionally detached in this situation than does the young Lieutenant.

Currita is generally more active and in more control of the situation in "La Generala." In "El canario," for example, it is Sandoval who responds to the immediate crisis of the General banging at the door by inventing the story of the canary's escape, while in "La Generala" it is Currita who, despite her shock at being interrupted by her husband, manages to create and carry out this delaying tactic.

While the title "El canario" suggests that the bird motif might be more significant in this version of the story, in fact it relates only to the fate of the General, and the canary in chapter 4 constitutes the only mention of a bird in the entire piece. "El canario" contains none of the references to hummingbirds, linnets, or parakeets found in "La Generala." In "El canario" Currita is not characterized as a creature whose lively chatter could come from a hummingbird's brain, but rather has the nickname of "mona inquieta" ["restless monkey"], thus providing a comparison with another member of the animal kingdom altogether. The reference to the nuns lamenting the loss of their "parakeet," and the implied comparison of Currita to the birdbrained seamstresses, are likewise missing from "El canario."

The comparisons of women and birds in "La Generala" occur with sufficient consistency and frequency to form a significant aspect of the story's imagery. The absence of these comparisons in the version of the story which focuses on the General's fate, confirms our suspicion that the female/bird equation in "La Generala" is used to promote an awareness of the position of women in society.

"La Generala" does not specifically promote feminist goals of equality between the sexes, but it does draw attention to the limitations of prevailing beliefs concerning the nature and role of men and women. The story calls into question the characters' unquestioning emulation of socially sanctioned ideal behavior. Both Currita and Sandoval are shown to be silly by clinging to cultural norms which designate certain values and qualities as natural and innate only in women. Thus, despite the narrator's propensity to compare the brains of women to those of birds in "La Generala," the story itself exposes the superficiality of such characterizations and subtly undermines many popular nineteenth-century gender-role ideals.

Notes

Carol Maier is responsible for the translation of passages quoted in this essay.

1. María Laffitte, *La mujer en España—Cien años de su historia. 1860–1960* (Madrid: Aguilar, 1964), 25.

2. Adolfo Posada in "Progresos del Feminismo," provides an excellent overview of women's social, political, and legal status in the late nineteenth century (*La España moderna* [1897]: 91–137). His views on equal rights for women, however, contrasted with those of many of his contemporaries. This attitude was not, of course, exclusively Spanish. For example, Joan Burstyn in *Victorian Education and the Ideal of Womanhood* (New Brunswick, N.J.: Rutgers University Press, 1984), provides details of the anthropological and anatomical evidence used in nineteenth-century England to prove that women were intellectually inferior. John S. Haller, Jr. and Robin Haller in *The Physician and Sexuality in Victorian America* (New York: Norton, 1974), discuss the studies of brain weight and skull capacity used to prove that women were the physical and emotional inferiors of men. Anne Harrington notes that "in 1874, Gaetan Delaunay, a French comparative biologist,' published what was to become quite an influential medical dissertation entitled *Biologie comparée du coté droit et du coté gauche.* He argued—and his dissertation cites a number of authors who apparently concurred—that differences between the two sides of the brain were analogous to, and *responsible for,* the differences presumed to exist between male and female brains. . . . It is interesting that, once one has given the two hemispheres sexual identities, the idea of cerebral dominance becomes a rather apt metaphor for the social and economic domination of men over women in 19th-century Europe" ("Nineteenth Century Ideas on Hemisphere Differences and 'Duality of Mind,'" *The Behavioral and Brain Sciences* 8, no. 4 [1985]: 620–31).

3. "La Generala" was first published in 1892 with the title "El canario" ["The canary"]. It appeared in an expanded form with the title "La Generala" in 1895, 1903, 1907, 1909, 1918, 1922, and 1936. In contrast to the major modifications made in transforming it from "El canario" in "La Generala," the variation in the editions entitled "La Generala" consists largely of minor changes in punctuation and wording and, in some cases, the division of the work into more chapters without, however, changing the text significantly. Sandoval is sometimes described as "un caballerete de miembros delicados" ["a young dandy with delicate limbs"] (1895), or as "un teniente bonito, de miembros delicados" ["a pretty lieutenant with delicate limbs"] (1909). The version in *Historias perversas* [Perverse stories] (1907) contains no chapter divisions whatsoever, while the version in *Cofre de sándalo* [Sandalwood chest] (1909) has nine chapters and that in *La novela corta* [The short novel] (1918) has ten. Most later versions have four chapters.

The version published in 1904 with the title "Antes que te cases . . ." ["Before you marry . . ."] contains several differences from other versions (*Colección de frases y refranes en acción* ed. Juan Cuesta y Díaz, vol. 1 [Madrid: Bailly-Bailliere e Hijos, 1904] 4 vols. 1–20). Though the descriptions of the characters are basically the same, their names have been changed. The old man is not a general but a "corregidor" ["mayor"] and the young man is a student rather than a lieutenant. The old husband's discovery of the young people alone together is very similar, but a small parrot rather than a canary supposedly escapes its cage. The ending is quite distinct, with the husband returning his young wife to the convent and going off to America. The wife dies of grief and the old man returns to find only the parrot which has been taught to say "Antes que te cases/mira lo que haces" ["Before you might marry / look out and be wary"].

This version features fewer comparisons between women and birds than "La Generala." In "Antes que te cases . . ." the young woman's brain is not compared to that of a hummingbird nor is there any mention of seamstresses with heads as empty as those of their canaries or linnets. At her departure from the convent she is referred to as a parakeet and there is a specific equation of birds with freedom since she "amaba la libertad como los pájaros" ["loved freedom like the birds"] (5). Like "El canario," this story stresses the fate of the old man more than that of the young woman and does not end with the image of a caged bird. For a detailed descussion of the various editions of "La Generala" see *La ficción breve de Valle-Inclán. Hermenéutica y estrategias narrativas* by Luis T. González del Valle (Barcelona: Anthropos, 1990), 121–22.

4. Ramón del Valle-Inclán, "La Generala," *Corte de amor. Florilegio de honestas y nobles damas* (Madrid: Sociedad General Española de Librería. Opera Omnia, 1922), 247–73, 251. All references to "La Generala" will be to this edition, which González del Valle finds to be definitive (122), and will be given in parentheses in the text.

5. Lourdes Ramos-Kuethe, "El Concepto del libertinismo en la narrativa temprana de don Ramón del Valle-Inclán," *Hispanic Journal* 4, no. 2 (1983): 55.

6. María Laffitte points out the similarity between convent and wedded life for the female in her observation that "en provincias, sobre todo, se exige a la mujer la obediencia a unas reglas sociales que tienen mucho de la obediencia exigida en las órdenes religiosas" ["in the provinces, especially, the obedience to social rules exacted from women closely resembles the obedience exacted in religious orders"] (*La mujer en España,* 79). Even some of those who favored more freedom for women acceded to the popular view that a woman's proper place was in the home. For example, the moderate British feminist Frances Power Cobbe (who once wrote a letter to the editor denying that female brains were smaller and less capable) also wrote, "The private and home duties *of such women as have them* are, beyound all doubt, their first concern, and one which, when fully met, must engross all their time and energies" ("Social Science Congresses and Women's Part in Them," in *Essays in the Pursuits of Women* [London: Emily Faithfull, 1863]).

7. Laura Mulvey, "Visual Pleasure and the Narrative Cinema," *Screen* 16, no. 3 (1975): 11.

8. Sara Delamont, "The Contradictions in Ladies' Education," *The Nineteenth-Century Woman. Her Cultural and Physical World,* eds. Sara Delamont and Lorna Cuffin (New York: Barnes & Noble, 1978), 135.

9. Alphonse Daudet's 1876 novel *Jack* was known for its sentimentality. López Bago's unsuccessful efforts at writing in the style of Zola are acknowledged in the observation that in his novels, "se nota el deseo de imitar a Zola, no consiguiéndolo sino en sus defectos" ["his desire to imitate Zola is obvious, although

he is successful only with respect to Zola's defects"] (*Enciclopedia Universal Ilustrada,* vol. 31 [Barcelona: Espasa-Calpe, 1928], 123).

10. Shlomith Rimmon-Kenan, *Narrative Fiction. Contemporary Poetics* (London and New York: Methuen, 1984), 87.

11. Lou Charnon-Deutsch, "Gender-Specific Roles in *Pepita Jiménez,*" *Revista de Estudios Hispánicos* 19, no. 2 (1985): 88.

12. Deborah Cherry and Griselda Pollock, "Woman as Sign in Pre-Raphaelite Literature: A Study of the Representation of Elizabeth Siddall," *Art History* 7, no. 2 (June 1984): 218.

The Novel as Feminine Entrapment: Valle-Inclán's *Sonata de otoño*

NOËL VALIS

A reading of the *Sonatas* (1902–5) is often an exercise in image-hunting: or expressed another way, it is a re-creation, on Valle-Inclán's terms, of the process of evocation. But in remaking the poet's images, the reader is beguiled by the hypnotic current of the words themselves, the narcissistic reflection of the aesthetic object. Deceived by the surface (or image making) of Valle-Inclán's art, we interpret the text as an act of homage to the cult of the author, metonymically (and ironically) embodied in the central figure of the Marqués de Bradomín. Indeed, the emphasis on memory, paramount in all the *Sonatas,* reinforces the notion of individual authorship, both within and outside the text. As an author of deeds, Bradomín extends his feats in time and space through "the cult of memory" ["el culto de los recuerdos"] just as the words on a white sheet of paper are made to last mnemonically by the process of repetition, alliteration, assonance, and adjectival expansion.

But this act of individual assertion conflicts with an older tradition, based on collective memory—the oral capacity for myth-making. Such distinctions are especially pertinent in *Sonata de otoño* [*Sonata of Autumn*] (1902), which can be considered as paradigmatic of the *Sonata* form. In this essay I will argue that Valle-Inclán, by endeavoring to surpass the temporal boundaries of narration through the creation of a mythic patterning of events and characters, paradoxically ends up fashioning a verbal labyrinth from which neither reader nor creator can extricate himself. The birth of the novel seems to make inevitable not only the death of the author, but of narration itself. Trapped in this pseudobiologic reductiveness—writing as an ending—Valle-Inclán will attempt to escape the temporal dimensions of authored fictions (i.e., the nineteenth-century realist novel) by returning to the prescriptural origins of storytelling, to myth itself. In this, ultimately, he fails. What he does do, instead, is place myth—ironically, the myth of the dying author—at the very heart of his discourse, by turning it into the supreme verbal artifact.

Most significantly, the mythic narrative frame which encloses this central discursive motif and even threatens to devour it ultimately, is largely conceived in feminine terms. What I hope to show is how Valle-Inclán's apparent acceptance and championing of myth as a modern response to conventional authored fictions, meets with his own resistance in the form of an opposing, gender-inhabited structure. Valle-Inclán, in an adversarial stance, will attempt to eradicate the feminine in his text by interiorizing the Other within himself as Bradomín. Like an actor, he will assume the feminine role for the purpose of submerging its presence. But this feminine alterity, or trace, will persist, dispersed paradoxically in its authorial guise throughout the work. Thus the struggle with the feminine will become a textual process in which author and work compete for verbal preeminence. My role as reader in this will be to provide a deconstructing feminist critique of the author's will to make of writing the supreme sexual act.[1] It is this tension between the feminizing impulse of unauthored, archaic storytelling and the masculine urge to reproduce self, and therefore history, which provides the basis for my dis-authorized version of *Sonata de otoño* as a creative failure. A failure, that is, only because the writer could not forget he was an author, and insisted on saving not the text, but himself, as the primary aesthetic object. The question which then suggests itself is: Was he worth saving?

Why Valle-Inclán fails—and magnificently so—is I think, of especial interest to us as readers and critics. His inability to create pure dream literature in the four *Sonatas*—the kind of writing which characterizes much of *modernismo* and the fin de siècle period as a whole—can be attributed not only to the corrosive satiric-ironic bent informing his style and vision, but to something else which is a driving force behind it. That force, I would suggest, is fear (to which I will return). To write successful dream literature one must believe in the illusion of the dream, or at least create the illusion of the illusion. But to do this the writer has to forgo his own life. He is forced to renounce biography and slip into the uchronic, mythy space of a motionless writing present. The re-emergence of myth in modern literature posits the disappearance of the authorial ego, for the ego, with its beginning, middle, and end, signifies mortality. The intimate and traditional connections between death and writing, as Michel Foucault has observed, have undergone a radical process of subversion. "The work," he writes,

"which once had the duty of providing immortality, now possesses
the right to kill, to be its author's murderer. . . ."[2] He is talking
about, of course, the Barthian contention that the author dies when
writing begins.[3] Yet one could argue that even when the author
vanishes, he does not surrender his immortality. If anything, he
spreads the notion about by creating a deathless text, one which
exists by virtue of the verbal sacrifice the authorial persona sustains, inflicting self-dismemberment into a thousand different
pieces, or words.

The avoidance of death in literary Arcadia—the blank page verbally inseminated—is as much an impossibility as escape from that
ego to which death always returns and, indeed traditionally, with
which it is identified, as Erwin Panofsky has beautifully illuminated.[4] The conflating of creative self and death, which I have
deliberately fostered here in alluding to the phrase, "Et in Arcadia
ego," could, however, be viewed as a textual decoy, drawing the
reader's attention away from authorial presence and deceiving
her—once again—into believing that she is reading words and not
the utterances of a human being. It may also be that we as readers
act as accomplices and willingly sacrifice the author in order to
assuage the demands of textual autonomy. What then can the
author do? He makes use of what any good strategist in defensive
tactics would advise: camouflage and deconcentration. Such devices decenter the notion of a single authorial presence through
dispersion and disguise, creating the effect of a plurality of writing
selves. The author thus proliferates, making it impossible to kill
him off. In this sense, the author doesn't simply make his final
appearance, but like any good actor with a meaty role, dies over
and over to the delight of his public. Unlike the American thespian
of the last century, Joseph Jefferson, who made a lifelong career
out of playing Rip Van Winkle, the author cannot exclaim at last,
"Then I am dead, and that is a fact."[5] He is not dead, and that is
not a fact.

I realize I have said several apparently contradictory things here,
not to mention the perilous mixing of the belicose and the bus-
kined. But the alternative is to simplify the relationship between
author-text-reader. As readers we blatantly adore the egotistic
qualities of writing as authorship, resuscitating the god-figure at
will each time we pick up a work with *that* name inscribed upon
it. But at the same time we attempt to annihilate the actor-author
when we collude with the text, turning it into a field of contention,
and the author into the adversary. Thus what occurs on paper and
in our heads is always a subtle form of maneuvering between

author-reader on the one hand, and author-text on the other, to establish priority. By the very act of reading we assume an authorial presence, one which, in the end, must be overcome in order to reach the text.

But in the process we continually run into the author richly and cunningly attired in a variety of verbal (dis)guises, all of which are ironically predicated on the lack of a subject. The author then is not a "fact," or thing *(factum)* within the text, and so cannot really die, even when writing as a linguistic and cultural code begins. He is too busy appropriating the text. Indeed, the Barthian concept is a paradoxical one, for as Patricia Waugh says, "The more the author appears, the less he or she exists."[6] The author's fictional status is always equivocal, since we are really talking about degrees of persuasiveness in our notions of authorial *splendeurs et misères.* As necessary points of reference acting for the reader, the author ends up reproducing himself, thus preempting the text.

Noticeable is my intentional use of the masculine pronoun here, first, because *Sonata de otoño* is plainly a male-authored text. But insistence on such gender preference also makes clear that we are dealing with a tradition, the dominant literary mode in which writing is always a test of the author's powers, of his ability to perform histrionically and otherwise. A nonperformance can be fatal. The god would have failed to make his appearance. This is precisely the threat posed in *Sonata de otoño.* Earlier I mentioned fear as a *force majeure* behind the ambiguities and instability of the *Sonata* form. Such insecurity plays upon an anxiety of authorship. By that I am not referring to the Bloomian angst of influence, but to the terror of authorial emasculation, the loss of the Verbum as a sign of sexual identity. Yet the first thing we notice about Valle-Inclán's text is the obviousness of its author.

Authorship in *Sonata de otoño* assumes the immediate shape of an aging and narcissistic Don Juan, the Marqués de Bradomín. This statement may very well offend, since clearly I am committing trespass against modern literary analysis by equating the first-person narrator to his very creator, the author (but see n. 3). But because we can never get at an author directly in his work,[7] we must discover him in his various metaphoric disguises. What startles us in the *Sonatas,* however, is the patent role-playing attached to the Bradomín creation. If the Marqués is Valle-Inclán's alter ego, then it is a bravura performance of the first rank. For like that damned elusive Pimpernel, we seek him everywhere except where he actually is, hiding in plain view. What I propose then is to take Valle-Inclán for what he ostensibly is, and to play out the performance for what it is worth, by reading his lines for him. This interpretation is doubtless suspect, for I will inevitably read him like a woman. Stated another way, regrettably, I shall be forced to point out his inadequacies. And it is precisely these weaknesses of his authorial persona which Valle-Inclán has taken such pains to cloak behind the shallow facade of a decaying Don Juan. Parody—the punctured myth of the dominant male—provides a protective screen behind which that same male is permitted nevertheless to strut and preen before an admiring audience of his peers and their women.

That the god figure as the source of sexual and creative authority remains essentially untouched, despite Valle-Inclán's tongue-in-cheek attitude, becomes more understandable if we place the *Sonatas* within the context of late nineteenth-century refined erotica. Like erotic art of the same period (and earlier), such writing is designed for male needs and desires. Until quite recently, no art existed which reflected a woman's sexual viewpoint. "The very term 'erotic art,'" Linda Nochlin points out, "is understood to imply the specification 'erotic-for-men.'"[8] The woman's role as art object is to puff up, to raise the male ego even as she is being flattened by brush or pen. One need only think of the physical passivity and lack of facial expression in most nudes, signs of an absent sexuality. Desire remains external to the canvas, but the strength of that desire is powerfully suggested by being transmuted into the creative act. Pygmalion, as man and as artist, will have his Galatea. In other words, authorship—like the underlying notion of possession—is supreme.[9]

This refusal to give up the author is, I believe, fundamental to our understanding of the *Sonatas* as narcissistic texts. For—ironically—even when the writer tries to kill himself off, his authorial image keeps on dying, with no end in sight. When the narrator finally exclaims, after Concha's death, "I wept like an ancient god as his cult is extinguished!" ["Lloré como un Dios antiguo al extinguirse su culto!"],[10] we wait in vain for that last flicker. But Valle-Inclán has already suggested his own sequel two lines before. "Would I again find another pale princess, with sad, enchanted eyes, who would admire my magnificence forever? Faced with such a doubt, I wept" ["Volvería a encontrar otra pálida princesa de tristes ojos encantados que me admirase siempre magnífico? Ante esta duda lloré"].

Concha's status as a sexual object, made for and by man, is in this instance unequivocal. She has been fashioned to please her owner-artist in all ways, and in so doing, to justify his talent. In dying, Valle-Inclán suggests, she also endangers his very existence. Without Concha, there would be no Bradomín. But without Bradomín, there would be no text. As we shall see, however, her death conceals something which had posed an even larger peril to Bradomín-Valle-Inclán, the artist lover: her very femaleness, which literally and figuratively will entrap him. In analogous fashion, the text itself will prove to be a labyrinth of female making, designed to unman by imprisoning the artist in his own words. In pursuing the female form, Bradomín ends up making love to yet another body, the text itself as evocation, that is, as a reflection of the memoirist's sexual capacities. In truth, he is making love to himself.

Approximately then, *Sonata de otoño* begins and ends with a dying body. The opening paragraph, like the ending, is written as a final exhalation.

> "My beloved, I am dying and wish only to see you!" Oh, that letter of poor Concha's went astray a long time ago. It was full of yearning and sadness, perfumed with violets and an old love. Without finishing it, I kissed it. She hadn't written me for nearly two years. . . . The three emblazoned sheets carried the trace of her tears, and preserved it for a long time.

> ["Mi amor adorado, estoy muriéndome y sólo deseo verte!" Ay! Aquella carta de la pobre Concha se me extravió hace mucho tiempo. Era llena de afán y de tristeza, perfumada de violetas y de un antiguo amor. Sin concluir de leerla, la besé. Hacía cerca de dos años que no me escribía. . . . Los tres pliegos blasonados traían la huella de sus lágrimas, y la conservaron largo tiempo.]

And a few lines later: "I had always hoped for the resurrection of our love. . . . It was the chimera of the future, the sweet chimera asleep at the bottom of blue lakes, where the stars of Destiny are reflected. . . . Poor Concha was dying!" ["Yo siempre había esperado en la resurrección de nuestros amores. . . . Era la quimera del porvenir, la dulce quimera dormida en el fondo de los lagos azules, donde se reflejan las estrellas del Destino. . . . La pobre Concha se moría!"] (121). Resurrection and extinction, the two principal rival motifs running throughout the *Sonatas,* shape the stylistic qualities of this beginning as well. In four sentences Valle-Inclán moves from an unsituated present (Concha's letter) to a remote preterite ("se me extravió hace mucho tiempo"), passing through a timeless imperfect ("era [not *estaba*] llena de afán . . ."), and thus into the narrative present ("Sin concluir de leerla, la besé"). The result of such temporal playing around is a confused chronos: a past wherein the narrator-lover kisses a nonexistent letter, or is it?

Significantly, these remembrances begin with a letter, that is, with writing upon writing in an attempt to overcome the ravages of time. The novel mix of tenses and the juxtaposition of differing narrative planes are effective rhetorical devices furthering the notion of textual supremacy. Thus it should come as no surprise to read right after this of the material existence of Concha's letter. The story, then, is put into motion by the act of writing itself. But more importantly, Concha's words have already been appropriated—in the act of reading—by the narrator-lover as *his* story. Without even bothering to finish reading her letter, he completes the rest of the text, leaving Concha's view of things a mere fragment.

But *Sonata de otoño* is as much Concha's story as the narrator's, we exclaim. Not so. It would be helpful at this point to examine the kind of character typology Valle-Inclán has created in Concha. On a first reading her consumptive state may strike us as little more than a late decadent manifestation of a well-known literary tradition. But that tradition of dying Camilles and Violettas is an extraordinarily vigorous one, reflecting more than a medical reality of the last century. Images of disease, real and fancied, are closely and repeatedly linked to the notion of womanhood as the unwell and weaker sex.[11] Illness kept woman in her place. Thus Concha's physical passivity mirrors a more radical quiescence, one which is in part responsible for her death.

It is of course quite true that the parodic overtones of Concha as the quintessential yielding woman are unmistakable. Both Bradomín and Concha are highly self-aware characters, playing out with relish, the traditional roles of dominant male/submissive female. But parody can not only disguise a serious purpose, it can also double back against itself, rewriting the text by giving the reader the option of choosing not simply an alternative model, but both simultaneously. Of course, in the process the original and its successor are both subjected to radical changes through ironic reflexivity.

Thus Bradomín/Valle-Inclán may trivialize Concha's status (as much as his own) by exploiting her typology and appropriating her very words, but he cannot do without her as text and as sex. Characteristic and highly revealing of such ambivalence is his treatment of her as an aesthetic icon. "Concha's neck flowered from her shoulders," he writes, "like an ailing lily, her breasts were two white roses scenting an altar, and her arms, their slenderness delicate and fragile, seemed like the handles of an amphora surrounding her head" ["El cuello (de Concha) florecía de los hombros como un lirio enfermo, los senos eran dos rosas blancas aromando un altar, y los brazos, de una esbeltez delicada y frágil, parecían las asas del ánfora rodeando su cabeza"] (135). The effect of such ecstatic contemplation is to turn Concha into a verbal objet d'art, an altar/amphora before which the adoring male viewer may feast his eyes or quench his thirst. He even dresses her like an image. "I dressed her with the loving, religious care that devout ladies use in dressing the images for which they are maids-of-honor" ["Yo la vestía con el cuidado religioso y amante que visten las señoras devotas a las imágenes de que son camaristas"] (129). This aesthetic-sensual worship of the female form, a familiar feature in pre-Raphaelite painting and fin de siècle literary texts alike, on the one hand pays quasi-spiritual obeisance to the power of woman. But on the other hand, such iconization of the feminine transforms her into a statuesque object, into text as sculpture, shaped lovingly if possessively by her owner-artist. To demonstrate that ownership Bradomín as Valle-Inclán—i.e., as metaphoric author—gives her the sort of permanence all art objects possess when they are hung on the wall, set at the proper angle on the table, or encased, enframed, and ensconced. In a word, he immobilizes her. And in so doing, once more he dominates not only Concha, but the text itself, by laying hands on word and thing, caressing them into being. The object—woman, text—has no existence outside the subject. The author then, in the guise of Bradomín, has become objectified as the internal lover to his own work.

But it would be a serious misinterpretation to see Concha merely as the victim of male predatoriness, for it is evident that she herself exerts a special authority over Bradomín. As Nina Auerbach notes of the Victorian period, beneath the image of woman as self-sacrificing domestic angel, there exists another myth, the myth of woman as powerful demonic being, endowed with a magical vitality which is essential to the way our very culture functions.[12] In *Sonata de otoño* the feminine as original source is also revealed negatively through metaphors of entrapment. The image will culminate in the nightmarish scene when Concha's hair is caught on a doorlatch as the Marqués, panic-stricken after fatal lovemaking, attempts to return the lifeless body to her own room. Valle-Inclán prepares us well for this moment by setting up first an entangling network of images suggesting intimate associations between Concha's long hair and the web of a spider. Hair as an erotic motif is

of course nothing new, but Valle-Inclán makes particularly deli-
cious use of it. "Amorous and obliging, [Concha] tossed the sweet-
smelling veil of her hair over me. I inhaled, with my face submerged
as in a holy fountain. . . ." ["Amorosa y complaciente, echó (Concha) sobre mí el velo oloroso de su cabellera. Yo respiré, con la
faz sumerigida como en una fuente santa. . . ."] (133). And then
that sublime seriocomic instant when her tresses become a literal
snare for Bradomín.

> At a doorway, her tragic, wavy hair became entangled. I groped in the
> dark to loosen it. I couldn't. It became more and more entangled. My
> hand, frightened and clumsy, was trembling over it, and the door was
> opening and closing, creaking interminably. With horror I saw that day
> was breaking. Vertigo overcome me and I pulled. . . . I had to yank
> brutally until her scented, beloved hair was torn away. . . .
>
> [En una puerta, su trágica y ondulante cabellera quedó enredada. Palpé
> en la oscuridad para desprenderla. No pude. Enredábase más a cada
> instante. Mi mano, asustada y torpe, temblaba sobre ella y la puerta
> se abría y se cerraba, rechinando largamente. Con espanto vi que ra-
> yaba el día. Me acometió un vértigo y tiré. . . . Tuve que tirar bru-
> talmente hasta que se rompieron los queridos y olorosos cabe-
> llos. . . .] (175–76)

Through the web of sexual entanglement, Concha's very femininity
has drawn Bradomín deeper and deeper into the center of her
weaving, imprisoning him within the fine-spun threads of her labyrinth. It is no coincidence that the labyrinth is psychologically
linked to the image of the spider's web. "Because of its dangerous
character," Erich Neumann remarks, "the labyrinth is also frequently symbolized by a net, its center as a spider."[13] Readers will
remember that Concha has a dream of being lost in a labyrinth, an
experience which is given a facile and unconvincing explanation
drawn from conventional Catholicism. But we are also given a
setting in which garden mazes, endlessly long corridors, protracted
hallways of mirrors, and receding interiors proliferate. Concha
does not simply dream a labyrinth, she lives in one. Thus when
she suddenly freezes over the dramatically prophetic appearance
of a spider in a dark corridor, we know we are reading a key
moment. "I saw a black spider!" she exclaims. "It was running
along the floor! It was enormous!" ["He visto una araña negra!
Corría por el suelo! Era enorme!"] (162)

The meaning of Concha's frightening encounter becomes even
clearer if we situate it within a specific literary tradition. For this
scene is reminiscent of an earlier, more naturalistic rendering of a

similar moment in Pardo Bazán's *Pazos de Ulloa* [*The House of Ulloa*] (1886), when the victimized and enfeebled Nucha espies "a spider of huge dimensions, a monstrous belly swaying on eight hairy stilts" ["una araña de desmesurado grandor, un monstruoso vientre columpiado en ocho velludos zancos"].[14] Later, the chaplain Julián will experience a nightmare in which Saint George in person violently stabs into the mouth of a dragon-spider. In the dream he feels the lance pierce his very rib cage, as though he himself were the monster under attack. But of course what is monstrous is his repressed sexuality, which must remain concealed before Nucha's desirability. Yet a third Galician writer, Torrente Ballester, would also exploit the intimate connections between the threatening nature of feminine sexuality and the image of the spider in *La isla de los jacintos cortados* [The island of floating hyacinths] (1980). When one of the three Fates—appropriately, "la Muerta"—is shot in the face, Torrente writes, "The face behind the face was revealed to be nothing more than the dark nest of arthropods: there, were jammed in, minute and enormous, all kinds, intermediate also, thousands of spiders" ["Quedó al descubierto la trascara, que no era más que el nido oscuro de los artrópodos: allí se apretujaban, mínimas y enormes, de todo, intermedias también, miles de arañas"].[15] One conclusion is inescapable: the kiss of the spider woman is fatal.

Thus too will the Marqués discover what lies in the center of the labyrinth. In the last scene as he stands on the balcony, he sees that "in the center of the labyrinth, a band of doves was circling, and out of the cold, blue sky a kite with long black wings descended, watching closely" ["en el fondo del laberinto, revoloteaba un bando de palomas, y del cielo azul y frío descendía avizorando un milano de luengas alas negras"]. He shoots the kite, which falls bloodied into the maze. If death is found in the heart of the labyrinth, it is because he has already felt it pulling at him like the snarls of Concha's hair. He has seen it staring at him in endless mirrors. "As I crossed in front of the mirrors I closed my eyes in order not to see myself" ["Al cruzar por delante de los espejos cerraba los ojos para no verme"] (175). Thus we cover up mirrors in the house or turn them to face the wall when someone dies, the soul having passed through to the other side.[16] The mirror in *Sonata de otoño* partakes of the labyrinthine, as an equally faithful duplication of reality's deceptions and ultimate, central truths.[17]

But like Tennyson, Valle-Inclán also finds enchantment in mirrors. "In the mirrors' depths the room was prolonged into a dream as in an enchanted lake" ["En el fondo de los espejos, el salón se

prolongaba hasta el ensueño como en un lago encantado"] (141).
"But in her web she still delights / To weave the mirror's magic
sights" are lines from "The Lady of Shalott" (1832).[18] With the
onset of sudden passion for Lancelot, "out flew the web and floated
wide; / The mirror cracked from side to side."[19] My purpose here
in quoting the Victorian poet is not to show literary provenance,
but to stress the connections between the web and the mirror,
between the labyrinthine and the specular which should also contribute to our understanding of *Sonata de otoño.* The weaver herself provides the link, creating the fictions—"a magic web with
colours gay"—which sustain her life, make it whole, until the advent of the shallow if brilliantly accountered knight unwittingly
shatters the illusion. The mirror, which reflects a secondhand image of the real world, also provides indirectly the means to fix that
reality through memory; and the memory is woven into the
threaded surface of the web. The mirror and the web thus become
symbols of artistic craft, as ways of connecting perception-mem-
ory-transcription. It is a threefold process in which the weaver
resurrects the transitory specular image threatened with extinction, that is, forgetfulness. The result is a weave which, textually,
surpasses the weaver. For as we know, the Lady of Shalott dies,
and the only thing remembered about her is her lovely face. "But
Lancelot mused a little space; / He said, 'She has a lovely face; /
God in his mercy lend her grace, / The Lady of Shalott.'"[20] Though
Lancelot may have the last word, he is not, however, the author
of his acts. Indeed it would be difficult to locate authorship within
this text, because as the author from without makes quite clear,
what the Lady of Shalott does, simply, is weave her web. He and
the reader provide the words for her. It is the story that counts.

Stated another way, Tennyson, like Valle-Inclán as we shall see,
harks back in this poem to a prescriptural tradition in which spinning, weaving, and similar womanly activities were the focal points
where oral storytelling took place. "I like to imagine," writes
Nancy Willard,

> that I have found my way to that room where stories as well as wool
> are spun. By the light of a candle an old woman is spinning, but it isn't
> wool she winds on her wheel. She is spinning straw into gold, so I
> know that this is the lady whom Hans Christian Andersen called his
> muse, his wise woman, the bringer of fairy tales. Her name is
> Anonymous.[21]

This collective spinning consciousness, which feminist criticism sees as crucial to our understanding of the relationship between art and the feminine, is also woven into Valle-Inclán's text. For critics like Mary Daly, Patricia Klindienst Joplin, and Carolyn Heilbrun, "the voice of the shuttle," though uniquely feminine, is all too frequently taken over by male authors.[22] Weaving is then viewed as subsequent feminine resistance, and a woman's silence as a manifestation of male supremacy.[23] Thus, seen in this light, the anonymity to which Willard refers, cloaks the bitter truth of feminine irrelevance. Nameless, she weaves a silent web, lacking the identity an author possesses. Some would even say she lacks language.[24]

If women have a voice in *Sonata de otoño,* it is through the discourse of preliterate modes of speaking and thinking. Feminine discourse threads its ways into Bradomín's memoirs, simultaneously resisting and assisting the process of literary reification of the feminine. Bradomín, we recall, doesn't need more than one sentence of Concha's letter. And later, when she shows him another letter full of recriminations from his mother, he calmly burns it. He pictures her in devout solitude, "spinning on her distaff of holy wood, sweet-smelling and noble. Upon her faded lips hovered a trembling prayer always" ["hilando en su rueca de palo santo, olorosa y noble. Sobre sus labios marchitos vagaba siempre el temblor de un rezo"] (163). This spinning image is sustained throughout the text (see, e.g., 125, 142, and 165). Valle-Inclán will also exploit the opposite effect, *el deshilar,* when an old servant and Concha's daughters pick apart, thread by thread, a large sheet of coarse linen called a *lenzuelo* (159–60). "The two girls applied themselves to unraveling the sheet. . . . Concha and Isabel were whispering to each other. . . . In their childish laps, within the luminous circle of the lamp, the lint was slowly forming a simple bundle" ["Las dos niñas se aplicaron a deshilar el lenzuelo. . . . Concha e Isabel secreteaban. . . . (S)obre los regazos infantiles, en el círculo luminoso de la lámpara, iban formando lentamente las hilas, un cándido manojo"] (160). As the *hilas,* or lint, drop into the girls' laps, little by little they begin to make connections, to form that "cándido manojo." It is a fitting backdrop to the "warm and fluid murmur of feminine conversation" ["cálido y fácil murmullo de la conversación femenina"] which then takes place between Concha and Isabel, with Bradomín the complaisant listener-observer to their talk. "It was a long and whispering commentary," he says, "on forgotten and remote kin" ["Era un largo y susurrador comento acerca de la olvidada y luenga parentela"].

Here we see how spoken language, even when indirectly re-

ported, forms the substratum, the underlying fabric of a highly
sophisticated and self-conscious piece of writing. In other passages
Valle-Inclán stresses the vigor and immediacy of vernacular, un-
written expression (123; 137, e.g.). This implied diglossia, or shuttle play between the oral and written registers of language, inevitably brings me back to spinning. I pick up a modern, bilingual
dictionary and read this definition of *hilar:* "to spin; to reason (of
discourse) to connect." Appropriately then, Concha and Isabel will
talk about family relationships, linking even the most remote member of their tribe to the rest of them. The moment may seem trivial.
It is not. For the best stories are about families.

Everyone in *Sonata de otoño* is related to everyone else. Even
the servants, devoted and unquestioningly loyal, are "family" in
the same way the incomparable Françoise is in Proust's *Combray.*
"Candelaria, Concha's nurse," we read,

> who like all the old servants knew stories and genealogies of her mas-
> ter's family, at one time used to tell us the legend of Captain Alonso
> Bendaña the way the old nobiliaries that nobody reads anymore tell
> it. Besides, Candelaria knew that two black dwarfs had carried the
> Captain's body off to hell. It was traditional that in the Brandeso family
> the men were cruel and the women pure of heart!

> [Candelaria, la niñera de Concha, que como todos los criados antiguos
> sabía historias y genealogías de la casa de sus señores, solía en otro
> tiempo referirnos la leyenda del Capitán Alonso Bendaña como la re-
> fieren los viejos Nobiliarios que ya nadie lee. Además, Candelaria sabía
> que dos enanos negros se habían llevado al infierno el cuerpo del Ca-
> pitán. Era tradicional que en el linaje de Brandeso los hombres fuesen
> crueles y las mujeres piadosas!] (169)

But Bradomín's mother also knows "the family history." ["la historia de todos los linajes"] (148). And Concha herself is a spinner
of tales. When Bradomín asks why she calls her servant "Florisel,"
she replies, "Florisel is the page a certain, inconsolable princess
falls in love with in a story" ["Florisel es el paje de quien se ena-
mora cierta princesa inconsolable en un cuento"] (140). All of these
women are storytellers, and whether or not they deal directly with
familial themes, their stories remain "all in the family," committed
as they are to the retention through oral repetition of this collec-
tively authored saga. Thus when Bradomín questions Concha further on the origin of Florisel's name, he asks: "Whose story?"
["Un cuento de quién?"] And she answers, "Stories don't belong
to anyone" ["Los cuentos nunca son de nadie"] (140).

It is evident that Concha's "culto de los recuerdos" is of a different nature from Bradomín's. For him, the appointed "chronicler of the family," or "cronicón de la familia" (160), the stories he hears, the story he is in, can only be remembered through writing.[25] The role of chronicler is to record events in history. Time becomes of consequence, and memory must therefore be fixed in some permanent fashion. But the storyteller can repeat the tale on every possible occasion, thus rescuing her words from oblivion, or death. Indeed, as Walter Benjamin remarks, "Death is the sanction of everything that the storyteller can tell. He has borrowed his authority from death. In other words, it is natural history to which his stories refer back."[26] With the rise of the modern novel (and modern society) death becomes a fearful thing, to be avoided at all costs. It signals an unacceptable ending with which the act of writing is forced to concur in despair. The shroud of writing accompanies the individual author everywhere, hence the urge to self-perpetuate, to possess at least the words themselves. The desire for domination—sexual and textual—in Bradomín the memoirist, is an implicit admission of his fear of death.

But in Concha we see how every one of her gestures, her words, are predicated on the knowledge of impending death. As death is in the midst of life, so Concha herself figures at the center of the labyrinth. For Bradomín then, whether he knows it or not, she is the heart of memory, linking past to present, remembering and retelling, as he says, "the most distant things" ["las cosas más lejanas"] (142). This "re-discovering hidden threads of connectedness," in Daly's words, forms part of woman's initiation "in the mysteries, threading her way through the Dreadful labyrinthine ways. . . ."[27] But, as we have seen, this "labyrinthe way" when viewed patriarchally, also becomes a frightening motif of disorder and confusion,[28] a convergence of the threads entwining Concha's death and Bradomín's male hysteria, to culminate in Concha's entangling hair, that web of feminine grace and power which Valle-Inclán has used euphemistically throughout for her undeniable sexuality (175).

Yet nothing of her remains, Bradomín says, except

a wave of perfume. That essence which Concha poured on her hair and which survives her! Poor Concha! She could leave nothing of her passage through this world except a trail of aromas. But is the palest and purest of lovers anything more than a small, divinely enameled bottle full of aphroditic and nuptial essences?

[una onda de perfume. Aquella esencia que Concha vertía en sus ca-
bellos y que la sobrevive! Pobre Concha! No podía dejar de su paso
por el mundo más que una estela de aromas. Pero acaso la más blanca
y casta de las amantes ha sido nunca otra cosa que un pomo de divino
esmalte, lleno de afroditas y nupciales esencias?] (176)

After reading this, we can hardly be surprised that Valle-Inclán
chose to call her Concha and that he never refers to her as María
de la Concepción. Her bivalvular name, with its wonderful mythic
and popular connotations of sexual enclosure and entrapment,
must have delighted a large number of Valle-Inclán's readers.[29]
And how in keeping with the innuendo of refined erotica is her
final appearance as an aphrodisiac.

Poor Concha! First to be subjected to the indignities of reification, only to be vaporized in the end. Yet this feminine trace—this
nameless aroma lingering like sky writing—is precisely what Valle-
Inclán cannot make disappear in *Sonata de otoño*. He even sets
up a patriarchal myth for explaining family origins to counter the
centrality of the feminine labyrinth in the work. Early in the text
Bradomín admits that the actual garden maze always frightened
and attracted him at the same time (126). Over the cornice of the
garden door are four coats of arms showing the lineage of the
founder. From the very beginning origins, or lineage, is linked to
the labyrinth itself, as if to point to the remote and fabulous nature
of human begetting. But it is his uncle, the arrogant Don Juan
Manuel, who best exemplifies the prevailing system of patriarchy.
As he explains it, the Bradomín line, particularly the title Señorío
de Padín, is an ancient and illustrious one, which goes back to Don
Roldán, "who did not die in Roncesvalles, as the Histories say"
["que no murió en Roncesvalles, como dicen las Historias"]. Don
Roldán, he goes on to say,

> was able to save himself, and in a boat reached the island of Sálvora,
> and attracted by a mermaid was shipwrecked on that beach, and had
> a child by the mermaid, who because he was Don Roldán's was called
> Padín, which is the same as Paladín. That's why you have a mermaid
> embracing and holding your coat-of-arms in the Lantañón church.

> [pudo salvarse, y en una barca llegó hasta la isla de Sálvora, y atraído
> por una sirena naufragó en aquella playa, y tuvo de la sirena un hijo,
> que por serlo de Don Roldán se llamó Padín, y viene a ser lo mismo
> que Paladín. Ahí tienes por qué una sirena abraza y sostiene tu escudo
> en la iglesia de Lantañón.] (153)

This beautifully silly passage, which anticipates the work of Alvaro Cunqueiro and Torrente Ballester, is of course pure *fabula,* storytelling at its most seductive. And that is precisely my point. To establish his claims of male firstness—Don Roldán as creator of the Bradomín line—he minimizes the feminine role in this great enterprise by keeping her anonymous and less than human. On the other hand, this miraculous union with a mermaid, typical of genesis mythmaking in its configurations, while legitimizing lineage through the extraordinary male powers implied in such an act, also strengthens the bonds between the feminine and the suprahuman. Stated another way, the *real* source behind the Bradomín mystique is woman as myth. Thus both family and storytelling emerge one out of the other as emanations of the feminine. Storytelling is family. Family is story. Is perhaps the only story told over and over. And it springs from that fabular center of weaving and spinning, the feminine labyrinth. But such feminine mythmaking is essentially used to serve patriarchal ends. So Candelaria spins stories in which traditionally the men are cruel and the women pure of heart.

Of course Valle-Inclán is satirizing here, creating a playful parody of traditional gender-imposed roles. Unfortunately though, he also perpetuates those same clichés by magnifying Bradomín's authority to the exclusion of all else. As narcissistic writing *Sonata de otoño* can only mirror the ego which is trapped upon its surface. And that ego, even when subjected to parodic intent, can never forgo itself. It is transfixed by the very desire which originally prompted the text into being. Stylistically, this immersion in the selfness of desire is rendered through a series of mnemonic devices of repetition (assonance and alliteration, e.g., as reiterative forms). Language becomes entwined, pregnant with self-praise. And sentences dilate, creating images within images. One morning as he contemplates the garden maze, Bradomín imagines all the memories contained in it. "Beautiful and far-away memories! I too evoked them one far-away day, when the golden autumn morning enveloped the garden, damp and green again by the constant rain during the night. Beneath the limpid sky, of a heraldic blue, the venerable cypresses seemed to emit the illusion of monastic life" ["Hermosos y lejanos recuerdos! Yo también los evoqué un día lejano, cuando la mañana otoñal y dorada envolvía el jardín húmedo y reverdecido por la constante lluvia de la noche. Bajo el cielo límpido, de un azul heráldico, los cipreses venerables parecían tener el ensueño de la vida monástica"] (139). The effect produced is that of a double evocation, of one set of memories stimulated by another, and situated within a landscape dreaming of itself. A moment later Concha bends her head over some roses fallen into her lap. Breathing in the fragrance, "she lifted her head and savored with delight, closing her eyes and smiling, her face covered in dew, like another rose, a white rose . . . she seemed like a Madonna dreamed by a seraphic monk" ["alzó la cabeza y respiró con delicia, cerrando los ojos y sonriendo, cubierto el rostro de rocío, como otra rosa, una rosa blanca . . . parecía una Madona soñada por un monje seráfico"] (139). This rose within the rose is also an image dreamed by someone else ("un monje seráfico"), who in turn is created by Bradomín, who is invented by Valle-Inclán.

The *mise-en-abyme* effect is not used here, however, to produce as expected confusion between reality and fiction, but to uncover the last rose, the last evocation. Valle-Inclán exploits memory in an attempt to make it all-inclusive, all-powerful, for in that reaching after the last image lies the original moment in time, which signifies the eradication of time itself. We are continually reminded in *Sonata de otoño* of distances and depths, with the word *fondo* functioning as a leitmotiv throughout. (See 126, 127, 130, 140, 174, 177, etc.) "In the mirrors' depths," we remember, "the room was prolonged into a dream as in an enchanted lake" ["En el fondo de los espejos, el salón se prolongaba hasta el ensueño como en un lago encantado. . . ."] (141). In prose which is both labyrinthine and specular, everything is made to sustain the erotic effects of prolongation, of deferment of desire. Sighs; the dragging of Concha's train; doors slowly opening; steps echoing; the length of the corridors; the labyrinth itself; the flickering light; Concha's long, entangling hair; are only a few examples of Valle-Inclán's prolonging motifs. But like the mirror of memory and dream, such enchantment is a reality which recedes continually before us.

Along similar lines, the roses emitted "that uncertain aroma which the melancholy of memory possesses" ["ese aroma indeciso que tiene la melancolía de los recuerdos"] (140). A "distant perfume" permeates Valle-Inclán's text, just as Concha's original letter, "perfumada de violetas y de un antiguo amor," contains the trace of her tears ("la huella de sus lágrimas," 121). And it is this feminine trace which is all that remains of *Sonata de otoño*. When Bradomín confuses and equates his lover's essence with her scent, or "esencia," he condemns his writing (and loving) self to the surface of desire. In the end, he can only possess *his* image of Concha, which is the text which is himself desiring. But beneath such specularity we sense the narrator's latent frustration, which is revealed in the tension between surface, or consciousness, and what lies behind consciousness, behind the written images informing his perceptions. That which makes the memory is *mythos*. But, as we have seen, Valle-Inclán as Bradomín is unable—or unwilling—to penetrate the heart of the labyrinth. He cannot reach that ultimate source of subjectivity, which is a form of knowledge, of connecting inner and outer worlds, past and present, death with life. Yet he follows its trace. And in so doing, he appropriates it, donning the perfumed guise, the feminine apparel, in what may appear an unsuitable role. In one scene we recall Bradomín murmuring to his lover, "Let me be your maid!" ["Déjame ser tu azafata!"] And a moment later, he opens her wardrobe from which "a delicate and faded fragrance was emitted" ["se exhalaba . . . una fragancia delicada y antiqua"] (128).

In scattering that delicate and faded fragrance throughout *Sonata de otoño,* Valle-Inclán demonstrates exquisitely how the writer's techniques of dispersion and disguise function to prevent a crisis of authority. For the feminine trace—in an ironic paradox—has become that narcissistic prolongation of self. Such authorial self-dismemberment, however, can only lead him deeper and deeper into a verbal labyrinth from which there is no escape. Gender as a doubling agent is thus interiorized within Valle-Inclán/Bradomín, and the conflict made to serve the oneness of the authorial subject. But if Valle-Inclán and the feminine are the same, then ultimately everything would appear to collapse into the prison construct of self. Such reductiveness is not, however, complete. There remains a difference within the identity: the feminine trace which becomes part of Valle-Inclán's verbal transvestitism and yet persists in being Other at the same time. This feminine alterity or trace—the Concha who resides in Valle-Inclán/Bradomín—will always signal a distorted version of woman because the male author sees her as an Image, an objet d'art, not as subject. The distortion, as we have seen, can reach the point of bankruptcy, the emptying of value until nothing remains but the cliché of femininity.

When Valle-Inclán/Bradomín as author actor assumes the woman's role, he acknowledges the diference he has tried to eradicate. If Valle-Inclán sees storytelling in feminine terms, it is because writing itself is Other. And that Other must be overcome, hence the significance of author as adversary. Acting the part of Other represents a verbal takeover, the merger between authorial self and the feminine Other. Nameless and collective, the feminine cannot be defined. But preempted, she not only paradoxically takes shape, she becomes her own Other: the masculine impulse to reproduce self.

Writing as power play (the author and authority one) desacralizes the centrality of myth, displacing the anonymous nature of story-telling with the individual *bios* of authorship. Stories don't belong to anyone, Concha declares, but *Sonata de otoño* is indisputably Valle-Inclán's. Yet the Galician writer's ambivalence toward the feminine and his parodic treatment of the Don Juan author under-scores a hidden conflict between two gender-inspired codes. Such tension has made inevitable the assumption of authorial masks and artful moves as Bradomín/Valle-Inclán carefully picks his way through a self-imposed narrative maze. It has also shaped my own reading of the work, in which I have shown myself to be by turns an adversary and a fellow actor, or sympathizer. As I struggled to come to terms with Valle-Inclán's attempt to save himself as text, I had to ask myself: Have I subjected him to a second feminine entrapment by a dis-authorized version of the text? Is this a case of sexual harassment in reverse? But then I ask: Could *Sonata de otoño* have been written by a woman? Just try to imagine it.

Notes

1. In the abundant bibliography of the *Sonatas* that I have consulted, to my knowledge, there is no such interpretation of the work. It goes without saying that I have read with pleasure and profited from earlier analyses such as those of Amado Alonso, Alonso Zamora Vicente, José Alberich, Eliane Lavaud, Robert Weber, Gerard Cox Flynn, Richard Callan, Enrique Anderson-Imbert, Rodolfo Cardona, Daniel Gulstad, Fernando de Toro-Garland, Guillermo Díaz-Plaja, and Antonio Vilanova. See also my article, "Valle-Inclán's *Sonata de otoño:* Refrac-tions of a French Anarchist," *Comparative Literature Studies* 22 (1985): 218–30.

2. Michel Foucault, "What Is an Author?" in *Textual Strategies,* ed. Josué V. Harari (Ithaca, N.Y.: Cornell University Press, 1979), 142.

3. Roland Barthes, "The Death of the Author," in *Image-Music-Text,* ed. Ste-phen Heath (New York: Hill and Wang, 1977), 142. Lest the reader think I am reading Barthes (or Valle-Inclán) "literally," I would like to make clear at the outset that my reading of Valle-Inclán is as metaphoric as Barthes's understanding of authorship is. If the way I refer to "author" seems as though I am talking of a vivid, corporeal presence, it is because as an "image," the "author" takes on a life of apparent literalness of his own.

4. Erwin Panofsky, "Et in Arcadia Ego," in *Pastoral and Romance,* ed. Elea-nor Terry Lincoln (Englewood Cliffs, N.J.: Prentice-Hall, 1969), 245–46.

5. Joseph Jefferson, *Autobiography* (New York: The Century Co., 1890), 228.

6. Patricia Waugh, *Metafiction* (London: Methuen, 1984), 133–34.

7. Georges Güntert, "La fuente en el laberinto: Las *Sonatas* de Valle-Inclán," *Boletín de la Real Academia Española* 53 (1973): 546.

8. Linda Nochlin, "Eroticism and Female Imagery in Nineteenth-Century Art," in *Woman as Sex Object,* eds. Thomas B. Hess and Linda Nochlin (New York: Newsweek, 1972), 9.

9. In this connection John Berger's comments are extremely illuminating. "I am in front of a typical European nude. She is painted with extreme sensuous

emphasis. Yet her sexuality is only superficially manifest in her actions or her own expression; in a comparable figure within other art traditions this would not be so. Why? Because for Europe ownership is primary. The painting's sexuality is manifest not in what it shows but in the owner-spectator's (mine in this case) right to see her naked. Her nakedness is not a function of her sexuality but of the sexuality of those who have access to the picture." See his article, "Past Seen from a Possible Future," in *The Look of Things,* ed. Nikos Stangos (New York: Viking, 1974), 215.

10. Ramón del Valle-Inclán, *Sonatas,* ed. Ramón Sender (New York: Las Américas Publishing Co., 1961), 177. Further reference to *Sonata de otoño* will be given in parentheses in the text.

11. Sandra M. Gilbert and Susan Gubar, *The Madwoman in the Attic* (1979; New Haven: Yale University Press, 1984), 53–59.

12. See chap. 1 in particular of Nina Auerbach's *Woman and the Demon* (Cambridge: Harvard University Press, 1982).

13. Erich Neumann, *The Great Mother* (1955; Princeton: Princeton University Press, 1972), 177.

14. Emilia Pardo Bazán, *Los Pazos de Ulloa* (Madrid: Alianza, 1966), 187.

15. Gonzalo Torrente Ballester, *La isla de los jacintos cortados,* 2d ed. (Barcelona: Destino, 1981), 273–74.

16. J. E. Cirlot, *A Dictionary of Symbols* (New York: Philosophical Library, 1962), 201.

17. Heinrich Schwarz, "The Mirror in Art," *The Art Quarterly* 15 (1952): 96–118.

18. Alfred Lord Tennyson, *The Poems of Tennyson,* ed. Christopher Ricks (London: Longmans, Green and Co., 1969), 357.

19. Ibid., 359.

20. Ibid., 361.

21. Nancy Willard, "The Spinning Room: Symbols and Storytellers," in *Angel in the Parlor* (New York: Harcourt, Brace, Jovanovich, 1984), 252.

22. See Mary Daly, *Gyn/Ecology* (Boston: Beacon Press, 1978); Patricia Klindienst Joplin, "The Voice of the Shuttle Is Ours," *Stanford Literature Review* 1 (1984): 22–53; and Carolyn Heilbrun, "Presidential Address 1984," *PMLA* 100 (1985): 281–86. Joplin's essay should be read in conjunction with Geoffrey Hartman's, which she attacks. "The Voice of the Shuttle: Language from the Point of View of Literature," *Beyond Formalism* (New Haven: Yale University Press, 1970), 337–55.

23. Joplin, "Voice of the Shuttle," 26; Heilbrun, "Presidential Address," 285.

24. Jean Franco, "Self-Destructing Heroines," *The Minnesota Review* 22 (1984): 106.

25. Valle-Inclán also links the chronicler, or literateness, with other male figures. Even the lowly page Florisel is "worthy of being the page of a princess and chronicler of a kingdom" ["digno de ser paje de una princesa y cronista de un Reinado"] (138). And Don Juan Manuel's fanciful re-creation of family origins is further legitimized by reference to an ancient book, "with large, clear print, where all these stories are told at great length" ["de letra grande y clara, donde todas estas historias están contadas muy por largo"] (153). (This, despite Don Juan Manuel's resistance to reading, 150.)

26. Walter Benjamin, "The Storyteller," in *Illuminations* (New York: Harcourt, Brace and World, 1968), 94.

27. Daly, *Gyn/Ecology,* 400–401.

28. Ibid., 413; Neumann, *Great Mother,* 29. I am well aware that women named Concepción are ordinarily called Concha in Spain. My point is that Valle-Inclán's particular choice of a name cannot have been arbitrary. I would also refer the reader to a curious—and revealing—incident in Spanish literary annals. In 1827 José Gómez Hermosilla wrote to Leandro Fernández de Moratín about the difficulties he was having in getting his *Arte de hablar en prosa y en verso* [*Art of Speaking in Prose and Verse*] past the censors. Among the items censored was a reference to Garcilaso's *concha de Venus." See Leandro Fernández de Moratín, Obras póstumas,* vol. 3 (Madrid: Rivadeneyra, 1868), 103.While Valle-Inclán did not have to contend with Fernando VII, Calomarde, and company, he, like other *fin de siglo* writers (Clarín in *La Regenta,* e.g.), played off Restoration Spain's pervasive and subterranean obsession with sex and sexuality as forbidden discourse. Berger's comments (n. 9) are also apposite here. I have since run across a poem entitled "A Concha" ["To Concha"], by Francisco Javier Godo, in *La Ilustración Ibérica* (Barcelona) 3, no. 153 (5 December 1885): 782–83, in which the Venus-conch topos appears as a double-entendre. "You are the sublime Conch(a)" ["Eres la Concha sublime"], Godo writes. And he continues: "A pearl, you are love transformed, / enclosed within your soul. / Oh, Concha, soul of mine / give me, for god's sake, that pearl!" ["En perla, Amor transformado / tú, dentro del alma encierras. / Oh Concha del alma mía / dame, por Dios, esa perla!"] (783).

The Role of Language in the Creation of Valle-Inclán's Female Characters

BIRUTÉ CIPLIJAUSKAITÉ

Translation by Kimberly H. Talentino and Carmen Gómez

When Valle-Inclán defined the aesthetics of his *esperpento,* he referred to a technique that, surprisingly, is also found in Luce Irigaray's explanation of current feminist practice. Max Estrella states in *Luces de Bohemia* [*Bohemian Lights*], "My present aesthetic approach is to transform all classical norms with the mathematics of the concave mirror" ["Mi estética actual es transformar con matemática de especjo cóncavo las normas clásicas"]; and he says later in the play, "Let's deform style with the same mirror that distorts our faces and contorts the whole miserable life of Spain"[1] ["deformemos la expresión en el mismo espejo que nos deforma las caras y toda la vida miserable de España"].[2] This *ars poetica* is a good example of what Adorno understands as "avant-garde art." Going beyond the premises of his teacher, Lukács, who demanded the faithful reflection of social reality in artistic work, Adorno claims that social protest can also occur as rupture. A novel or drama is not necessarily what the normal mirror reflects, a total image of the social world, but monads that contain within themselves the outside world in synthesis, without depending on intercommunication. Instead of the organic totality that would be obtained by returning to the epic, as Lukács wished, what occurs is almost a parody of the epic, in which technique and form become more important than content. This art is based on abstraction, not on exact reflection. It is a subversive art that seeks renovation, one desired at the artistic as well as the social level.[3]

Feminist writing also employs subversion in order to reach absolute truth. If the artists of the avant-garde protested against the total reality in which they were forced to work, women narrow their focus to explore principally the feminine condition. The method they propose is similar to that of Valle-Inclán: existing

limits must be exceeded. Like Valle-Inclán, women see an intimate
connection between social and linguistic aspects. They claim that
a society governed by rules made by men also uses a language
men have established, one in which there is no room for feminine
"specificity." Luce Irigaray, likening the theory of the novel to
the mirror, comes to the conclusion that all this mirror reflects is
something incomplete, something that is therefore a misrepresenta-
tion: "its impossible reappropriation 'on the inside' of the mind, of
thought, of subjectivity. Whence the intervention of the speculum
and of the concave mirror, which disturb the staging of representation according to too-exclusively masculine parameters"[4] ["son impossible réappropriation, 'à l'intérieur' de l'esprit, de la pensée, de
la subjectivité. D'où l'intervention du speculum et du miroir concave, qui dérangent le montage de la représentation selon des para-
mètres exclusivement 'masculins'"].[5] She urges women to seek the
essence denied them by the coating on the glass that makes it a
mirror, because only through a reformed language will that essence
become accessible.

The difference between the role Valle-Inclán attributes to the
concave mirror and the role attributed to it by women writers, lies
in the fact that, as a man, Valle-Inclán has a command of language
and enjoys more freedom to experiment with it. This enables him
to move away from everyday bourgeois reality and to use shock
to uncover a deeper truth. "The image in the flat mirror had worn
out and become false, and Valle-Inclán's new realism aimed cruelly
at truth" ["la visión del espejo plano había venido a parar en
falsedad y el nuevo realismo valleinclaniano aspiraba cruelmente
a la verdad"].[6] Verity Smith notes a similar purpose for his invention of an "Hispanic language" ["idioma hispánico"].[7] The need for
renovation arises from the falseness prevalent in language used
in daily life, a fact Valle-Inclán himself stressed in *La lámpara
maravillosa* [*The Lamp of Marvels*]. "Day by day over the years
I have been toiling within the areas of my concerns to dig a pit in
which to bury that hollow, pompous, high-flown prose; it is a style
of writing we can no longer afford if we are to be receptive to
the moment's urgency."[8] ["Desde hace muchos años, día a día, en
aquello que me atañe yo trabajo cavando la cueva donde enterrar
esta hueca y pomposa prosa castiza, que ya no puede ser la nuestra
cuando escribamos, si sentimos el imperio de la hora"].[9] Valle-
Inclán seems to follow Nietzsche's motto, "Destroy to create." The
new creation incorporates fragments that already exist.

Women writers emphasize "masculine corruption" and use subversion to reach women's reality and to vindicate a repressed lan-

guage. This is to say, they start from scratch, having to create what has yet to be acknowledged. This difference, together with the context within which they create, explains the ways in which their strategies diverge from Valle-Inclán's, and the fact that he never created what could be considered a specifically feminine discourse. In the discussion that follows, I shall try to depict those divergences more precisely, focusing on the discourse of female characters rather than on discourse per se. In Valle-Inclán's case, this discourse is almost always that of the narrator, and it has already been studied in great detail.[10]

Some statements from *La lámpara maravillosa* will be helpful in understanding the approach to spoken language found in Valle-Inclán's novels. Many studies have demonstrated that Valle-Inclán's concept of time influenced the overall structure of his work and the creation of his characters. One of his maxims reads, "In the creations of art, images of the world are accommodations to memory, wherein they present themselves to us beyond time in an immutable vision" (100) ["En las creaciones del arte, las imágenes del mundo son adecuaciones al recuerdo, donde se nos presentan fuera del tiempo, en una visión inmutable"] (685). This goal of "aesthetic quietism" ["quietismo estético"] leads to a tendency toward the archetype, a "technique of stereotyping and synthesis" ["técnica tipificante y sintetizante"].[11] This emphasis on the eternal quality of words eliminates the need to particularize the differences between men and women or between generations. "I conceived a dream, that words emanated without age, like eternal creations filled with the secret virtue of crystals" (107) ["Concebía como un sueño que las palabras apareciesen sin edad, a modo de creaciones eternas, llenas de la secreta virtud de los cristales"] (689).[12] Many characters appear only as shapes and shadows.

The draped figure might have been some spirit of a thousand centuries ago. Her flesh was quivering and her eyes burned hotly beneath the folds of the mantle.[13]

[Así, arrebujada, parecía una sombra milenaria. Temblaba su carne, y los ojos fulguraban calenturientos bajo el capuz del mantelo.] (*SO*, 17)

She was a motionless shadow in the middle of the locutory, and it seemed she had appeared there from the depths of some chapel where she had been buried.

[Era una sombra inmóvil en medio del locutorio, y parecía haber llegado allí desde el fondo de alguna capilla donde estuviese enterrada.] (*CC*, 39)

These figures frequently speak through their gestures or their eyes. Feminist writers also consider body language significant, but their idea of that language is very different from Valle-Inclán's. In Valle-Inclán's work, the gesture and the gaze *replace* words. Today's women writers want words to acquire body and to include the gestures and sensations that are *enunciated* when this occurs. Eva Llorens points out that eyes are the most provocative feature for pre-Raphaelite painters and for Julio Romero de Torres. One of Romero de Torres's portraits of a woman hung in Valle-Inclán's home and it was Romero de Torres who prepared the illustrations for the first edition of *Voces de gesta* [Epic cries].[14] According to Francisco Madrid, Valle-Inclán himself used to say that "before I start writing I need to see the characters bodily and in detail."[15] This explains why, in his early works, we *see* more than *hear* the female characters, who sometimes function like decorative art nouveau props. Ildefonso Manuel Gil cites Rosarito from *Jardín umbrío* [Shadowy garden] as an example. "More than a 'being' she is a 'pretext' for aesthetic play" ["Más que un 'ser' es un 'motivo' para el juego estético"] (69). What is more, in Barbey d'Aurevilly's *Les Diaboliques* [*The She-Devils*], which has been cited often as one of Valle-Inclán's sources, the language of gestures is also found more frequently than the language of words.[16] In the work of both authors, women are treated as objects which do not need a language of their own. (Sophocles once said that silence is women's greatest charm.)[17] Finally, the reliance on the gesture and the gaze can be linked with another statement from *La lámpara maravillosa*. "Something will always be hermetic and impossible for words" (14) ["Hay algo que será eternamente hermético e imposible para las palabras"] (644). Words must be supplemented. Paralanguage and kinesics are important elements of Valle-Inclán's technique, and they are primarily associated with women, whose linguistic consciousness has not yet awakened.

In Valle-Inclán's early works, women frequently assume the role of the chorus. As Zamora Vicente suggests, women are voices "of a distant, collective nature, whose function is to provide a background—almost like an anonymous, plebeian chorus—against which actions and atmosphere stand out better" ["de aire colectivo y lejano, que se encargan de dar como un fondo—como un coro casi, anónimo, plebeyo—sobre el que resaltan mejor los ambientes y las acciones"].[18] Even when they are protagonists, like Adega in *Flor de santidad* [Flower of holiness], women do not attain sufficient importance to be seen as the Other instead of "the other to be used by man" ["el otro para el uso del hombre"]. Keeping in mind Pérez de Ayala's insistence on the importance of the chorus in Valle-Inclán's work, García de la Torre points out that at times women do not even have their own names. They are presented as "old women" ["mujerucas"] or as a "group of village girls" ["cortejo de mozas"] who form part of a religious backdrop. "As they heard the tales of the old women mending their ponchos in the afternoons, they felt the times of the ancient ballads return. Those were the old women who could be sisters to vine shoots" ["Sentían renacer el tiempo de los romances viejos, oyendo el relato de las mujerucas que por las tardes les remendaban los ponchos. . . Eran aquellas las abuelas que parecen hermanas de los sarmientos"] (*GA*, 271).[19] This presentation involves more than mere stylization. The voice heard almost always speaks ungrammatically and it betrays its social origin. The Galician village girl represents the most "underdeveloped" social class; she is almost without consciousness, and consequently she lacks a language of her own. It is important to point out that in these works the voice of women is *described* rather than *heard*.

> The voice of the maid was monotonous and singsong: she spoke the archaic, almost Visigothic tongue of the mountains.
>
> [La voz de la sierva era monótona y cantarina: hablaba el romance arcaico, casi visigodo, de la montaña.] (*FS*, 465)
>
> Her voice was soft and melodious, the voice of a priestess, a princess. (91)
>
> [Su voz era queda, salmodiada y dulce, voz de sacerdotisa y de princesa.] (*SE*, 411)

When a woman's voice is heard, many times it occurs as ritual repetition or superstitious incantation. "I cast a spell on you, at one, by the brightness of the sun!, I cast a spell on you, at two, by the face of the moon!, I cast a spell on you, at three, by Moses' stone decrees!" ["¡Yo te conjuro, a la una, por la cara de la luna! ¡Yo te conjuro, a las dos, por el resplandor del sol! ¡Yo te conjuro, a las tres, por las tablas de Mosén!"] (*CC*, 56). The effect produced by words is more important than the words themselves. This effect is used more than once to close a chapter. "In the silence of the garden the voice has a painful clarity, and the nun appears as a misty figure, completely veiled in the shadow of the laurel trees" ["En el silencio del huerto, la voz tiene una claridad dolorosa, y la monja parece una figura de niebla, toda velada en la sombra de los laureles"] (*CC*, 93).[20]

The trilogy *La guerra carlista* [The Carlist War] represents a work of transition: some *modernista* techniques still remain and the *esperpento,* as process, begins. One of the central characters in this trilogy is Mother Isabel, a figure both female and remarkable. (Following nineteenth-century tradition, the work opens and closes with scenes dominated by masculine figures.) Some observations by Anne Robinson Taylor in *Male Novelists and their Female Voices* suggest an approach to female protagonists.[21] Taylor proposes that when a male author writes a narration in the first person using a woman as a central figure, this woman generally adopts his own voice and ideology: it is easier for him to reveal himself behind a mask. Although the autobiographical elements of Valle-Inclán's Mother Isabel will not be analyzed here, it is important to note that she is the character who speaks most clearly and articulately. This allows her to undergo a process of "awakening" and, toward the end of the novel, to become the voice of protest against what is happening in Spain. Within a few pages, the nun is transformed from an idealist to a skeptic who exchanges prayers for admonitions. Her speech sparkles with clarity and determination rather than manifesting such "typically" feminine qualities as indecision, repetition, irrationality, hyperbole, understatement, euphemism, and indirectness. Other characters exhibit at least one supposedly feminine characteristic, the repetition of parallel expressions.

> God will that you find her blooming like a rose! . . . Like a rose on a rosebush! (151)
>
> [¡Quiera Dios que se encuentre sana a la señora y con los colores de una rosa! . . . ¡Así la encuentre como una rosa en su rosal!] (*SO,* 16)
>
> I am well punished . . . I am well punished . . . (205)
>
> [¡Bien castigada estoy! . . . ¡Bien castigada estoy!] (*SO,* 70)
>
> Well spoken, Mother! . . . Well spoken!
>
> [¡Qué tan bien lo pinta, madre! . . . ¡Qué tan bien lo pinta!] (*CC,* 65)
>
> You would have the nerve to kill him! Yes, you would![22]
>
> [¡Tendríais alma de matarlo! . . . ¡Pues tendríais alma!] (*RH,* 157)

In Mother Isabel, on the other hand, a reversal of one of the characteristics typical of her gender occurs. Recent linguistic analyses show that when women speak they are frequently interrupted by men and, therefore, cannot complete what they intend to say.[23] In *El resplandor de la hoguera* [The bonfire's blaze] the voice of the abbess interrupts that of the courier to affirm her superiority.

> It is a tight spot, and if women are not able . . . !"
> "Women are capable, brother," the old woman replied from the cart.
>
> ["¡Mal paso es, y si las mujeres no son capaces . . . ! Habló desde el carro la vieja:
> —Las mujeres son capaces, hermano."] (99)

A large step forward with respect to spoken language is taken in *El ruedo ibérico* [The Iberian ring], where the proportion of dialogue has increased considerably. In these novels, the techniques of Valle-Inclán's *esperpento* come into their own. This is especially true in passages of stage directions (*las acotaciones*)— a theatrical term seems most appropriate for defining the narration here—and the breaks, reversals, and abrupt changes in speech. Valle-Inclán's women are no longer silent. The evolution of their language follows that of the male characters: their replies are lively, eloquent, and categorical. They are ladies of the court accustomed to manipulating from behind-the-scenes. This role, common to almost all of them, retains something of the function of the chorus, which is composed of voices more individualized than those of the Galician servants. Queen Isabel stands out among all the ladies of her court. There is nothing shadowlike about her, nor does she use the submissive and self-denying language predominant in the speech of women in earlier novels. What is more, like the Celestina, Queen Isabel uses diverse languages, depending on her interlocutor. The variation in her speech serves as an indication of the relationship with different characters. Of Valle-Inclán's female characters, Queen Isabel is the one who manifests the greatest linguistic awareness, as she speaks to her duenna Pepita, to the Marquis of Torre-Mellada, and to the Duke of Valencia, respectively.

> You've done the right thing, because you're nothing but an old chatterbox. Look what you've just said!
>
> [Haces bien, porque eres un badajo cascado. ¡Mira que con lo que sales!] (*CM,* 122)
>
> I sincerely appreciate the token of love and loyalty of my subjects. The one who loves me is spitting at me now. What I want is to make the Spaniards happy and I want them to love me.

[Yo agradezco mucho las muestras de amor y lealtad de mis súbditos. El que me quiere, ya me tira tierra a los ojos. Mi deseo es hacer la felicidad de los españoles y que ellos me quieran.] (*CM*, 130)

Are you really sick? You're not lying to me? You look terrible! Let me feel your hand. You're burning up! Take good care of yourself. Spain and the Queen need you. You may leave now. Fortunately, it is probably nothing major.

[¿De veras estás enfermo? ¿No me engañas? ¡Tienes muy mala cara! Dame la mano. ¡Ardes! Cuídate mucho. Te necesitan España y la Reina. Retírate. Afortunadamente, no será nada.] (*CM*, 133)

In his explanation of the techniques Valle-Inclán employed in order to achieve "total speech" ["un habla total"], Antonio Risco refers to an earlier study by Amado Alonso and explains that "Valle combines, therefore, all these elements so arbitrarily that it is absurd to look for either a philological or documentary interest in his language. He is all style, just style" ["Valle combina, por tanto, todos estos elementos tan arbitrariamente que es absurdo buscar en su lenguaje un interés documental o filológico. Todo él es estilo, sólo estilo"].[24] It is interesting to note that, in the case of Isabel's speech, there are many elements drawn from reality, even within this stylization. The Queen's Castilian sounds "pure" and self-confident, and she has a voice of her own. Documents gathered by Leda Schiavo prove that *El ruedo ibérico* and the character of the Queen have a firm base in reality. These documents confirm the "affection and fondness people had for her because of her good nature, her appearance, which we could not call sophisticated, her common way of speaking, and her 'Spanish charm'" ["el afecto y simpatía que le tenía el pueblo por su modo campoechano, su figura, digamos, no sofisticada, su hablar populachero, su gracia 'española'"].[25] Schiavo's documents also demonstrate that the Queen did not always use an elevated language and that she expressed herself in a way similar to the language attributed to her in Valle-Inclán's novel. "I am a typical Spanish woman, one of those who prays to the Virgin of the Dove and carries a knife in her garter" ["Yo soy muy española y de las de la Virgen de la Paloma, que llevan la navaja en la liga"].[26]

When trying to determine Valle-Inclán's contribution to spoken feminine language, it is important to remember that he wrote at a time when misogyny was very prevalent. According to Segundo Serrano Poncela, this period produced "novels abounding in nothing but sexual appetites, fantastic females, or man eaters" ["novelas por donde sólo circulan apetitos sexuales, fantasmáticas féminas o devoradoras de hombres"].[27] The concept of woman as an archetypal figure in Valle Inclán's early novels stands in opposition to the feminine characteristics advocated by contemporary feminist critiques: fluency, uniqueness, clear awareness of everyday details, and direct expression of intimate perceptions. Valle-Inclán's female protagonists have been endowed with more silences than words. It would be difficult to argue that the authentic elements of speech predominate in his fiction or that a unique, individual language is developed by each character. The masculine voice, or the faked voice of the puppeteer who controls the puppets in Valle Inclán's later works dominate in his dialogues. The secondary characters often appear as types who use codified language. The presentation of the female protagonists is seldom achieved through their own speech. They are more frequently created through stylized description, through the "stage directions" that accompany the dialogue, and through ambience that surrounds them; these are all techniques in which the narrator's perspective prevails. Female figures and voices are sometimes used to open or close a chapter, where they adopt the role of the Greek chorus, or to express a collective awareness. Whether this awareness is expressed through the "chorus of old women" ["coro de mujerucas"] or through well-crafted, nuanced reflections of Mother Isabel's individual awareness, its purpose is clearly that of synthesizing the Spanish situation and the spirit of Spain's people.

Notes

1. Ramón María del Valle Inclán, *Luces de Bohemia* [*Bohemian Lights*], trans. Anthony N. Zahareas and Gerald Gillespie (Austin: University of Texas Press, 1976), 183–85 [trans. note].

2. Ramón María del Valle-Inclán, *Luces de Bohemia* (Madrid: Espasa-Calpe, 1961), 106–7.

3. See Theodor W. Adorno, *Asthetische Theorie* (Frankfurt/Main: Suhrkamp, 1970; and *Zur Dialektik des Engagements* (Frankfurt/Main: Suhrkamp, 1973), discussed by Peter Hohendahl in "Lukács and the Frankfurt School," a lecture delivered at the University of Wisconsin-Madison, 9 March 1986.

4. Luce Irigaray, *Ce sexe qui n'en est pas un* [*This Sex which Is Not One*], trans. Catherine Porter with Carolyn Burke (Ithaca, N.Y.: Cornell University Press, 1985), 155 [trans. note].

5. Ibid., 150.

6. Ildefonso-Manuel Gil, "La base del esperpento," in *Valle-Inclán, Azorín y Baroja* (Madrid: Seminarios y Ediciones, 1975), 95. [Trans. note: All of the translations that follow in both the text and the notes are ours unless otherwise noted.]

7. Verity Smith, *Valle-Inclán: Tirano Banderas* (London: Grant & Cutler, 1971), 78.

8. Ramón María del Valle-Inclán, *La lámpara maravillosa* [*The Lamp of Marvels*], trans. Robert Lima (West Stockbridge, Mass.: Lindisfarne Press, 1986), 48. The translations of other quotes from *La lámpara maravillosa* have been taken from this book. Page numbers follow the quote [trans. note].

9. Ramón María del Valle-Inclán, *Obras escogidas* (Madrid: Aguilar, 1965), 661. The following works from this same edition will be abbreviated with the page references given in parenthesis: *La lámpara maravillosa (LM)* [*The Lamp of Marvels*]; *Flor de santidad (FS)* [Flower of holiness]; *Jardín umbrío (JU)* [Shadowy garden]; *Sonata de estío (SE)* [*Sonata of Summer*]; and *La corte de los milagros (CM)* [The court of miracles]. Other abbreviations are *La guerra carlista (GC)* [The Carlist War]; *Los cruzados de la causa (CC)* [Crusaders of the cause]); *El resplandor de la hoguera (RH)* [The bonfire's blaze]; *Gerifaltes de antaño (GA)* [Falcons of yore] (Madrid: Aguilar, 1970); and *Sonata de otoño (SO)* [*Sonata of Autumn*] (Buenos Aires: Losada, 1938).

10. José Manuel García de la Torre is perhaps the critic who has studied the speech of Valle-Inclán's characters most thoroughly. Even he, however, has analyzed mainly the quality of voice, the sounds, and the characters' demeanor while speaking, rather than their language itself. When referring to their language, he offers general observations concerning Valle-Inclán's technique of "derealization" ["desrealización"] (*Análisis temático de "El ruedo ibérico"* [Madrid: Gredos, 1972] 209–21, 255ff., 327). The chapter on taxonomy, "Análisis sistemático de personajes a través de su habla," from Carlos Alvarez Sánchez's *Sondeo de "Luces de Bohemia," primer esperpento de Valle-Inclán* (Sevilla: Universidad de Sevilla, 1976) does not add much on this topic. Alison Sinclair's interesting study, "Nineteenth-Century Popular Literature as a Source of Linguistic Enrichment in Valle-Inclán's *Ruedo Ibérico*," *Modern Language Review* 70 (1975): 84–96, does not attempt to analyze the process of linguistic individualization of Valle-Inclán's characters.

11. María Eugenia March, *Forma e idea de los esperpentos de Valle-Inclán* (University of North Carolina: Estudios de Hispanófila, 1970), 43. The author notes that "in *Luces de Bohemia,* all the female characters are described in practically the same terms; physically, they correspond to the description of a certain 'type' of woman" ["en *Luces de Bohemia* todos los personajes femeninos son descritos prácticamente en los mismos términos; físicamente responden a la descripción de un cierto 'tipo' de mujer" (114)].

12. The translation of this passage has been modified slightly [trans. note].

13. Ramón María del Valle-Inclán, *Sonata de Otoño* and *Sonata de Estío* in *The Pleasant Memoirs of the Marquis of Bradomín,* trans. May Heywood Brown and Thomas Walsh (New York: Harcourt, Brace & Co., 1924), 151–52. The translation of other quotes from *Sonata de otoño* and *sonata de estío* have been taken from this book. Page number follows the quote [trans. note].

14. Eva Llorens, *Valle-Inclán y la plástica* (Madrid: Insula, 1975), 49–66. I owe the reference to the portrait to Melchor Fernández Almagro, *Vida y literatura de Valle-Inclán* (Madrid: Taurus, 1966), 117.

15. Francisco Madrid, *La vida altiva de Valle-Inclán* (Buenos Aires: Poseidón, 1943), 116.

16. Claudine Herrmann interprets this as evidence of women's silence at that time. *Les voleuses de langue* (Paris: éditions des femmes, 1976), 110.

17. Sophocles, *Ajax* 1.293.

18. Zamora Vicente, *Las sonatas de Valle-Inclán* (Madrid: Gredos, 1969), 167. The English quote is our translation.

19. Cf. "The voices of old women murmured beneath the mystery of their mantles" ["Voces de viejas murmuraben bajo el misterio de los manteos"] (*CC*, 11). "All the church bells were tolling his death and there was the sound of old women weeping rhythmically" ["Tocaban a muerto todas las campanas, y se oía un acompasado plañir de mujerucas"] (*CC*, 87).

20. Cf. another chapter that ends with a sense of timelessness. "The shadow of the walnut tree fell on the four women, immobile in the middle of the road, and in her intonation Josepa de la Arguña conveyed the frightening uncertainty of that hour and a tragic, mysterious, popular feeling" ["Sobre las cuatro mujeres, inmóviles en medio del camino, caía la sombra del nogal, y Josepa de la Arguña ponía en su acento la vaguedad medrosa de la hora, y un sentido popular, milagrero y trágico"] (*RH*, 186).

21. Anne Robinson Taylor, *Male Novelists and Their Female Voices: Literary Masquerades* (Troy, N.Y.: The Whitston Publishing Co., 1981).

22. Ramón María del Valle-Inclán, *El resplandor de la hoguera. Obras escogidas.* (Madrid: Aguilar, 1965).

23. See Marina Yaguello, *Les Mots et les femmes. Essai d'approche sociolinguistique de la condition féminine* (Paris: Payot, 1979); Robin Lakoff, *Language and Woman's Place* (New York: Harper Colophon Books, 1975); Cheris Kramarae, *Women and Men Speaking* (Rowley, Mass.: Newbury House Publisher, 1981); and Mary Ritchie Key, *Male/Female Language* (Metuchen, N.J.: The Scarecrow Press, 1975).

24. Antonio Risco, *La estética de Valle-Inclán en los esperpentos y en "El ruedo ibérico"* (Madrid: Castalia, 1980), 176.

25. Leda Schiavo, *Historia y novela en Valle-Inclán. Para leer "El ruedo ibérico"* (Madrid: Castalia, 1980), 358.

26. Ibid., 359. Quoted by Miguel Villalba Hervás, *Recuerdo de cinco lustros (1843–1868)* (Madrid, 1896), 219.

27. Segundo Serrano Poncela, *"Eros y tres misóginos," El secreto de Melibea y otros ensayos* (Madrid: Taurus, 1959), 140.

Valle-Inclán: Modernity, Heterochrony of Gender Constructs, and Libidinal Economy: A Dialogic Reading

IRIS M. ZAVALA

> From the vantage of this laughter and this dance, from the vantage of this affirmation foreign to all dialectics the other side of nostalgia, what I will call Heideggarian *hope,* comes into question.
>
> —"La différance," Derrida

Nowhere is the dialogue of popular discourse and fantasy life more enriching than in Valle-Inclán's texts, where the popular and the libidinal interact and intersect. Valle-Inclán's fantasy life is replete with metonymies and metaphors from the domain of newspapers and journals (what recently Linda Hutcheon identifies as the "postmodern collage"), icons, photographs, and movies. Jean F. Lyotard's (1974) description of the "libidinal economy of popular culture," or the infiltration of popular discourses into fantasy life, provides a good understanding of the complex plurality of Valle-Inclán's texts,[1] and serves as a meaningful frame for rereading his free-floating gender constructs. The plurality of images and signs creates a complex polyphony of social discourses that enrich and feed on each other, thus favoring multiple associations on different semiotic levels. These interwoven images and sounds, which relate discourses, come from the domain of the printed word and the images of fashion, as well as from the rhythms of popular songs; they are sounds and images that celebrate emotions and pleasure, as well as modes of experience, enjoyment, and hidden obsessions.

Valle-Inclán reappropriates these discourses and reaccentuates them, meaningfully integrating "trash" magazines and newspapers, street signs, and what is now called mass media into aesthetic pleasure, while destabilizing exhausted notions of personal and collective identities. He breaks down hierarchies, while reintegrating these discourses (which are laden with power struggles), into political and ethical frontiers, in a fruitful exchange which reinscribes heteroglossia into an otherwise monological cultural discourse. This multiplicity provides destabilizing strategies while it simultaneously uncovers the ensemble of beliefs and practices that form the symbolic economy of Valle-Inclán's specific time. Consequently, we may speak of his texts as the battleground of the entire spectrum of limits and models of social behavior of turn-of-the-century Spain, and as the open space of disrupting boundaries that open new grounds for liberating the web of static definitions engulfing class and gender, whose hegemony has not been questioned previously. Through their constraints and mobility, Valle-Inclán's texts articulate the cultural codes of behavior; within the openness of the "both/and" of dialogism. His verbal language provides an entrance to the symbolic economy by moving through boundaries, traveling in circuits, and advocating the accretion of verbal, social, cultural, and individual sign systems against systems that are arid and static. He gathers motifs irreverently, reaccentuating ambivalent signs and relying on indeterminacy to suggest marginal meanings away from the unavoidable social control of his time and the rigidity of norms. He specifically encourages associations from the margins with feelings, emotions, and sensations to convert all elements of experience into fluid, mobile meanings, disrupting centralized authoritarian forms of control.[2]

The first consequence to be drawn from this is that Valle-Inclán conjures the general symbolic economy in the topical signs that excite desire, and/or create fear, and aggression. He draws on the symbolic material of language, from one zone of culture to the other (the "elite" and the "popular"), in intersections without boundaries (Myriam Díaz-Diocaretz's distinction is pertinent here),[3] altering meaning and understanding. Within the historical dimension of Valle-Inclán's symbolic practice, his texts are situated at the very limits and borders of what could be said in turn-of-the-century Spain, where they juggle symbolic material so as to unfurl the imaginary identities (generic and social) in everyday speech. And Valle-Inclán does this by displaying the entire variety of symbolic dimensions, whose knowledge normative authorities seek to suppress.

This principle of libidinal economy is neither a concept nor a word among others if translated to the Bakhtinian "heteroglossia." What is written as heteroglossia will be the movement that produces the densely overlaid traces of historical usages of the sign in the chain of signification. It includes the multiplicity of languages or dialects, which creates and uncovers social positions. In Valle-Inclán, this political combat over signs reveals the social logic of a projection of collective desires, based on a thorough demystifing of the political and ideological structures that channel desire (the symbolic dimension) in oppressive ways. He speaks to the deepest desires and fantasies as a "shared territory" (to employ Bakhtinian terminology) of social voices.[4] Valle-Inclán reminds his reader of pleasure and desire, at the same time acting in concert with that reader in pursuit of social goals as shared territory of the pleasure principle. He projects the inert weight of social systems and repressive powers, indicating openings for their subversion.

Such glimpses of collective freedom are shared with gender constructs, in opposition to the conventional and normative semiotic (and therefore political) representation, and its taboos. If a collapse in conventions of representation—lyric, drama, narrative—is in itself an act of representation,[5] it could be argued that the symbolic processes that participate in the construction of genre (among other constructs) are deconstructed in Valle-Inclán, showing them to be essentially contingent and dependent. Valle-Inclán is particularly drawn to the ambivalent character of social and gender structures. He thus leaves an openness of responsive understanding, assuring the possibility of a new hermeneutics in the "contesting" meanings of the world of heteroglossia.

This very powerful ideological vision can be tested and grasped though the explanatory powers and perspective of a Bakhtinian "dialogic criticism."[6] From this evaluative axis, Valle-Inclán's textual strategies can be read as reflections about identity and Otherness through the collapse of conventions, and the ratios of Otherness privileged through the mastery of chronotopes. The chronotopes (units of analysis) allow for critical perspectives, which serve as outsidedness and values. Simultaneously, they are categories of knowledge, which can be perceived in the context of a larger time/space relation that obtain meaning in the social and historical context. Thus, it becomes necessary to introduce yet another time/space component of chronotopes: those of gender constructs. As such, gender constructs can be diverse in their ideological forms, and they are textually constituted by acquiring the languages and discourses of their world. Taking this concept a step further, gendered selves are hybrid syntheses of institutional and discursive practices that bear on "imaginary identities" produced and reproduced by class, generation, and situatedness.

As complex networks of ideological signs, gender constructs can be recognized as voices representing distinct socioideological positionings. Taking Bakhtin's concept still a step further, there is a "heterochrony" of conflicting representations mediated through positionings in time and space, determined by the dynamic circumstances of communication. I am tempted to say that gender constructs are not only determined by heteroglossia but by heterochrony, i.e., competing descriptions of gender combining time/space with value.[7] In short: value attached to the observed world of difference. One such general direction can be described dramatically throughout Valle-Inclán's writing, which aims (often successfully) to "break the chain"[8] of the symbolic economy of liberal realistic narratives, regulators, and guarantors of sexual (and gender) social order. His *anamorphistic mirror* (to use a term I have suggested elsewhere) unleashes the limits of the ensemble of beliefs and practices of tradition and its technologies of control.[9] He disturbs the rhetorical signification in terms of a libidinal economy against the perceived essentialism of gender identities. His symbolic practice introduces the logic of supplementarity in the fetishization of the female body, widening the gap between realism and avant-gardism through the ironic critical distancing from and within the libidinal economy of representation; that is, with the tropological status of gender symbolic difference.

Here it is possible to address only a few competing gender representations in Valle-Inclán's texts that combine time/space with value: (1) the tropological sequence of the *Sonatas;* (2) the bodies of history: hysteria, sexual/social cannibalism; and (3) disruption of the symbolic structures of his *farsas* [farces] and *esperpentos.*

What must be observed first, however, with respect to Valle-Inclán's early work, even before considering the contents of the tropological sequence of the *Sonatas* (and other early texts), is that Valle-Inclán inscribes himself in the ironic structure in the figure of an ambivalent Don Juan with pathogenic qualities. This is a powerful operation for situating his ironic utterances in a performance of what could well be called *aphanisis* (in the Lacanian sense), since the subject disappears in term of self and sexuality. In an attempt to localize and historicize sexual relations, the Marquis of Bradomín is here represented as a sexually ambivalent identity in the public forum. Simultaneously, Valle-Inclán is ironic (and parodic) of the cheap vulgar romantic fiction that flows in the Don Juan chronotope, creating a *pastiche* (in the sense Adorno gives to this term). The detachment and ironic critical distancing serves the purpose of problematizing the semiotic representation of aristocratic erotic games.

What seems more certain is that the traces of the traditional
practice of romantic aristocratic Don Juanism linked to a precapitalist cultural order are released, ensuring a loss of their symbolic
dimension. The texts "disarticulate," one could say, cultural codes
of behavior, as the narrator ironizes the repertoire of models, aug-
menting the contingencies of cultural representation. (There have
been numerous studies of this ironic distancing.) Valle-Inclán
throws into question the roles by which men and women are expected to pattern their erotic lives. These roles are further demol-
ished in the *farsas*, where they are modeled as deconstructions of
the bodies of history. The bodies of canons and norms are recognized no less strategically. (*La enamorada del rey* [The girl who
fell in love with the king] can be read in this light.)

What seems clear to the contemporary reader is Valle-Inclán's
ironization and his ironic blow to the construct of woman as the
healing panacea of men against the alienation brought to the modern world by the cult of reason (found in Bécquer, e.g.). His women
are not temptresses promising trascendence to deal with alienation
and fear. The unbridled sexuality of la Niña Chole [Mistress
Chole], for instance, endowed with all the exoticism of the Renaissance, the luxuriousness of the Orient, and the enigmatic nature
of the New World Other, serves to demystify the symbolic, namely,
the incest taboo and homosexual denouement, both of potential
significance in the development of modern sensibility and modern
erotic idioms. A writing blind to love, sexual encounters as power
relations, and erotic behaviors and sexual deviances previously
restricted to pornography, would entail turning its back on forty
or fifty years of Western exploration of sexual imagination, an important modifying element of modern literary freedom.[10]

Valle-Inclán moves further than many of his contemporaries in
exploring sexuality, violence—power, the promiscuous power
games of the modern world—by virtue of irony, pastiche, mime,
and parody. He explores this symbolic world through verbal and
representational erosion, as well as through the multiplication of
different forms of knowledge. The heterochrony of gender constructs is further enhanced by a reshaping of conventional genres
and an alteration of the way cognitive images of time and space
are used in them. The idyllic, romantic chronotopes, as well as the
adventure chronotope are reaccentuated here in a dialogy through
a complex of political, theological, and cultural questions. The
form-shaping ideology of speech and the typical generic form of
prose and finalization (novella) includes a view of the language of
heteroglossia and a dynamic way of understanding time and space.

As a chronotopic motif or motives (the Don Juan topic, libertine literature, and modernist forms of representation), as they structure Valle-Inclán's ironic and distanced narrative, the events of the past (precapitalist and rural Spain, as well as prerevolutionary rural Mexico) were compressed reminders of the kind of time and space in which these symbolic economies originated.

To fully appreciate this heterochrony of gender constructs, it is helpful to refer to "realist" poetics and its laws of a Ptolemaic universe. In the architectural logocentrism of realistic narratives, matters of primary concern were texts articulating cultural codes of behavior. Spain's principle examples are works by Galdós and Clarín. Gender in both writers is correlated with sex and associated with forms of "imaginary" identity and behavior; the symbolic processes that help constitute gender (and social) contrasts show compatibility with forms of normative and institutional authorities. This is the explicit social lesson taught to Fortunata/pueblo [Fortunata/the people] in Galdós's *Fortunata y Jacinta* [*Fortunata and Jacinta*]: "entrar por el aro" ["fall into line"]. Women "connote and condense" the production of the subject on the basis of a chain of paradigmatic discourses, determined by the closure of the social and the fixed character of the signifier.

Realist texts invariably construct the feminine as a pole subordinated to the masculine; for this reason one can speak of a sex/gender system that reinforces the imaginary signification of a subordinate immutable feminine essence. For example, Don Juan (a major chronotopic motif for Clarín as well as for Valle-Inclán) functions as limits in the general symbolic economy,[11] to stabilize both gender and nature. Realists see women within a history of unrelenting victimization, a stasis of patriarchal victory that projects a disabling view of women's transgressions.[12] It is important, however, to be sensitive to the formal limiting situations of realist (liberal) symbolic practice, which explains, to an extent, the collapse of conventions of representation among modernists, particularly Valle-Inclán, whose antimaster narrative projects a demystification and liberation of the symbolic, as I have already suggested elsewhere.[13]

Valle-Inclán readjusts his language to the abrupt turn in history signified by Spanish political affairs after 1868 and 1898, World War I, and the Russian and Mexican revolutions. The dead styles of the past become vehicles for new works (what Adorno calls pastiche) and at the same time he explores parody, to mock not only literary styles, but also social absurdities and mendacities. Clearly, shallow social relations, standardization, and the emptiness of the nascent comodification of his own time, all present Valle-Inclán with a wealth of content. From it, he unfolds unexpected, precise combinations of forms of struggle and the alignment of forces.

History provided Valle-Inclán with new conditions of possibility and an exact discursive location from which to undertake his symbolic practice. The symbolic processes that helped constitute class and gender (and even ethnic) contrasts propose to intensify and even generate group consciousness among both dominant hegemonic forces and suppressed collectivities, so as to project hostile confrontation. Valle-Inclán embodies the violent buggery of the modern world in a dramatic form by virtue of irony and/or parody, portraying new idioms for the savageries of the so-called respectable (bourgeois) conditions of modernity.

The immediate sense of the monotonous and intolerable conventional descriptive features of romanticism and realism are rewritten or defamiliarized by rethinking them in terms of abstract thinking and knowledge. Valle-Inclán ironizes and parodies institutionalized forms of evaluation of symbolic representations of a cross-class gender categorization as he carnivalizes the bodies of history into hysterical constructs and projects the sexual/social cannibalism of the monarchs, the Church, the army, and the politicians. The harmonious hegemonic relation of these social groups surfaces as a dissolution of such constructs, for the relational character of every social identity implies a breaking-up of social/sexual constructs. Consequently, it follows that Valle-Inclán's contesting symbolic practice is dominated by an articulation of the fragments of a now lost totality, that of both Imperial Spain's absolute monarchy, and its cross-cultural metaphors as well as the muddled claims of Spanish liberalism since 1834.

There is no social edifice more appropriate for expressing the anachronism of the pastiche and parody of the social than the cannibalistic (in the Freudian sense) discourse of the Spanish monarchy itself. Valle-Inclán sums up the whole of the social as ghosts, dying generations possessed by history, formal afterimages of dismembered voices. King and queen are gendered, hysterical constructs, while other semiotic representations of the military, the Church, and politics breach the social agreements that constitute representation. Valle-Inclán's anaphormistic mirror redirects the institutionalized forms of evaluation of symbolic representation: a cuckold-"fairy" king, a cannibalistic queen devouring the political body, the monoglot and monological forms of official and dogmatic truths aimed at one-dimensional constructs. In this particular historical moment (the "esperpentos," like the *Ruedo Ibérico* [The Iberian ring] trilogy are structured around the 1868 Revolution), the institutions and practices through which the categories of gender are produced are themselves being deconstructed in a dispersion of subject positions.

Valle-Inclán's reader can perceive the struggles against oppressive forms of constructing and producing sexual differences in relation to one another. Symbolism linked to gender reinforces political and ideological questions. The sexed-body becomes a carrier of various discourses, an exchanged signifier uniting public and private. Bodies become the central element in the working out of a new ideology and new social constructs: the sexual bodies of the oppressors are a necessary semiotic exchange to demystify the dominant cultures. At this point, the libidinal economy of popular culture intersects along boundaries in explosions of metonymies and metaphors aimed against the Manichaean projections of symbols.

Walter Benjamin's *Angelus Novus* comes to mind as Valle-Inclán's demystifications of gender, social, and cultural constructs project new identities and texts that inscribe the storm of destruction. The ensemble of posters, icons, newspaper rhetoric, visual arts, and written and oral texts—all the literary and nonliterary series that enter into a heteroglossic text. M. M. Bakhtin's words describe similar semantic treasures embedded in Shakespeare's works.

> [These] were created and collected through the centuries and even millennia; they lay hidden in the language . . . also in those strata of popular language that before Shakespeare's time had not entered literature, in the diverse genres and forms of speech communication, in the forms of a mighty national culture (primarily carnival forms) that were shaped through millenia, in theater-spectacle genres (mystery plays, farces, and so forth) in plots whose roots go back to prehistoric antiquity, and, finally, in forms of thinking.[14]

Such semantic wealth and heterochronies, with their specific forms of thinking enter Valle-Inclán's polyphonic orchestration of interrelated cultural worlds.

Questions of sexual ideology and gender categorizations are part of Valle-Inclán's national project and social imaginary. These demystifications are grounded in the power of the allegorical, which Benjamin identified as crucial in modern (baroque) drama, and which Paul de Man designates as the rhetoric of temporality.[15] De Man suggests that the successful combination of allegory and irony (or "permanent parabasis," to use Schlegel's definition) captures the experience of the present as a distance (critical distance), and an interrogation of subjectivity and identity in the present.

Such interrogations are a site of contest to disclose the overlapping contradictions of power, the manipulations and constructions of sexual behaviors (so central in the figuration of gender), whose underpinning is the entire false normative and authoritatian relations of the fragmented political body, and the social/sexual cannibalism of the rulers. Valle-Inclán aims at disclosing how human nature and society had changed on or about 1830 and 1868 (with liberalism), actualizing that society and allowing us to reread and rewrite the past.

In fact, the privileged historical content of this symbolic practice seems to have been largely constituted in those turn-of-the-century decades which entertain a semiotic binary opposition in stereotypes of European and Spanish history. Signs form a coherent dichotomous class and economic system (high versus low, urban versus rural, privileged versus poor). In the upper-class component the nostalgia of its characters for class content and elegance is staged. Valle-Inclán does this through modernism and stylized, ironic, mimed forms which underscore the dependency on earlier cultural language of romantic precapitalism (the ironic distance).

In his work (the *Sonatas,* e.g.), the various chronotopic motifs of elegance and leisure (the *Sonatas*) are coordinated as ironic allegories to indicate the ludic exercise in futility of that old power. He problematizes the transition from "feudalism" to "capitalism" since the liberal or bourgeois narrative of progress (the ascension of Isabella II and the death of Carlism), to indicate the extinction of that master narrative with the Revolution of 1868. The proposition projected symbolically is the end of traditional society in all its forms; the heterochrony of female sexuality and women's representation in the four polyphonic texts of the *Sonatas* is ironically projected, and the characters speak their sexuality.

It becomes clear that none of these projections is innocent, and that all pass through the body, filtered and symbolically invested in the narrative significance. Through varying strategies, Valle-Inclán models the reification and fragmentation of the social, approached initially by way of traditional problems on whose permutation his originality depends. All this formal reorganization consistently invokes optics and ocular conceptions of knowledge. The syntax of this demystifying intention, is finally supplemented and modified by techniques, the organization of matter, and the languages of representations.

This marriage of style and logos is patterned through the disruption of the symbolic (more evident in the farces and "esperpentos") is accompanied by the total disruption of representation (gender and genres) in cross-cultural and transsemiotic contacts, incorporating all the cultural series (past and present). Allegory (in Benjamin's modern *Trauerspiel* sense) and irony are the rhetorical temporal devices that Valle-Inclán privileges to strengthen the "libidinal economy" or political fantasy. The social symbolic meaning of his writing practice at his point conjoins irony and parody as the great sociophilosophical issues.

My point here is that there is a close connection between women's bodies and these sociosymbolic issues. It is women, more than men, who are the carriers or filters of history (similar to Benjamin), as either images of violation or the alternative (but simultaneous) history that runs beneath the history of the cannibals of the political body.[16] This "poetry of the future" (to use Marx's words), of an epic without heroes, is framed by ironic distancing, comic estrangement (the farces), the unbounded laughter of parody, and the tragic montage of some *esperpentos*.[17]

It is no accident that Valle-Inclán stages a hallucinatory phantasmagoria of symbolic figures of violation, corpses, prostitutes, and carnivalized rulers as the living expression of the body's insertion as signifier into the zone of social space and time. The images of the body in Valle-Inclán are not positive; on the contrary, they are often inscribed as disemembered—*das unheimliche*. That is, they manifest a crisis of representation that points to the once familiar now uncanny, through castration, fragmentation, and division. His metaphors of the body project the ills of liberal bourgeois metanarratives, and they can be read as ambivalent revolutionary undecidable categories. He rewrites the body so as to organize promises (however ambivalent) of transformed material forces. The body is language, libidinal images speak the materiality of history;[18] through allegorizing he aims to unleash another collective libido.

Divinas palabras [*Divine Words*] seems to be the strongest libidinal image of such materiality and their link with theological tradition. The *Trauerspiel* takes here its other modern vision of the turning wheel, in its ceaseless succession of masks not only of the powerful and mighty, but also of the dance of death of the lowly (already present in early short stories and poems). The empty acts and words of the Church's immobilized Latin, are divested of visible and social function. Moreover, the ballads, *consejas* [tales], and other forms of oral culture that Valle-Inclán inserts in his heteroglossic texts as part of what has been called "gender generics,"

merit further study, since women were custodians of ballad tradition.[19] In fact, ballads are old wives' tales that were able to develop
and change in feminine ways. On the other hand, and to contextual-
ize *Divinas palabras,* Latin (and Greek) were forms of class and
gender exclusionist practice in androcentric (and Catholic) cultures. In Valle-Inclán, this practice becomes contested from the
margin.

What I have been seeking to demonstrate, in short, is that Valle-
Inclán avoids implicit gendering situations (where the masculine is
active and the feminine passive, e.g.), or presenting trascendence
as a masculine endeavor. He does not succumb to the belief that
sexes possess sets of essential possibilities, and does not promote
and project either female or male values. What is particularly relevant is that the body (both political and private) is a dynamic exotopy, and he recognizes its changing positions and relation (what
we would today call its subject positions), eschewing a monolithic
view of the lower classes as a subversive force.

In this respect, Valle-Inclán's attempt to subvert the categories
of semiotic representation and the collapse of conventions situates
his symbolic practice on the very edges of the constraints and
contingencies of history. My claim is that his writing is an elegant
rebuttal of the romantic sentimental narrative of behavior, nation,
identity, and sexual relations. His writing has something to do with
the convergence of the problematic of nation with that of subject-
formation. Female sexuality is not projected through the one-dimensional view of male domination (here his treatment is akin to
that of Joyce); both sex and gender stereotyping, when projected,
are interwoven with their material conditions in history.

His signifying practice makes every brutality explicit and explores verbal and representational taboos, teasing out types of sexual behavior previously unstated and identified with what was
called *sicalipsis* or straight pornography (the texts of Alejandro
Sawa or Felipe Trigo, e.g.). The richest erotic idioms were shown
in his modern fiction and drama.

Two things follow from this. First, Valle-Inclán's symbolic economy is oriented toward Otherness; all axiological determinations
and characterizations of the world, to paraphrase Bakhtin, are oriented with reference to the Other, in answerability, Second, his
outsidedness (the famous points of view) gives him a unique position from which to distance himself so as to produce undecidable
images and indeterminant constructions from the margin. His gender constructions make accessible the profoundly ambivalent nature of social life, since in the modern world there is no fixed place

from where to look, and any form of systematic system falls under suspicion. Style is inseparably linked not only to particular thematic and compositional unities, but to representation and, therefore, to gender constructs or what I have addressed as the heterochrony of gender constructs. Changes in speech genres and historical changes in language styles and chronotopes constantly interact.

It might be argued that Valle-Inclán dissolves boundaries in order to capture more directly, clearly, and flexibly, the historical changes taking place in social life, changes inseparably linked to the semantic exhaustion of a theme (i.e., the erotic cultural capital of the Bradomín series, the choral architectonics of *Flor de santidad* [Flower of holiness], and other utterances). The condition of boundaries becomes determined by changes in speaking subjects: from the function of an anonymous chorus (similar to that of classical Greek tragedies) in his early work, to the untypically strong-voiced Madre Isabel of the Carlist War trilogy, to the articulate female voices in the *Ruedo Ibérico*.[20] It would be difficult to identify Valle-Inclán with the one-dimensional characters, the predictable plots, or the reactionary values of the normative authority of institutionalized norms.[21] Nor is it possible to ascribe to his symbolic practice the prescribed double standard; the projection of passive heroines and masterful heroes; suicidal disintegration of women; the focus of chastity as women's identity; procreation as a political and religious act; domesticity as an imperative; or the triumphs of marital, heterosexual bliss except as ironic or parodic registers. All of these potent imaginary constructs and fictions are often deconstructed through irony, farce, or parody, or at least through indeterminacy.

What I feel the need to stress is that "voice" and "body" are in intersections, in dialogicality, and, more specifically, that "voices" refer to the "speaking Other" and not "speaking the Other." The language games of gendered bodies are linked to form-shaping ideologies and to authoritative discourses themselves. In Valle-Inclán's textual world there exists no single monolithical uniform region of representation, rather the "uncanniness" of the Other which allows for dialogue.

More important, perhaps, Valle-Inclán's constant rethinking of old and previously explored cultural capital brings to focus the challenge of unfixed signs which are, simultaneously, situated in the events of the concrete social world. If so, his inverted form of "politics of style" dramatizes both venerable scenarios of stereotypes (within the rhetoric of temporality I have previously suggested), and the critical awareness of exotopy to give voice to characters who utter the different languages of heteroglossia.

The hidden agenda (the "unuttered" or "not-said") of his symbolic practice is that ethics are undecidable in the political arena and, therefore, political decisions must be made in this contingency. He opens the terrain of decision as he solicits correction, modification, even collaborative disagreement in rejoinder and continuation: understanding and meaning are, in his world, explicitly provisional.

My underlying concern has been to produce a theoretical space to indicate that there is an ethical as well as a political dimension in Valle-Inclán's competing versions.[22] The pleasure principle was to him a point of departure for a journey into the seas of undecidable meanings and margins. It involved him in a "game" of uncanny repetitions outside authorized circles. A game of absences, silences, and deaths, contrary to the discursive power games of his contemporaries and their strongly marked gendered program both in culture and in social life.

The point is contentious, since I believe Valle-Inclán articulates a new symbolic capital outside the dominant order, disrupting the symbolic power through dialogy and indeterminacy. He sustains a multiplicity of various levels of speech and meaning and relinquishes the romantic "I" as the subjective center of speech. This is worth pursuing.

As gender criticism and Valle-Inclán's modes of cultural production are retheorized, it is important to stress that the surfaces of the political bodies of women he rewrote and reinscribed were not politically constructed as frail beings to be tamed nor barbarian lusty cannibals to be enslaved. A whole performative political theory of identifying acts proliferates, in flight from the Manichean allegory that normally describes patriarchal colonialist discourses and textual and epistemic imperialisms.

A second proposition is also being suggested here: namely, that the emergence of the modern world is not projected through raptures of submission in Valle-Inclán's symbolic practice, nor through the cult of invalidism, mirrored Venuses, or women of glass.[23] These erotic fantasies are often deliberately ironic projections for purposely reorienting his reader toward a recognition of stereotypical forbidden male erotica to which Valle-Inclán's own textual production of meaning did not conform. The language games of his modes of cultural production underscore his independence from contemporary cultural language, and they enabled him to exercise his political imaginary in a variety of openings of the social. The interpretive problem is that his interconnections are not transparent and the hermeneutic approach ought to work "between the blinds," making enigmatic what one thinks one understands (to borrow from Derrida).

Valle-Inclán's whole writing practice constituted a determinant mode of cultural production of knowledge and is constitutive of a problematic inscribed in the invisible questions posed in his texts. The questions of epistemological status of his literary discourse projected new sets of answers to old sociocultural questions. His cognitive cultural fantasy has the willed quality to unfix and invert the hegemonic structures of power, and something no less courageous, to mount an attack against the epistemological imperialism of a fixed, sutured, symbolic economy. This would be, the "nonsaid" or "unuttered" of his signifying practice, which both creates a vision and constitutes the means for knowing it.

Notes

1. Jean-Françoise Lyotard, *L'Économie libidinale* (Paris: Minuit, 1974). It should be obvious that my account here is very sketchy and is in fact a prologemonen to a theory of the heterochronies of gender. It goes without saying that a study of gender entails an analysis of the constructions and meanings of masculinity and femininity in history and culture.

2. It should be clear that I draw on but adapt Derrida's *Margin of Philosophy* (1972), trans. Alan Bass (Chicago: University of Chicago Press, 1982).

3. "The Bakhtinian Text as Intersections," lecture given in May 1991 at the International Seminar on M. M. Bakhtin, Institute of Semiotics, University of Amsterdam.

4. I would like to stress here that when I speak of "voices" and the "intertextual" in Valle-Inclán, I do not refer, in polemic or assent, to the system of direct or indirect citations, which is the stuff palimpsestic texts are made of. I employ the Bakhtinian "voices" in a very specific sense: that of a dynamic relation between signifying practices, as well as subject positions of the utterances. See my book, *La musa funambulesca. Poética de la carnavalización en Valle-Inclán* (Madrid: Orígenes, 1990).

5. On this idea, although his discussion is sketchy, see J. T. Mitchell, "Representation," in *Critical Terms for Literary Study,* eds. Frank Lentricchia and Thomas McLaughlin (Chicago: University of Chicago Press, 1990), 11–22. The category of representation cannot be thought without reference to presence (genre), as the perception of self in presence.

6. I should like to remind the reader that a dialogic criticism is concerned with identifying and arranging relations between voices, further understood as articulations of value, thus bringing together time and space in their simultaneity and inseparability.

7. The reader will rightly conclude that I am enlarging Bakhtin's concept of the chronotope to include gender constructs. On the chronotope in general, an excellent analysis can be found in Gary Saul Morson and Caryl Emerson, *Mikhail*

Bakhtin: Creation of a Prosaics (Stanford, Calif.: Stanford University Press, 1990).

8. I am obviously adapting Naomi Schor, *Breaking the Chain: Women, Theory, and French Realist Fiction* (New York: Columbia University Press, 1985).

9. See my book, *La musa funambulesca.*

10. I refer to George Steiner's compelling essay, "Eros and Idioms," in *On Difficulty* (New York: Oxford University Press, 1980), 95–136.

11. I am aware that I am writing against the grain as I suggest that the master narratives of Galdós and Clarín do not batter against the boundaries of their culture, and that both augment the emotional force of fear and submission to gender constructs. An exception should be made for *Tristana.*

12. In contrast, transgressions must have been frequent, as the multiplication of repressive institutional discourses since the 1830s suggests. See Iris M. Zavala, "Infracciones y transgresiones sexuales en el romanticismo hispánico," *Journal of Interdisciplinary Studies/Cuadernos Interdisciplinarios de Estudios Literarios* 1, no. 1 (1989): 1–18.

13. I refer specifically to my book, *La musa funambulesca,* where I stress (against current Lacanian usage) that Valle-Inclán's project is a liberation from the symbolic, understood in its materiality of social fear.

14. Mikhail Bakhtin, *"Speech Genres" and Other Late Essays,* trans. Vernon McGee, Caryl Emerson, and Michael Holquist (Austin: University of Texas Press, 1986), 5.

15. See, in particular, Paul de Man, *Blindness and Insight: Essays on the Rhetoric of Contemporary Criticism* (Minneapolis: University of Minnesota Press, 1983), 187–228.

16. It should be obvious that I am employing the term *discursive cannibalism* in the sense given to it by Freud, namely, that it devours and takes the place of the history lost to it.

17. The references to this poetry are to be found in the often-quoted *Eighteenth Brumaire of Louis Bonaparte* (1848).

18. It could be argued that Valle-Inclán (like Bakhtin and Benjamin) understand the body in its theological tradition. On this last issue and Bakhtin, see Charles Lock, "Carnival and Incarnation: Bakhtin and Orthodox Theology," *Journal of Literature and Theology* 5, no. 1 (1991): 68–82.

19. I adapt this term from Kathleen Blake, "'Pure Tess': Hardy on Knowing a Woman," *Studies in English Literature* 12 (1978): 700. If my suggestion is accepted, this would seem to problematize Noël M. Valis's heuristics ("The Novel as Feminine Entrapment," essay in this volume).

20. For a complementary yet different perspective, see "The Function of Language, . ." Biruté Ciplijauskaité's synoptic article on the representation of women (in this volume). Also, see Noël Valis's "Novel as Feminine Entrapment" (in this volume), a perceptive reading based on the assumption that the parodic "can also double back against itself." This is precisely what I call undecidability and ambiguity meant to undo the symbolic. I suggest, therefore, that Valle-Inclán's demystification of the symbolic includes setting the boundaries and intersections just mentioned so as to subvert traditional gender roles.

21. The female body and Western cultural imagination have been addressed in the well-known collection of essays, *The Female Body in Western Culture: Semiotic Perspectives,* ed. Susan Rubin Suleiman (Cambridge: Harvard University Press, 1986).

22. Versions that compete, in short, to legitimize different agendas, which is

indicative of the problem of appropriation, since the production of texts is never completed and they are reappropriated with different political effects and purposes. On this point, see Tony Bennet's *Formalism and Marxism* (London: Methuen, 1979), 136, passim. I fully agree with John Frow, who suggests that a text is marked by multiple temporality: the time of its production and the times of its reception, and that the serial or lateral movement between systems produces new texts, and new kinds of texts. See *Marxism and Literary History* (Oxford: Basil Blackwell, 1988), 171. It would seem, following this line of argument, that the questions Valle-Inclán left open are our contemporary questions; this is a Bakhtinian agenda.

23. I adapt these libidinal fantasies liberally from Bram Dijkstra, *Idols of Perversity: Fantasies of Feminine Evil in Fin-de-Siècle Culture* (Oxford: Oxford University Press, 1988).

Modernism and Margins: Valle-Inclán and the Politics of Gender, Nation, and Empire

MARY K. ADDIS and ROBERTA L. SALPER

As the nineteenth century clicked over into the twentieth, Valle-Inclán's literary project emerged, Janus-like, at the waning of one historical moment and the beginning of a new one. Valle-Inclán started to write in the late 1880s, at the close of the period during which an ascending bourgeoisie had struggled to impose an alternative vision for society as a whole. Part of the realization and coming of age of this new worldview was an increase, in the twentieth century, in the social significance of sectors of society, initially marginalized by that very bourgeois rule, principally the working classes and women. In the wake of the Bolshevik Revolution, Europe (and Spain was no exception) experienced an acceleration of working-class militancy, the reverberations of which became a major factor in the complex aesthetic configurations often classified as the European post-1917 avant-garde. As we show in the following pages, part of Valle-Inclán's literary production—in particular his subversion of reigning gender discourses in texts such as *La hija del capitán* [The captain's daughter]—is related to the facet of the European post-1917 avant-garde that moved from bourgeois dissidence to a certain affiliation with, or overt sympathy for, the working class and marginalized.[1]

Valle-Inclán's "transgressions" from the mode of "seeing" characteristic of his contemporaries—from the Eurocentric or, more specifically, the peninsular gaze—led him, in comparison with others of the so-called Generation of '98, to encompass a broader scope of the totality of contradictions that were prevalent at the turn of the century in the Hispanic world. If his fiction is a textual site of Spain's cultural, linguistic, and social struggles, his literary production is also implicated in the articulation (within, and addressed to, the metropolis) of the margins of Spain's empire, of the "Other," that is, Hispanic America. Valle-Inclán's corpus of texts is a projection of a contradictory totality—the plurality of interests and projects of competing social classes and groups[2]—encompassed in the dissolution of the Spanish empire and its belated entrance into the modern fraternity of twentieth-century nationhood.

In the early years, we find in Valle-Inclán a preoccupation with the fashioning of masculine identities, a kind of self-fashioning, that we will examine in some detail in the short story "Octavia Santino" (1892). An important aspect of Valle-Inclán's early constructions of masculine identities constitutes a rejection of bourgeois manhood that is part and parcel of his early bourgeois dissidence. While he continues throughout his career to experiment with the fashioning of what some critics have called "alter egos" (the poet-figure Max Estrella of *Luces de Bohemia* [*Bohemian Lights*] is a notable example), his early constructions of masculinity take a decidedly narcissistic and subjectivist turn. In "Octavia Santino," Pedro Pondal's unconscious need to liberate himself from domestic entrapment (and also, therefore, from women) in order to achieve poetic stature suggests a vision of the male artist as standing outside (or above) a social world essentially hostile to, and dismissive of, the creative genius and true art. Pedro Pondal's self-marginalization and solipsism will contrast dramatically with the political commitment Max Estrella admires in the Catalan revolutionary (scene 6).

While any number of Valle-Inclán's early texts, from other stories in *Femeninas* [*Feminine portraits*] (the book's title notwithstanding) to the *Sonatas* or even the *Comedias bárbaras* [*Barbaric Comedies*] could be used to illustrate his various preoccupations surrounding masculine identity in the bourgeois world of Restoration society, we have chosen the short story "Octavia Santino" because Valle-Inclán's rewriting of the Octavia-Pedro love story in his first play, *Cenizas* [*Ashes*] (1899) and its subsequent revision, *El yermo de las almas* [*Wasteland of souls*] (1908), registers with particular clarity important shifts in his thinking, especially regarding the family. One of our principal interests in the following pages is to trace Valle-Inclán's revisioning and reworking of what we will call "the domestic paradigm" in texts that span most of his opus. We see in the revision of the Octavia-Pedro love story a shift on Valle-Inclán's part, from a certain "modernista" solipsism in the short story, to a less male-centered representation of domesticity in the two plays, which begins to question the very foundations of the family as social institution and that sees those foundations as distinctly patriarchal. We will argue that the shift to a critique of patriarchy as it operates through the family structure challenges, at least implicitly, the whole notion of distinct and dichotomous private and public spheres. That such a dichotomy is both pernicious and gender oppressive lies at the very heart of Valle-Inclán's attack on the military and its nationalist rhetoric in *Martes de carnaval* [Shrove Tuesday]. In *La hija del capitán* (1927), the last of the three plays of *Martes* and the last text of Valle-Inclán's we analyze, the military establishment invokes the family (and "la familia militar" ["military family"]) constantly in the face of threats to its status and power. In fact, it is through the family's least powerful member, the daughter, that Valle-Inclán challenges both the integrity of the military state and its dependence on a rhetoric of the family to legitimate its authority.

As Nancy Armstrong and Leonard Tennenhouse posit, no representation of the family is politically neutral,[3] and, as feminist scholarship has long insisted, representations of the family have been, and are, potent ideological vehicles. Valle-Inclán's critique of Restoration society through the familial or domestic paradigm in *Yermo* has widened by *La hija del capitán* to encompass a regressive yet still dominant ideology of nationhood articulated in this play by the military and its allies, the Church, the King, and even a "conservative feminist" named, aptly, Doña Simplicia. In *La hija del capitán* Valle-Inclán interrogates and deconstructs the complex configurations of gender, nation, and empire implicit in the military's nationalist rhetoric and bid for power. In this play, the family quite literally emerges from the "household" and moves to the center stage of national politics. Valle-Inclán therefore demonstrates clearly, especially in the drama's final scene, that the family is not a self-enclosed unit but the very basis upon which a concept of the nation can be constructed and defended. Women in particular, while always "marginalized," from public life, are not "marginal" to nationalist ideology and the power structure it sustains. The demeaning and violent consequences of not being marginal— Captain Sinibaldo prostitutes his own daugher in order to keep his corrupt business practices afloat—dramatizes this point. Valle-Inclán utilizes the daughter (in concert with others likewise "marginalized") as a potent ideological vehicle of his own, as a means of rewriting not only the discourse of the family but also the discourse of official Spain.

As J. C. Mariátegui observed long ago, a "nation" is always a fiction, something more imagined than real insofar as definitions or representations of nations often serve to conceal internal divisions and hierarchies of class, gender, and race.[4] For Tim Brennan, a nation is above all a "discursive practice and an imaginary projection."[5] Nationalism invents nations where they do not exist. The nationalism of the military in *La hija del capitán* is both reactive and reactionary. It tries to shore up an outdated concept of Spain in the face of intensifying working-class militancy and the bankruptcy of the Restoration "turno" system [alternating two-party system]. It also attempts to mollify a nagging uncertainty about Spain's status as a modern nation among national leaders and some intellectuals.[6] Indeed, the military did succeed temporarily and partially in reimposing its vision of Spain with the Primo de Rivera coup of 1923, to which Valle-Inclán's play plainly alludes. That the military hierarchy recognized Valle-Inclán's historical references and antimilitarist and hence antinationalist stance accounts for the government's censorship of *La hija del capitán*.[7]

We are particularly interested in the ways in which gender categories operate in *La hija del capitán* to deconstruct nationalist ideology. It is therefore well worth remembering, as Mary Louise Pratt has demonstrated, the resolutely androcentric character of modern nations as "imagined communities." Pratt finds in her analysis of Benedict Anderson's study of nationalism that

> women "don't fit" his descriptors of imagined communities. Rather, the modern nation by definition situates or "produces" women in permanent instability with respect to the imagined community. . . . What bourgeois republicanism offered women [was] "republican motherhood," the role of producers of citizens. . . . As mothers of the nation [women] are precariously other. . . .[8]

It is precisely this otherness, women's marginalization from the sphere of public life and national politics, that *La hija del capitán* exposes and exploits. What Pratt calls the "uneasy coexistence of nationhood and womanhood" is what permits Valle-Inclán to deconstruct an outmoded nationalism and, at the same time, to move toward a more internationalist vision.

Throughout his texts Valle-Inclán diverged from many of the hegemonic social categories of gender propagated in his time by advocates of conservative Spanish traditions. He also remained removed from the hypocrisy inherent in the gender warp characteristic of certain Spanish liberal thought in the 1920s, as exemplified by the *Revista de Occidente* and its close affiliation with two of Spain's leading intellectuals, José Ortega y Gasset and Dr. Gregorio Marañón.[9] Valle-Inclán's gender subtexts probed beyond Spain's generally accepted middle-class codes of conduct. With characteristic verve and originality, he gazed "against the grain" both on the Peninsula and in the New World.

Domestic Ideologies: From "Octavia Santino" to *El yermo de las almas*

This section examines three texts in the Octavia-Pedro Pondal series[10] in order to illustrate a major ideological shift in Valle-Inclán's representation of bourgeois domesticity.[11] In retelling the story of the love affair between the young poet Pedro Pondal and an older woman, the single Octavia Santino of the short story of the same name and the unhappily married Octavia Goldini of *Cenizas* and *El yermo de las almas,* Valle-Inclán moves from a male-centered vision in which the female functions primarily as a projection of male desire, to a more critical focus on the social construction of gender in connection to the bourgeois division of the world into public and private spheres. We have not chosen these three texts because they are necessarily representative of different stages in Valle-Inclán's literary production, but rather because they enable us to trace significant changes in Valle-Inclán's handling of what we are calling the "domestic paradigm" or familial trope. We will argue that the representation of domesticity in Valle-Inclán's work acquires increasing social and political resonance as he moved from an early sui generis bourgeois dissidence to a more conscious affiliation with the marginalized and disenfranchised. Valle-Inclán thus provides us with an ever-widening angle on the family that not only identifies the private sphere of the home and family as the primary site for the reproduction of bourgeois ideology, but also links family relationships with specific forms of political power and control.

From the very beginning of Valle-Inclán's opus, gender and the notion of gendered spheres are vehicles for social critique. This is not surprising because, as Rita Felski reminds us, "gender, as one on the central categories of social and symbolic organization, provides a key terrain on which to challenge dominant definitions of the real."[12] As Noël Valis has noted,[13] gender in fact structures many of Valle-Inclán's early narratives, and there is in these texts at least a partial awareness of gender's social constructedness, its contingent or arbitrary nature. The short stories of *Femeninas,* for example, treat gender identities not as essences but as roles people play. By holding gender constructs up to subtle ridicule in some of these stories, Valle-Inclán shows them to be based on social convention: they are contingent, disputable, and thus linked to forms of social authority and control. Valle-Inclán's awareness of the contingency of gender constructs would not, however, have been a radically new observation in turn-of-the-century Europe. At the center of late nineteenth-century Naturalism, for example, and according to Raymond Williams, "was the . . . proposition that human nature was not, or at least not decisively, unchanging and timeless, but was socially and culturally specific."[14]

Critics have observed that Valle-Inclán's overriding concern in his early narratives is with the male subject and his subjectivity.[15] Female characters, consequently, function primarily as mirrors for men, mirrors which refract a masculine identity, allowing Valle-Inclán to play with different styles of manhood. If, however, and as Felski points out,[16] there is something liberating in the recognition that gender identities are constructed and not "natural" or fixed, Valle-Inclán's insistent experimentation with the fashioning of masculinity betrays a certain anxiety over male gender roles.[17] Three of Valle-Inclán's recurring male characters—the young poet Pedro Pondal; the mature aesthete, the Marqués de Bradomín; and the aging feudal patriarch, Juan Manuel Montenegro—diverge from the conventional model of male bourgeois identity insofar as they stand outside the cycle of capitalist production and refuse the bourgeois male ethos of individual competitive achievement for material ends. The intensified ideology of manhood these male characters reflect, while certainly associated with Valle-Inclán's rejection of the values of Restoration society, also suggests that gender pressures, a struggle with what it meant to be a "man," played a role in his literary production. Valle-Inclán's preoccupation with a masculine self-fashioning also involves, as we will show in the discussion of "Octavia Santino," a misogynistic dismissal of women as subjects in their own right.

In "Octavia Santino," the Spanish bourgeois female remains trapped within, and identified with, the private sphere and an ideology of domesticity that the Modernist Valle-Inclán criticizes and seeks to escape. The second text in the Pedro Pondal series, this short story ostensibly narrates the pain and anguish the young poet Pondal suffers as a result of the grave illness and finally the death of his lover Octavia Santino. At a deeper level, however, the narrative can be read as the story of the freeing of the Modernist poet from the shackles of domesticity. In this sense, it participates in that male Modernist critique of the bourgeois family that Williams has described.[18] Octavia's death at the end of the story symbolizes the liberation of Pedro's subjectivity and desire, which can then be used at the service of his art, as Octavia herself tells him:

> ¿Qué era yo para ti más que una carga? ¿No comprendes? Tú tienes por delante un gran porvenir. Ahora, luego que yo me muera, debes vivir solito; no creas que digo esto porque esté celosa. . . . Te hablo así, porque conozco lo que ata una mujer. Tú si no te abandonas, tienes que subir muy alto. Créeme a mí . . . Dios que da las alas, las da para volar solo (97)

> [What was I for you but a dead weight? Don't you understand? You have a great future in front of you. When I die, you ought to live alone; don't think I'm saying this because I'm jealous. . . . I'm speaking to you in this way because I know how a woman ties a man down. If you're careful, you're sure to go far. Believe me . . . God gives you wings, but you have to fly alone].

Octavia's words reinforce the social construct of the middle-class Spanish woman as inferior to, and appended to, the male. It is clear from her perspective that domesticity or indeed any established intimate relationship will inhibit Pedro's development as a poet. Domesticity would, to borrow a phrase from Williams, "tame his genius." That virtually all of the action of the story takes place in a stiflingly hot and dark bedroom smelling of medicine, only reinforces the notion of the home as an oppressive enclosure.

Though Pedro and Octavia are not married and have been secretly living together for a year, their relationship, we argue, still coincides with the paradigm of bourgeois domesticity. It is confined to the home, shut off from the outside world, and thoroughly privatized in a way that other amorous liaisons in Valle-Inclán's early work are not. As if to emphasize a conventional domesticity, Pedro remembers that he first met Octavia two years earlier, at precisely that moment in which his childhood home was being dismantled ("¡Ay, fue al deshacerse aquel hogar cuando conociera a Octavia Santino!" (99) ["It was when that home disappeared that I met Octavia Santino!"] Because Pedro draws this association between the two households and because the narrative suggests at different points that the relationship between this young man and his older female lover has shades of a mother/son relationship,[19] the reader might conclude that Pedro has merely moved, on some level, from one bourgeois home to another and has yet to really "leave home."

Valle-Inclán does not represent the female, Octavia Santino, as a sovereign individual in her own right, and she acquires an identity only in terms of the home and as the object of Pedro's desire. Octavia, therefore conforms to that nineteenth-century idealized construct of Spanish womahood, the "ángel del hogar" ["angel of the hearth"] that Bridget Aldaraca has described. In this construct, woman can be idealized only by "taking as a starting point the negation of the real presence of woman as individual, i.e., as an autonomous social and moral being."[20] Valle-Inclán's male Modernist quest for liberation, metonymically expressed by a rejection of the bourgeois family, barely masks a disdain of women. In this story Valle-Inclán is therefore immersed in a Spanish variant of a kind of androcentrism particular to turn-of-the-century European literature. By registering in this story and others a vision of women as special examples of the weak who hold back the strong, he is participating in an *artistically dominant* vision, what Williams has called Modernism's "cultural Darwinism," "in which the strong and daring radical spirits are the true *creativity* of the race."[21]

Unlike the short story "Octavia Santino," Valle-Inclán's first play, *Cenizas* (1899) and its 1908 revision, *El yermo de las almas,* critique the dominant construction of Spanish bourgeois womanhood of the time, as well as the ideological foundation of that construct, the bourgeois home and family. In these two texts, Valle-Inclán looks at the family not as some natural and transhistorical entity, but as the product and reflection of bourgeois political power. It is important to remember, furthermore, that he is in both dramas criticizing an institution that during the first decade of the twentieth century was being vehemently defended in the face of an emergent yet still very weak feminist movement. Valle-Inclán examines some of the particularly dark areas of the bourgeois family, especially its control and manipulation of women, and in the process adopts a critical perspective on the family whose political implications acquire heightened significance in *Martes de carnaval.*

Cenizas and *El yermo de las almas* rewrite and substantially revise the love story narrated in "Octavia Santino." For our purposes, they can be considered identical, though we will cite only from *El yermo de las almas.*[22] Both plays reverse the thematic emphasis of the short story. First, the setting shifts from Galicia to Madrid. It is also significant that the Octavia/Pedro liaison is now an adulterous one, with all the legal, religious, and social implications adultery had in the early twentieth century.[23] Unlike the short narrative, the dramas examine concretely, different facts of bourgeois family life: the roles of fathers and husbands and the social construct of the Catholic bourgeois wife as well as institutions that have a decisive influence on the family, most significantly the Church and, because it insisted on a specific definition of female biology that facilitated the subjugation of women, medical science. Each of these forces acts on, and attempts to, control Octavia. Even the adulterous lover is complicitous with dominant ideology, for we see in the plays that Pedro, while still a poet, is an established (and establishment) figure rather than an aspiring writer, and he counts among his admirers even members of the clergy. Pedro's bourgeois affiliations are also made clear in the descriptions of both the exterior and interior of his house.[24]

All individuals act in a self-interested way to determine what Octavia should and should not do, and the action revolves around the psychological torment this produces in Octavia. The cuckolded husband, Don Juan Manuel, has complete legal authority over Octavia. Having discovered his wife's affair, he has determined that she will be shut up in a convent, never again to see her young daughter. We learn shortly after this pronouncement that Octavia escapes from her house, which she frequently refers to as "una cárcel" ["a prison"], to see Pedro one last time. He insists she stay with him, assuming in his own way the authority Spanish law grants husbands.[25] Oppressive and conflicting ideological prescriptions and demands emanating from patriarchy's various representatives—Octavia's husband, her priest and doctor, even her lover, Pedro, and her mother, Doña Soledad (closely allied with the priest, she is described as "la mujer española, apasionada y devota que sueña con el Infierno" [202] ["the Spanish woman, passionate and devout, who dreams about Hell"])—cause Octavia to fall gravely ill. The relentlessness with which these individuals pursue their own agendas culminates, at the play's end, with Octavia's death.

Thus we see in the transformation of the love story a move away from the Modernist poet's rejection of domesticity as potentially damaging to his creativity in the short story "Octavia Santino," and a move toward a fuller appreciation of the political significance of the bourgeois ideology of family and the gender system it prescribes in Cenizas and Yermo. We see in the theatrical texts, moreover, what happens to a woman, weak though Octavia is, who dares defy patriarchy as she seeks to satisfy her desire outside marriage. While the Octavia of the narrative rejects Pedro's pleas that a doctor and a priest be brought to the home—Octavia rejects the priest in particular, because she knows a confession would force Pedro from her side, leaving her to die alone—the Octavia of the two plays must endure oppressive treatment from both a doctor and a priest, and the priest succeeds in convincing a cow-ardly Pedro to abandon his lover only moments before her death. The female is the victim of domestic arrangement in *Cenizas* and *El yermo de las almas,* not the male. Another difference between the story and the plays is instructive. In the prose version, Octavia does in fact "confess," but not to a priest. Just before her death, she confesses to Pedro that she has been unfaithful. Whether or not this is true remains a mystery. The confession would serve, if so intended, to assist the more sensitive Pedro of the story in overcoming his grief in order to get on to the more important business of writing poetry. Thus this confession was another action carried out with the male's interest in mind.

The only character in the plays who is cognizant of the workings of bourgeois patriarchy is someone who stands partially outside this structure, the old Galician servant, Sabel. At different mo-ments in *Cenizas* and *El yermo de las almas,* she confronts patri-archy's representatives,[26] even trying to block Doña Soledad's attempts to remove her daughter from Pedro Pondal's house. In addition, she is the only character who understands the reasons for Octavia's illness. As in *Martes de carnaval,* it is a woman on the margins who is best able, precisely because of her marginality, to see through and demystify dominant ideology.

By 1908, Valle-Inclán had moved beyond his initial preoccupa-tion with a masculine self-fashioning and had adopted a more de-tached and critical stance toward Restoration society. *El yermo de las almas* would, in Williams's periodization of late nineteenth- and twentieth-century drama, be categorized as "modernist Natural-ism," the work of a dissident faction of the bourgeoisie that ex-plored the environment, the bourgeois household, "within which human lives were formed and deformed," and in which the social and financial insecurities and above all the sexual tensions [of the bourgeois order of the time] were most immediately experi-enced."[27] Williams emphasizes that "modernist Naturalism" very soon came up against the limits of its form and thematics. It quickly discovered that there were "crucial areas of experience which the language and behavior of the living room could not articulate or fully interpret."[28] As we previously noted, two tendencies devel-oped out of this discovery: on the one hand, a theater that moved toward a more intense exploration of subjectivity and, on the other, a more openly political theater that required "a decisive reoccupa-tion of that public space which the bourgeois domestic drama had evacuated."[29] With his *esperpentos,* Valle-Inclán participates in the second tendency, discarding what Valis has called his "modernist discourse of interiority" in order to confront fully the political culture of early twentieth-century Spain.[30]

Social and Familial Inversion: *La hija del capitán*

In *Cenizas* and *El yermo de las almas,* Valle-Inclán deconstructed the canonical middle-class marriage, reworking turn-of-the-century Naturalist conventions in the locus of the bourgeois home, within the private sphere of bourgeois intimacy. In the process, he shattered the illusion of separate, privatized, and public spheres by showing how outside forces create and control the family's existence. In the *Comedias bárbaras,* Valle-Inclán focused on the paradigmatic father/son relationship in a traditional, rural landowning family. In the interaction between Don Juan Manuel Montenegro and his sons, Valle-Inclán dissected the degenerate remnants of Galician feudal organization. In addition, as Michael Predmore astutely suggests (see his article in this collection) strong female characters begin to emerge, pointing the way to a new kind of female subject who will appear in *Martes de carnaval,* and most strikingly in *La hija del capitán.*[31] As Valle-Inclán shifts from a focus on corrupt individuals and provincial authorities and begins to reveal the injustices of Spain's entire social system, women outside the parameters of the feudal rural oligarchy and bourgeois urban centers of power move into the public sphere of his universe and speak with ever-increasing authority. With the appearance of the trilogy of *Martes de carnaval* (*Los cuernos de don Friolera* [1921], *Las galas del difunto* [1926], and *La hija del capitán* [1927]),[32] the marginalized female moves to center stage.

Before engaging in a gendered reading of *La hija del capitán,* a few words on the trilogy as a whole are in order. Over two decades ago Joaquín Casalduero pointed out that *Martes de carnaval* is a unified work that records specific events in Spanish history between 1898 and 1923, noting, in addition, that the trilogy is a chronology of "la más completa desmoralización: período de incubación del mal [*Las galas del difunto*] [The dead man's regalia] seguido de su plena manifestación [*Los cuernos de don Friolera*] [*The Grotesque Farce of Mr. Punch the Cuckold*] y por último su consecuencia natural [*La hija del capitán*]. Pasamos del soldado de *Las galas* a los oficiales de *Los cuernos* y vamos a parar al General"[33] ["the most complete demoralization: a period of incubation of evil is followed by its full manifestation and, finally, its natural consequence. We move from the soldier of *Las Galas* to the officers of *Los Cuernos* and we end up with the General"]. It is generally recognized that all three "esperpentos" deal with Spain's colonial wars, with specific aspects of contemporary Spanish militarism, and with what Casalduero termed "la abulia del Imperialismo" (690) ["imperialism's exhaustion"], an expression of historical exhaustion linked to the complex realignment of Spain within the global framework at the beginning of the twentieth century. What has not been noted by critics is that the status of women is a central concern throughout *Martes de carnaval*. In this trilogy, Valle-Inclán shows, on the one hand, how the military appropriates the rhetoric of family relations, and how it directly intervenes into family affairs, in order to "save" the nation.[34] On the other hand, he repositions the daughter as subject, simultaneously dramatizing and disassembling the asymmetries of gender and power that conventionally controlled the daughter/father bond.[35]

According to Lynda E. Boose and Betty S. Flowers, this focus in itself is noteworthy because there is a general absence of daughters in Western cultural discourse.

> It says something telling . . . that of the possible structural permutations of parent-child relationships inscribed in our literary, mythic, historical, and psychoanalytical texts, the father and son are the first pair most frequently in focus, and the mother and son the second. . . . Of all the binary sets through which we familiarly consider family relationships, the mother-daughter and father-daughter pairs have received the least attention, a hierarchy of value that isolates the daughter as the most absent member within the discourse of the family institution.[36]

Yet daughters problematize the story of patriarchal exchange in many ways. In the Western narrative of family, the father is the figure who controls the exogamous exchange of women, and the exchangeable figure is the daughter. (The mother belongs sexually to the father and the sister comes under the jurisdiction of her own father.) By reading the erasure of a topic to illuminate what is not included in the cultural text, the discourse of daughter and father becomes particularly significant. As Boose and Flowers emphasize, daughter relations to fathers, both familial and cultural, are a paradigm of women's relations to male culture.

Although this study focuses only on *La hija del capitán*, the daughter/father paradigm is an issue in all three *esperpentos*. In each play, aspects of outmoded gender constructs that devalorize the female and valorize the male are mercilessly scorned, and the traditional sexual hierarchy of Spanish society is inverted: the male, a despicable "Pater familiae," is ridiculed, and the least powerful female, the daughter, defended and supported either because she is an innocent victim *(Cuernos, Galas)* or, as in the case of *La hija del capitán,* because she fights back. In *Los cuernos* Don Friolera mistakenly kills his daughter while attempting to assassinate his wife for her alleged extramarital trysts. This grotesque event becomes Valle-Inclán's vehicle for satirizing not just outmoded Calderonian codes of honor, but, more pointedly, the Spanish practice of punishing only *female* adultery. The wife is condemned, and the daughter is an expendable commodity.[37] In *Las galas del difunto,* La Daifa, abandoned by her boyfriend who is conscripted to fight in Cuba, is relegated to prostitution because her father, the pharmacist Sócrates Galindo, threw her out when he discovered she was five months pregnant. The military has deprived La Daifa of socially condoned partiarchal protection: marriage. Then, her father, obeying his (petty) bourgeois code of honor, casts her permanently out of the parameters of "respectable" society—in Cardona's words, "la actitud bestial del padre en quien se caricaturiza la actitud del burgués español ante el pecado de la carne" ["the bestial attitude of the father in whom the attitude of the Spanish bourgeois toward sins of the flesh is characterized"].[38] Valle-Inclán's scathing satire of the inhumanity of social norms regarding female sexuality continues in this daughter/father paradigm as he takes another swipe at gender systems that denigrate the female and value the male: in the letter in which the supplicant daughter pleads for money to travel to Lisbon (from the father who forced her into prostitution) because she has heard Spanish prostitutes fare better there, La Daifa writes that she changed her name, in order to leave her father's "patronymic" honor in tact.[39]

La Hija del capitán, a satirization of Primo de Rivera's coup d'état in 1923, recounts how "El golfante," in love with "La Sini," the Captain's daughter, abandons his studies to follow her to Madrid. When he finds out the Captain has given his daughter as a mistress to the General as payment for the latter's protection in a lawsuit, the "golfante" kills "El Pollo de Cartagena," believing it was the General. In order to avoid a press scandal, the Captain suggests to the General they get rid of the body by sending it off to North America. Meanwhile, "La Sini" removes a wallet and valuables from the corpse, delighted that she will be able to finance her (and her boyfriend's) escape ("¡Pues que se remedie 'La Sini'!" [199] ["So that La Sini can get free!"] she says delightedly, pocketing the dead man's money), and through an intermediary, she informs the press of the crime. A scandal ensues that promises dire complications for the military. In the face of the loss of prestige the consequences of the scandal would mean for the army, the General proposes and executes a diversionary measure: a military coup d'état to take charge of the nation. The play ends in a train station in Madrid as the King arrives triumphantly, and "La Sini" and her boyfriend wait to depart.

Valle-Inclán's last "esperpento" departs from the other two plays of *Martes de Carnaval* in that it is complexly and concretely rooted in real life actual events.[40] In this sense it is more like *Ruedo ibérico* than *Las galas del difunto* and *Los cuernos de Don Friolera*. Therefore, it is not surprising that this last "esperpento" inscribes the unequal and asymmetrical gender system of Spain in the 1920s more directly than other texts.

La hija del capitán registers a new level of disintegration of the bourgeois family unit that culminates in allowing a marginalized woman to occupy public space and reconstruct herself with an open-ended possibility for liberation. In doing this, Valle-Inclán merges gender, class, nation, and empire in a novel way. However, in the final scene, "La Sini's" potential "ride to freedom" is contingent on the recognition of more than just her own marginalization. It requires an awareness of the marginalized colonial other. The play's opening words, the parroting (literally) of "Cubanita canela" (177) ["Little cinnamon-colored Cuban girl"][41] is the polyvalent expression of that colonial other, of a gendered dissolution of empire that Valle-Inclán began exploring in *Femeninas*.[42] "La Sini's" freedom is also contingent on further layers of the Spanish post-imperial situation: namely, the challenge to (and parodic dissection of) empire and metropolitan forms of authority expressed in the play in gendered terms—boyfriend, father, army general, king, bishop, conservative feminist.

By 1927, when Valle-Inclán wrote *La hija del capitán*, not only had the Western world and Spain undergone drastic changes, but Valle-Inclán had too, and this last *esperpento* belongs to one facet of the political crises of the post-1917 world. When Valle-Inclán wrote *La hija del capitán* he knew that the image of a fully empowered female citizen (of any class) was as inaccessible in 1927 as it was in 1892, but Michael Predmore is correct in pointing out that "Valle is experimenting . . . through the characer of "La Sini" with the creation of a new social type, a more emancipated human being, who will gain entrance to a more liberated world."[43] In contrast to the earlier texts we examined, this is a more overt drama of nation, of dissolution of empire, of new roles for traditional "others," played out in gendered relations. In this process women are important both as symbols and agents.[44]

Embedded in Valle-Inclán's political evolution during the first decades of the century is a subtext which reveals that gender and politics intersect in important ways. With the creating of "La Sini," Valle-Inclán works more overtly on gender in a politically critical fashion. "La Sini" is empowered to reconstruct herself. Significantly, Valle-Inclán does not empower an upper-(or middle-) class woman—someone like Doña Simplicia—campaigning for female emancipation in Spain at the time to write her own narrative, but rather, chooses a young woman belonging to a sector of society that is decidedly not bourgeois. "La Sini" is part of the displaced poor that became an urban underclass in post–World War I Spain. In this last *esperpento*, women are not totally immobilized in that they leave the traditional private sphere of the home to act in the public sphere. At the end of *La hija del capitán* both Sini and Doña Simplicia are in the train station. The "Dama intelectual" ["Intellectual Lady"] stays to welcome the King and uses a thoroughly coopted feminism to reinforce the political status quo of Church, militarism, and monarchy. "La Sini," however, may ride off in a train to construct a new life. Her newly acquired public space stands in sharp contrast both to the situation of Octavia who died hemmed in by the claustrophobia of her bedroom, and to the socially prescribed space of the conservative feminist Madame Simpleton who remains immobilized, protecting the status quo.

La hija del capitán has seven scenes: the first six take place in one afternoon and evening, and each scene, as the following discussion shows, has a different locus. In each of the seven scenes certain facets of gender codes are deconstructed as Sini, before leaving, moves to challenge the authority of boyfriend (female as individual); father (female as daughter and member of family unit); general (female as citizen of nation); and of the triumverate, bishop/king/"feminist" (female as social category defined and controlled by ecclesiastical and political authorities).

The play's opening words, "¡Cubanita canela!" (177), come from the parrot's mouth ("un loro *ultramarino*"; emphasis added ["a parrot from overseas"]). They link gender and race in ways that are "other" to Spain and create new textual spaces. "Cubanita canela" becomes a metonym for colony and colonized within the empire as Valle-Inclán shows the complex political configurations of postimperialism. The marginalized colonial comes to the capital of the "empire," epitomized here with the "negra mucama" ["black servant"] in Madrid. She is the conquered territory (Cuba), a female Creole. Introduced in the first *acotación*, she is a constant reminder of the Cuban war and Spain's territorial loss. "La mucama mandinga, . . . lipuda sonrisa, penetra en la sala" (189) ["The Afro-cuban maid . . with her full-lipped smile, gets into the living room"]. The rot of the colonial empire, Valle-Inclán tells us, comes home to roost in the form of the corrupt military and politicians, inflation, and economic crisis.

The "golfante" was able to find "La Sini" in Madrid because "el lorito en tu ventana ha sido como un letrero" (183) ["the parrot in your window was like a road sign"]. This is the parrot her father (one supposes) has brought back from Cuba, from Spain's colonial war. Valle-Inclán is opening up new space here for the reverse trip—the colony coming back to reside in the metropolis—Cuba, the periphery, the new female, the colony inserted into empire. By reversing the conventional pattern of the colony mimicking the metropolis, Valle-Inclán's utopian and liberatory impulse includes America.[45]

From the beginning, the text is penetrated not just with "nostalgias coloniales de islas opulentas . . . del trópico" (185) ["colonial nostalgia; for opulent tropical islands"] and *la negra mucama/mandinga* (Afro-Cubanisms; emphasis added). It is also saturated with subversive "other" elements from Spanish history. "Están más penados que entre *moros* comer tocino" (179) ["They are in worse shape than Moslems forced to eat pork"]; *"¡Marrano!"* (193) [Spanish Jew forced to convert to Christianity; a pejorative term and metonymically, the outsider]; Don Alfredo *Toledano,* the Director of El Constitutional (210); Toledano has been historically, and still is, a well-known patronym of Sephardic Jews. In short, otherness is present linguistically as well as thematically.

In the opening scene "La Sini" is given masculine power to "see" (and narrate)[46] what makes society function. Immediately after we learn that Captain Sinibaldo has prostituted his daughter to save his own neck ("la dormida de la hija por la dormida del expediente" [181], ["his daughter's body in exchange for squashing the lawsuit"]), "el horchatero" gives us the social construct for this father/daughter relationship. "Hay mucho vicio y se cultiva la finca de las mujeres. . . . Te casas y pones la parienta al toreo" (181) ["There is a lot of vice around and women are used for the most profitable ends . . . you get married and send a female relative out to work as a prostitute"]. "La Sini" then reveals, by mockery, the female social construct. In "el que dirán" [public opinion] language of social hypocrisy appropriate perhaps to describe actions of Doña Simplicia but not to protect the illicit relationship pimped by her father, Sini states, "La mujer, en mi caso, con un amigo que nada le niega, está obligada a un miramiento que ni las casadas" (181)

["A woman in my situation, with a boyfriend who doesn't deny her anything is obliged to watch her p's and q's even more than married women"]. "La Sini" knows the "rules of the game" better than the "golfante." Like Valle-Inclán, she knows about conventional gender construction. "¿Tú has podido sacarme de la casa de mi padre? ¿Qué no tenías modo de vida? . . . ¿Lo tienes ahora? Pronta estoy a seguirte" (182) ["Could you get me out of my father's house? You had no way to earn a living? You do now? Well, then I'm ready to follow you"]. "La Sini" also knows how ridiculous the conventions are. "¡Vaya un folletín" ["What sentimental garbage!"] she responds to her boyfriend's clichéd declarations of love and fidelity. In fact, instances abound of Sini mocking bourgeois sentimentality (of Octavia and Pedro Pondal's world), such as when the "golfante" wants to hold her hand and begin a classical seduction, and she says, "¡Adiós, y que me recuerdes!" (184) ["Come on, remember who you're dealing with!"].

In scene 2 "La Sini" mocks the authority of the Código Penal [Penal code] (188–89) and then questions the authority of the General—unthinkable behavior for any female.

La Sini.	¿Le sería a usted muy molesto oírme una palabra, general?
El General.	Sini, no me hagas una escena. Sé mirada.
La Sini.	¡Vea usted de quedarse!
El General.	Es intolerable esa actitud. (191)

[*Sini.*	Would it be a great deal of trouble for you to listen to me for a moment, General?
The General.	Sini, don't make a scene. Watch your behavior.
Sini.	You better sit down and listen!
The General.	That attitude is intolerable.]

The General tries to control her with a traditionally male way of silencing females. "Ensaya una sonrisa despreciando a la Sinibalda" (192) ["He attempts to smile disdainfully at Sinibalda"], but she intensifies the challenge to male authority, now including her father. "¿Cuándo has tenido para mí entrañas de padre? . . . Si la mano dejas caer, me tiro a rodar. . . ." ["When have you been a real father to me? . . . If you so much as lay a hand on me, I'll leave"]. In fact, however, Sini did not have the legal right to leave home without parental permission until she was twenty-five years old, according to article 320 of the Spanish Civil Code,[47] part of the legal system to which she has disparagingly referred.

Scene 3 underlines the indignity of this law (article 320) as Valle-

Inclán shatters the credibility of this aspect of the legal foundation for the father/daughter paradigm. The Captain, resplendent in military decorations, invokes the law in order to pillage money from his daughter. "¡Mi general, no puede consentirse que esa insensata se fugue del domicilio paterno con una cartera de valores!"[48] (199) ["My General, you cannot allow this crazy girl to flee the paternal domicile with a wallet full of money!"] When the General tells Sini to have a cup of tea to calm her nerves and not to be so rude to her father or otherwise he'll be ashamed of loving her, she retorts, "¡Abur y divertirse! . . . Voy libre" (200–201) ["Get off my case . . . I'm a free person"]. It would be hard to find a more gripping example of a daughter problematizing patriarchal exchange.

Scene 4 is Sini's "trial run" at independence. In the Café Universal she enters alone "y llama al mozo con palmas" (201) ["and claps for the waiter to take her order"], a forceful masculine gesture. She now has the experience of being a woman alone in public. "¿Pero cuando van a dejar de mirarme esos pelmazos?" (202) ["When are those pains in the neck going to stop staring at me?"] Part of being a woman is to be looked at; not to look. The waiter then replies, "¡Que no estará usted acostumbrada a que la miren!" (202) ["I can't believe you're not used to being stared at!"] Part of the social structure of a young female is to receive passively the male gaze. In addition, as the waiter further clarifies, "¡Raro que siendo usted una hembra tan de buten, no la haya seguido alguna vez por esas calles!" (203) ["It's strange that being such a good-looker you haven't been followed some time on the streets!"]

Scene 5 takes place in the Círculo de Bellas Artes; this is the public sphere of the press so no women are present. Three *socios* [pals] talk and joke about women in a traditionally vulgar way (212–13) as the latest edition of the newspaper is distributed and the crime commented on. The public (male) power of the press enhances the reigning male/female hierarchy as the men reify the absent women in their conversation as well as in their writing. The Camastrón's question, "¿Ustedes creen en esas saternales con surtido de rubias y morenas?" (212) ["Do you believe in these all-night orgies with an assortment of blonds and brunettes?"] and phrases in the press like "la rubia opulenta" (213) ["the opulent blond"] reinforce traditional gender structures as Valle-Inclán ridicules a concept of honor that leads to a duel "por la rubia"[49] ["for the blond"].

In scene 6 the military is planning a coup. The military resides in the "public" sphere so, again, no women are present. Embedded in the frantic political scrambling that Captain Sinibaldo and the

General plot to keep themselves in power is the equally frenetic effort to try and hold onto traditional gender constructs that Sini has been challenging in the first five scenes. In the face of press revelations about his "lío de faldas" ["sexual scandal"] the General is "outraged" at the invasion into his sacrosanct family life. "Esta intromisión de la gacetilla en el privado de nuestros hogares es intolerable" (221) ["This intrusion of the press into our private life is intolerable"]. The attempt to restore the traditional bourgeois family is now utterly preposterous. "I am a patriot motivated only by 'el amor a las Instituciones' [institutional love]" (223) the General pronounces. "No me guía la ambición, sino el amor a España" (223) ["I am not motivated by ambition, only by love for Spain"]. However, the patriotic fervor has been supplanted in importance by the General's "lío de faldas." The outcome of the sexual scandal—revealing the interconnectedness of gender, nation, and empire—is nothing less than the fall of the government. "Si ha de salvarse el país," the General pontificates, "si no hemos de ser una colonia extranjera, es fatal que tome las riendas el Ejercito" (225) ["If the country is going to be saved, if we are not to become a foreign colony, it is absolutely necessary for the army to take charge"]. That is, if Spain is not to be emasculated (colonized), the army (signifying "real" peninsular men) must take power. Valle-Inclán's characterization of Totó, one of the General's aides, subtly pokes fun at the military's claims to virility by equating its actual degeneracy with the loss of "masculinity." "Totó aparece en la puerta: Rubio, oralino, pecoso, menudo. . . ." (223) ["Totó appears in the doorway: Blond, golden, freckly, delicate"]. This is hardly the image of the male warrior the military wishes to project. Several moments later, Colonel Camarasa bemoans the military's (and the nation's) loss of prestige due to the sexual scandal by a belated and hollow-sounding return to a language of family and masculine virility. "Mi General, la *familia* militar llora con *viriles* lágrimas de fuego la mengua de la *Patria*" (227; emphasis added) ["My General, the military family laments the decline of the Fatherland with burning virile tears"].

In the final scene both "La Sini" and Doña Simplicia, "Delegada del Club Femina [*sic*]" ["Women's Club Delegate"][50] have moved into the public sphere of the train station, and stand alongside traditional masculine figures of authority: the monarchy, the military, the Church, and the press.[51] Here Valle-Inclán contrasts "La Sini's" gradual struggle for freedom with the conservative "feminism" that Doña Simplicia advocates. "Nosotras, ángeles de los hogares, juntamos nuestras débiles voces al himno marcial de las

Instituciones Militares . . . ofrecemos fervientes oraciones . . . fortalecidas por la bendición de la Iglesia. . ." ["As angels of the hearth, we join our weak voices to the martial hymn of the Military Institutions . . . we offer our fervent prayers . . . we are strengthened by the blessing of the Church."] (231). Simplicia conjoins the traditional construct of the "angel of the hearth" with the patriarchal establishment that enforces that construct, reinforcing in her own way the intricate connections between gender and nation that the play emphasizes and dismantles.[52] Valle-Inclán's understanding of the political chaos in Spain in the early twentieth century, chaos which led to the 1923 coup, as well as his perception of the bungling corruption and inept leadership of the military establishment overlap, in his last "esperpento," with a clear consciousness of gender asymmetries and how these asymmetries underlie and are implicated in the politics of nation and nationalism. (Recall that Valle-Inclán constructs the drama such that a sexual scandal, the "lío de faldas," will necessitate the military coup.)[53] Valle-Inclán's satire of the military and its intervention in national affairs can therefore be most forcefully expressed through a daughter figure like "La Sini," for it is her freedom to roam outside the father's home that most dramatically challenges the patriarchal structure. According to Lynda E. Boose, "When the threat of insurrection comes from the son, it fits into the authorized structure of society. When it comes from the detached daughter, it engenders a vision of social inversion that must be vehemently quashed. . . ."[54] But "La Sini's" insurrection against the whole cast of patriarchal representatives is not suppressed. Standing on the train platform in the final scene, and on the brink of constructing a new narrative, she has the last word and the last laugh which hints at the extent of her new freedom. "¡De risa me escacho!" (232) ["This cracks me up!"].

Notes

1. Raymond Williams discusses the different tendencies coexisting in the 1920s European avant-garde in "Theatre as a Political Forum" in *The Politics of Modernism—Against the New Conformists,* ed. Tony Pinkney (London and New York: Verso, 1989), 81–94. For our purposes it is helpful to note that one strain characterized by the Surrealists (Artaud, Dali, etc.) moved to explore subjectivity more intensively, rejecting conscious representation and reproduction of public life in favor of the dramatization of an inner consciousness or the unconscious. The other trend (German Expressionist drama, Brecht, etc.) experimented with socially grounded theater, presenting "the bourgeois world as grotesque, haunted by dead customs and laws, choked by its self-repressions" (86).

2. This is an idea that is also present in Catherine Davies, "'Venus impera'? Women and Power in *Femininas* and *Epitalamio*," essay in this volume.

3. Introduction to *Ideology of Conduct, Essays in Literature and the History of Sexuality,* eds. Nancy Armstrong and Leonard Tennenhouse (London: Methuen, 1987), 8.

4. This idea is present throughout J. C. Mariátegui's classic text, *Siete ensayos de interpretación de la realidad peruana,* originally published in 1928.

5. In Tim Brennan, *Salman Rushdie and The Third World* (New York: Macmillan, 1989), ix.

6. For further details on this period see Raymond Carr, *Modern Spain: 1875–1980* (New York: Oxford University Press, 1980), especially chaps. 4–7.

7. This has been amply documented. See, for example, A. Zahareas and R. Cardona, *Visión del esperpento. Teoría y práctica de los esperpentos de Valle-Inclán* (Madrid: Castalia, 1970), 196–98.

8. Mary Louise Pratt, "Women, Literature and National Brotherhood," in Emilie Bergmann, Janet Greenberg, Gwen Kirkpatrick, Francine Masiello, Francesca Miller, Marta Morello-Frosch, Kathleen Newman, and Mary Louise Pratt, *Women, Culture and Politics in Latin America* (Berkeley: University of California Press, 1990), 51.

9. The biologic/social construct of "womanhood" was, for Marañón and Ortega, synonymous with what is now widely considered to be a prototype of a sexually repressed and intellectually passive bourgeois woman. Marañón, Spain's most celebrated turn-of-the-century medical intellectual, adopted the liberal stance of popularizing modern theories about sexual taboos and about advocating sexual education, yet he believed that sexual pleasure was not important to women even though, according to his writings often published in the *Revista de Occidente* in the 1920s, women were primarily defined by their sexual functions. Ortega, for his part, believed that women were essentially confused beings, but should remain so, otherwise they "equivaldría a aniquilar la delicia que para el varón es la mujer gracias a su ser confuso" ["would be equivalent to annihilating the delight that women, thanks to their confused state, are to men"] [quoted in Geraldine M. Scanlon, *La polémica feminista en la España contemporánea 1868–1974* (Madrid: Siglo veintiuno de España, 1976), 189]. For an insightful exploration of Ortega's views on women see Scanlon, *La polémica feminista,* 187–92.

10. In Valle-Inclán's corpus, six works, written between 1892 and 1908, revolve around Pedro Pondal and an Octavia: "El gran obstáculo," two chapters of an unfinished novel published in *Diario de Pontevedra,* 3, 4 1892; "Caritativa" ["A Charitable Woman"] June 1892; "La confesión" [The confession] July 1892, in addition to "Octavia Santino," *Cenizas,* and *El yermo de la almas.*

11. See Susan Kirkpatrick, "From 'Octavia Santino' to *El yermo de las almas:* Three Phases of Valle-Inclán," *Revista Hispánica Moderna,* 39, nos. 1–2 (1972–73): 56–72, for an earlier examination of these three texts.

12. Rita Felski, "The Counterdiscourse of the Feminine in Three Texts by Wilde, Huysmans and Sacher-Masoch," *PMLA* 106, no. 5 (October 1991): 1099.

13. Noël Valis, "Two Ramóns: A View from the Margins of Modernist *Cursilería*" *ALEC* 17 (1992): 325–43.

14. Williams, *Politics of Modernism,* 84.

15. See, for example, the essays in this volume by Valis, "The Novel as Feminine Entrapment. Valle-Inclán's *Sonata de Otoño*", and Catherine Davies, "'Venus impera'? Women and Power in *Femeninas* and *Epitalamio*".

16. Felski, "Counterdiscourse of the Feminine," 1097.

17. Valle-Inclán's preoccupation with the fashioning of a masculine identity was also a concern, though perhaps an unconscious one, of other Spanish writers at the turn of the century. Fictional surrogates created by his contemporaries include Antonio Machado's Juan de Mairena, Gabriel Miró's Sigüenza, and Martínez Ruiz's Azorín.

18. See "Toward an Understanding of History and Gender in Valle-Inclán's Spain," n. 13, essay in this volume.

19. Examples abound. Octavia caresses Pedro, "como a un niño" (96) ["like a child"]; "Ponía ella algo de maternal en aquel amor" (95) ["She invested that love with maternal concern"], to cite but two.

20. Bridget Aldaraca, "'El ángel del hogar': The Cult of Domesticity in Nineteenth Century Spain," in *Theory and Practice of Feminist Literary Criticism,* eds. Garbriela Mora and Karen S. Van Hooft (Ypsilanti, Mich.: Bilingual Press, 1982), 67.

21. Williams, *Politics of Modernism,* 50.

22. The only major revision of *Cenizas* was the addition in 1908 of the prologue. For a detailed discussion of this and other textual changes, see Kirkpatrick, "From 'Octavia Santino' to *El yermo de las almas.*"

23. For an explanation of the prejudice in the Spanish Penal Code against women regarding the definition of, and punishment for, adultery, see Scanlon, *La polémica feminista,* 131. For more information on the role of the Church and medical profession in controlling women's behavior, see the section on "Feminism in Spain" in the article, "Toward an Understanding of History, Gender, and Valle-Inclán's Spain," essay in this volume.

24. The first *acotación* ["stage direction"] describes the exterior. "Una casa nueva, con persianas verdes que cuelgan por encima del balconaje de hierro florido, pintado de oro y negro con un lujo funerario. . . ." (13) ["A new house, with green blinds that hang over a series of balconies made of florid iron, painted gold and black with lugubrious luxury"]. On the bedroom: "[Octavia] yace sepultada en el vasto lecho, una cama antigua, en forma de góndola, sostenida por sirenas doradas. Pedro Pondal la había comprado para trono de sus amores. . . ." (51) ["Octavia lies entombed on the huge bed, an antique piece in the shape of a gondola, held up by golden mermaids. Pedro Pondal had bought it as a throne for their love. . . ."].

25. Pedro tells Octavia that she has come to his home as would his wife. "Has venido aquí para quedarte, como el día de las bodas va la mujer a la casa del marido" (37) ["You have come here to stay, just like a wife who moves to her husband's house on the wedding day"].

26. At one point, Sabel insists that doctors are interested only in profit, not in their patients' well-being (77). At another point she tells the priest that it would be impossible for Pedro to abandon Octavia by leaving the house, as the priest demands (79).

27. Williams, *Politics of Modernism,* 85.

28. Ibid.

29. Ibid., 89.

30. Kirkpatrick makes a similar observation on the direction Valle-Inclán's work will take. *El yermo de las almas,* in her view, "represents the exhaustion of a set of themes. *El yermo de las almas* is the last of the cycle of decadent, fin de siècle writing which began with *Femeninas.* . . . From now on, his hostility to the bourgeois establishment will express itself more directly in grotesque stylization

of the real world. . . ." "From 'Octavia Santino' to *El yermo de las almas,*" 71. The "real world" in this citation refers to the public sphere.

31. It is noteworthy that Biruté Ciplijauskaité also posits that in the Carlist trilogy Madre Isabel "becomes the voice of protest against what is happening in Spain," in "The Role of Language in the Creation of Valle-Inclán's Female Characters," essay in this volume.

32. First published as a trilogy in 1930. It is important to note that in 1927, the year that *La hija del capitán* appeared, Valle-Inclán also published *La corte de los milagros* [The court of miracles], the first volume of the *Ruedo ibérico* [The Iberian ring], with a daughter/father paradigm similar to La Sini and the Captain: Sofi and her father. See *Corte,* iii, titled "Ecos de Asmodeo" ["Echoes of Asmodeo"]. Valle-Inclán rewrote this section of *La corte de los milagros* shortly before his death and it was published in the Madrid newspaper *Ahora* some months after he died. This final version of "Ecos de Asmodeo" with Sofi and her father, first appeared in book form in 1975 titled *El trueno dorado* [Golden thunder] (Madrid: Bruguera).

33. "Sentido y forma de *Martes de Carnaval,*" in A. N. Zahareas, ed. *Ramón del Valle-Inclán: An Appraisal of His Life and Works* (New York: Las Americas, 1968), 689–90.

34. Valle-Inclán did not need to invent the connection between nationalist rhetoric and a discourse of the family. It was common in the 1920s for the military to refer to itself as a "family" and to speak of the need to preserve "the harmony of the military family" threatened by dissension among officers. For references to this use of the familial trope and for details on problems within the military see Carr, *Modern Spain,* chaps. 5 and 6.

35. In 1921 with the publication of *Los cuernos,* Valle-Inclán takes direct swipes at Spain's outmoded gender and legal codes by suggesting divorce (illegal in Spain at the time) to be a plausible solution for an untenable matrimony. In these lines from the concluding "romance" ["ballad"], "A la mujer y al querido/ los degüella con un hacha /. . . . Tiene pena capital / el adulterio en España" (171) ["The woman and her lover get their throats cut with an ax . . . adultery is punished by death in Spain"] he alludes to Spanish law and how it punished adulterous women much more harshly than it dealt with unfaithful husbands.

36. Lynda E. Boose and Betty S. Flowers, eds., *Daughters and Fathers* (Baltimore, Md.: Johns Hopkins University Press, 1989), 2.

37. Stephen M. Hart discusses *Los cuernos* in light of its subversion of Calderonian honor and undermining of Lacanian "Law-of-the-Father" and "Name-of-the-Father" in "A Tale of Two Genres: Puppet Show and Caleronian Honour Play in *Los cuernos de don Friolera* and *Amor de don Perlimplin,*" in *Golden Age Spanish Theatre. Studies in Honour of John Varey by His Colleagues and Pupils,* eds. Charles Davis and Alan Deyermond (London: Westfield College, 1991), 106–17.

38. Rodolfo Cardona, "Las Galas del difunto," in Clara Barbeito, ed. *Valle-Inclán: Nueva evaluación de su obra* (Barcelona: PPU, 1988), 249.

39. "Y debo decirle no ser verdad que yo arrastré su honra, pues con esa mira cambié mi nombre, y digo en todas partes que me llamo Ernestina." *Las galas del difunto* (60) ["And I ought to tell you that it is not true I stained your honor, because, in order to prevent that, I changed my name and say everywhere that my name is Ernestina"].

40. See Juan Antonio Hormigón, *Ramón del Valle-Inclán: La política, la cultura, el realismo del pueblo* (Madrid: Industrias Felmar, 1972), 377–80; and Ro-

dolfo Cardona and A. N. Zahareas, *Visión del esperpento*, 198–219, for documentation of actual events that Valle-Inclán used in constructing *La hija del capitán*. For a detailed scrutiny of the different versions of the play, see Javier Serrano Alonso, "Las tres versiones de *La hija del capitán* (1927–1930)," in *Valle-Inclán (1866–1936): Creación y lenguaje*, ed. J. M. García de la Torre (Amsterdam: Rodopi, 1988), 99–130. For further incisive comments on the play see Cardona and Zahareas, "La función histórica del espectáculo: El arte de Valle-Inclán," in *Busca v rebusca de Valle-Inclán*, ed. Juan Antonio Hormigón (Madrid: Ministerio de Cultura, 1989), vol. 2, 126–27.

41. *La hija del capitán* in *Martes de carnaval* (Madrid: Espasa-Calpe, Austral, Novena edición, 1984). All references will be from this edition and will be given in parentheses in the text.

42. "La Niña Chole" (1893) ["Mistress Chole"], and "Tula Varona" (1893), for example, "gender" relations of empire and colony. Gender hierarchies are inverted in both stories. In both, a Latin American woman is able to exercise a degree of power over a young Spanish male aristocrat, and in so doing, she problematizes not only the normative hierarchy of gender, but also the geopolitical hierarchy of empire and colony. Although it is beyond the scope of this paper to elaborate further, we believe a careful reading of these stories justifies this interpretation.

43. Michael P. Predmore, "The Central Role of Sabelita in *Aguila de blasón*: Toward the Emergence of a Radical Vision of Women in the Later Art of the 'Esperpento,'" essay in this volume.

44. In this context one must question Verity Smith's dismissal of *La hija del capitán* as a work that "deserves little attention . . . an inferior work arising out of a particular scandal which happened to anger the author," in *Ramón del Valle-Inclán* (New York: Twayne Publishers, Inc., 1973), 96. Cardona and Zahareas, on the contrary, recognize the particular importance of this text. See Cardona and Zahareas, *Visión de esperpento*, 217.

45. Indeed, only in his novel about Spanish American dictatorship, *Tirano Banderas* (1926) does Valle-Inclán manage to portray revolutionary movement that successfully overthrows a repressive economic and political regime. The imaginary dictatorship of Santos Banderas is buttressed by both new and old imperialist powers, and the revolutionary forces led by Filomeno Cuevas overthrow what is an essentially neocolonialist regime. Only in America, in other words, does Valle-Inclán locate forces capable of effecting revolutionary change. See Mary K. Addis, "Synthetic Visions: The Spanish American Dictator Novel as Genre," in *Cultural Studies: Crossing Boundaries, Critical Studies* Book Series, Guest editor Roberta L. Salper (Amsterdam: Rodopi, 1991), 189–219.

46. Maryellen Bieder explores this concept in "Woman Transfixed: Plotting the Fe/male Gaze in 'Rosarito,'" essay in this volume.

47. "Las hijas de familia mayores de edad [twenty-three years] pero menores de veinticinco años, no podrán dejar la casa paterna sin licencia del padre o de la madre en cuya compañia vivan. . . ." Scanlon, *La polémica feminista*, 125. ["The daughters of a family who are older than 23 but younger than 25 cannot leave the paternal household without permission of either the father or the mother, depending on which one they live with."]

48. Unlike La Daifa in *Las Galas*, "La Sini" does not have to beg for money from patriarchal sources to travel; she subverts the order by stealing money to pay for her own train ticket as well as her boyfriend's.

49. "¡La gran bomba! Voy a telefonear a mi periódico. Se ha verificado un

duelo en condiciones muy graves entre el General Miranda y Don Joselito Benegas. / ¿Por la rubia? / Eso se cuenta" (217–18) ["The big scoop! I'm going to telephone my paper. It's been verified that there was a very serious duel between General Miranda and Don Joselito Benegas. / Over the blond? / That's what they're saying"].

50. Doña Simplicia is not only the delegate from the Club Femenina [Women's Club], she is also "Presidenta de las Señoras de San Vicente y de las Damas de la Cruz Roja, Hermana Mayor de las Beatas Catequistas de Orbaneja" (230) [President of St. Vincent's Ladies Club and of the Red Cross Dames (and) Senior Sister of the Catechist Fanatics from Orbaneja]. In the person of Doña Simplicia Valle-Inclán satirizes the conservative traditionalism characteristic of Spanish bourgeois Women's clubs in the 1920s. For documentation and analysis of these organizations, see Scanlon, *La Polémica feminista,* 197–210.

51. According to Raymond Carr, homages to Primo de Rivera, literally staged at train stations, signified to the Dictator that he had broad public support and could therefore ignore opposition leaders' calls for a return to parliamentary democracy. Carr, *Modern Spain,* 105–7.

52. Primo de Rivera supported "conservative feminism." While saying he was concerned with women's rights, he was also outraged by the participation of young women in student demonstrations protesting his government. Carr indicated that Primo de Rivera linked this participation of women in politics with the rise of pornography. Ibid., 103 and 108.

53. To create this causal connection, Valle-Inclán took some liberties with history. The sexual scandal to which the play alludes historically took place in 1913, some ten years before the Primo de Rivera coup. For details see Cardona and Zahareas, *Visión del esperpento,* 198.

54. Lynda E. Boose, "The Father's House and the Daughter in It: The Structures of Western Culture's Daughter/Father Relationship," in *Daughters and Fathers,* 34. Boose adds, "Patriarchal ideology has always imagined that women—and especially the unstructured daughter—pose the ultimate threat to its power," 34.

"Venus impera"? Women and Power in *Femeninas* and *Epitalamio*

CATHERINE DAVIES

This essay explores how Valle-Inclán's early narrative subverts the modernist aesthetic through its representation of female sexuality. In this context, Rubén Darío's *Prosas profanas* [Profane hymns] provides a useful contrast because, despite obvious thematic and stylistic resemblances between these early texts, the subversive strategy employed by Valle-Inclán is quite distinct. Indeed, as we shall see, *Epitalamio* [Epithalamium] engages with *Prosas profanas* itself, undermining its claim to seriousness by means of a counterrepresentation of the female figure.

Valle-Inclán's first book (*Femeninas* [Feminine portraits], Pontevedra, 1895) contains six stories dated between April 1892 ("La Generala" ["The General's Wife"]) and April 1984 ("Rosarito"); it was followed by the novela *Epitalamio* (Madrid, 1897). In the intervening year, 1896, Darío, one year younger than Valle-Inclán, published *Prosas profanas* (Buenos Aires), the majority of the poems of which were also written after 1892.[1] The short stories of *Femeninas* are dated in Galicia, Mexico, Paris and on board a ship as Valle-Inclán traveled to Mexico through Cuba and back to Spain. Darío's first trans-Atlantic journey took him in the opposite direction, from Argentina, through Cuba to Spain and Paris to return to South America. While he was in Spain (1892) Valle-Inclán was in Mexico; they subsequently met in 1899. Their crossing paths point to the cultural interconnections of Hispanic "modernismo" and imply a similar critique of what was considered a decaying Hispanic society and culture in the crucial years leading up to 1898. The key to their dissimilarity, however, is perceived in their recreation of woman.

In a previous article I argued that the female figure in *Prosas profanas* functioned primarily as a "scientia sexualis," a means to reach truth through knowledge, as well as an exotic "ars erotica" involving ecstasy leading to the conquest of death. The polyvalent female sign appears in a series of superimposed images, always under the control of the masculine gaze of the poet-creator who seeks transcendent truth, oneness, and harmony through female allegory. Masculine sexual activity stands as a metaphor for creative endeavor and the female form (muse, art, and poetry), both passive inspiration and the final product of this mystical, erotic quest. It is not surprising, then, that despite the narrativity of the poetry, there is little interaction between characters, male or female, or that women never speak (the exception being in "Mía" [Mine]). Despite the proliferation of female names, types, and attributes, woman remains anonymous, reified (as precious object, vessel, or mask) and aestheticized out of real existence. The poet cannot reconcile the contradictions of the sign and, having denied the body, takes up a position of androgyny.[2] In *Prosas profanas*, of the five categories into which female types can be divided, classical, mythical, the exotic, the aristocratic, the plebian and the family circle, the least important is the latter.

In *Femeninas* and *Epitalamio,* on the other hand, the female is not only sign, but also woman as social and familial subject and agent. Here, the kind of three-dimensional model of cross-classification favored by categoricalists would be needed to map the complex power and gender relations. The society in question is that of Spain, more precisely Galicia, during Cánovas's Restoration (1876–97); a traditional agrarian system based on landed property and tenure, experiencing the impact of capitalism. Above all, it is a patriarchal society in the most traditional sense, "one in which power is held by male heads of households. There is also a clear separation between the 'public' and the 'private' spheres of life. In the 'private' sphere . . . the patriarch enjoys arbitrary power over all junior males, and females and all children. No female holds any formal public position of . . . power. Contained within patriarchy are two fundamental nuclei of stratification: the household/family/lineage and the dominance of the male gender."[3] The dominant mode of representation is that of the white, male, adult, heterosexual of the Spanish establishment. Peripheral are women, animals, children, and foreigners. The ironic and open-ended narrative of Valle-Inclán's short fiction exposes the unsustainable and unresolved inner contradictions of a decadent social structure and the ambiguities inherent in the concentration and exercise of power therein, particularly from the point of view of gender.

All the female characters, with the exception of Octavia Santino (a governess), belong to the wealthy upper crust, are respected, and enjoy social status. All but Niña Chole belong to the powerful Spanish landed (often absentee) elite, that confluence of titled aristocracy and bourgeoisie so typical of Restoration society. The female protagonists are, often as not, the active desiring subject indulging in "female profligacy" ["libertinismo femenino"], more adept at seduction than useful production.[4] They are decadent "femmes fatales"; tantalizing, aggressively beautiful, perverse, and without conscience, women who lure weaker men to their ruin and wield the upper hand. As far as the male characters are concerned, about half could be classified as ruling class and as such politically powerful. But several qualify as petty-bourgeois (Aquiles Calderón, Pedro Pondal—both students, and the officer Sandoval). Although they are male, their class position is inferior to that of the female characters. Indeed some interesting heterosexual relationships are articulated along this axis (Sandoval/la Generala; Aquiles Calderón/la Condesa de Cela; Niña Chole/her husband and the yankee).

Other categories are equally important and mediate across this simple gender/class framework. These are nationality and ethnicity, age, family and lineage, and religion. Aquiles Calderón, Tula Varona, and Niña Chole are South American and hence in the position of (post) colonial subjects which attenuates their power potential (the blacks and the "Indio" provide an interesting contrast). Similarly, Sandoval, Rosarito, Beatriz, and la Generala are children or young persons, hence minors, despite their gender or their noble birth. Only the two Condesas de Cela (mother and possibly daughter-in-law) and, to a lesser extent Augusta (belonging to the nouveau riche), represent apparently unmediated female participation in the power elite.[5] The Condesas are especially important because they typify matriarchal linkage within and between families and lineages. Through them the stories of *Femeninas* are interrelated. Conversely, the representatives of the all-powerful patrician patriarchy are flawed in some way: the General is old; the Duquesito young; the Principe foreign (Italian); and Don Juan Manuel, a liberal atheist. The siting of a center of power is problematic. One source of power, inferred in the text, is the absent biological father and/or the legitimate husband. These (the Condesa de Cela's husband, father of Rosarito and son of the elder Condesa; the husbands of Tula Varona and Augusta [father of Beatriz]; the fathers of la Generala and the Duquesito de Ordax) are the very perpetrators and conduits of patrimony and patriarchal power. None of them appear in the stories but they are alluded to and indeed are crucial to their respective plots. Arguably, the site of power is occupied by the narrator himself, whose apparently objective commentary belies on one level a smug male-centred, paternalistic perspective.

The problem with such cross-classification is that it freezes the individual character within a static framework and makes no allowance for the dynamic constitution of either those categories or the characters as subjects *en procès*. As Roberta Salper points out, "The organic nature of Valle-Inclán's narrative universe discounts any kind of static, definitive group division" ["la misma naturaleza orgánica del universo narrativo de Valle-Inclán descarta todo tipo de agrupación estática o definitiva"].[6] Yet such an analysis does not seem entirely inappropriate; although the characters interact, they do so as if in a pantomime of set pieces. Having but a sketchy individual psychology they verge on types and, with a twist of irony, become the kind of puppetlike *esperpentos* found in Valle-Inclán's later work. Irony inverts even the narrator's assumed control and credibility. Manuel Bermejo Marcos observes that the stories are usually read seriously "when what the author wanted . . . was to give his personal version—ironic and biting, it's true—of the fashionable literary themes and styles of his time" ["cuando su autor lo que pretendía . . . era dar su versión personal—irónica y mordaz, es cierto—respecto a temas y modas de la literatura de su tiempo"].[7] The characters are deformations of those in vogue and the stories are satiric subversions of the modernist aesthetic. As several critics have pointed out, *modernismo* is the reverse side of *esperpento*; in which case *Femeninas* and *Epitalamio* are related antithetically to *Prosas profanas*. What becomes clear is that, as with the *Sonatas,* "they reflect the kind of criticism associated with the Generation of 1898 as well as the disrespect and iconoclasm of the later works. . . . Valle-Inclán begins his ferocious but healthy attack on all things pertaining to 'Old Spain,' the dead weight of which had turned the Spain of the Restoration into a grotesque anachronism" ["reflejan tanto el espíritu crítico de la Generación del 98 como la irreverencia y el sentido iconoclasta que caracterizan las obras posteriores . . . inicia Valle-Inclán su feroz pero saludable ataque a todos los aspectos de la 'vieja España,' cuyo peso muerto ha convertido en grotesco anacronismo gran parte de la España de la Restauración"].[8] However, in making this point Michael P. Predmore rejects the notion of ambiguity in the *Sonatas.* In my view, it is the very ambiguity and inconclusiveness of the earlier stories and the interpersonal relationships they articulate (subsuming questions of gender and power distribution and the dismantling of hierarchies) which distinguishes this narrative. It points to a gaping power vacuum in a corrupt society of anachronistic institutions set up by the puppet-figures of the dominant classes, themselves crisscrossed by conflicting interests.

In what appears to be woman-centered narrative, each story involves heterosexual relationships which fall foul of the prevalent moral code; hence the term *decadent* so often used to describe them; "woman is the protagonist of these stories. She is above all the lover, the seductress, the don Juan . . . these are easy women and more or less cruel, with the inconsistency and fickleness of (their) sex" ["es la mujer en estas historias el protagonista. Ella es ante todo, la amante, la seductora, el don Juan . . . son mujeres fáciles [sic] y más o menos crueles, con la inconstancia y veleidad del sexo"].[9] The norm the stories undermine is, of course, monogamy as laid down by the Roman Catholic Church according to whose tenets sexual acts are morally acceptable only if with the same partner within matrimony (marriage and motherhood) for reproductive purposes. Five stories involve the adulterous relationships of (usually) an older married woman with a younger single man, the woman being the seducer. In two stories the same age gap appears but the woman is unmarried and dies. Human sexuality is explored not only at a moral but also at a psychological level. Erotic heterosexual relationships based on clear gender distinctions often involve sexual drives which in a Freudian analysis implicate the Oedipus complex and incestuous desires, yet they are focalized principally from a female perspective. The older mistress is often cast as a mother-figure; her lover as her son. The Don Juan Manuel of "Rosarito" is an obvious father-figure to his young female relative. Maternal feelings conflict with erotic pleasure, to the extent that in *Epitalamio* a mother aims to marry her lover to her daughter, suggesting interesting new configurations of kinship structure. Bisexuality is a major theme; several women are endowed with male attributes, the most extreme case being Tula Varona who seems to be lesbian, while men are often feminized. Clearly, not only are commonly assumed social hierarchies involving class, kinship, and community brought into question, so too is the conventional Western understanding of appropriate gender roles. The narrative also shows an awareness of the significance of the unconscious and of the relation between sexuality and age. Valle-Inclán deconstructs common social and cultural conceptualizations of gender and sex and plays them out within a framework of similarly disarticulated concepts of class. This almost exclusive focus on private lives and personal relationships and awareness of the unconscious, although in some ways a shift away from society, could be seen as a further "symptom of the disintegration and decline of the bourgeois world."[10]

"La generala" (1892) deals with the institutionalized rank and authority of the army (and, by analogy, of patriarchy) undermined by a young girl within the enclosure of her domestic space. General Miguel Rojas is the epitome of the father-figure. Invested with wealth, status, rank, and seniority, he is the personification of Spanish masculinist gerontocracy; the "saintly warrior" ["santo guerrero"] and "saintly gentleman" ["santo varón"] (137). His wife, Currita (note the diminutive), has some personal claim to power through her noble birth, but she is young and female and is referred to continually as a child—her legal status would indeed be that of a minor. She is likened to pet animals (cat, kitten, bird, and monkey) which associate her with childlike play; she herself is a plaything. She is also compared to a plant raised in the dark, an obvious allusion to her convent education. Whether child, animal, or plant, as a woman she is under the control of the General, her fatherlike husband. On one level the text expresses a clear political allegory: women (representing the powerless masses) may well escape the repressive clutches of the Church, but (like birds) will be finally caught and tamed by the "armed force" of paternalistic authority and enclosed in their "proper" space. The daring, dangerous Other is assimilated into the dominant social formation. But the narrative also maps out strategies that women in particular can follow to undermine the law of the father. Although Currita is forced to assume a dependent role and adopt the identity allotted to her by borrowing male attributes such as her husband's status and rank as a "militar" with three gold braids, she is, as a result, in a position to express her female desire and to exercise power as "matron" ["matrón"], "formal lady" ["señora formal"], "madame" ["dama"], and "general's wife" ["generala"] (142, 146) over the equally young corporal, Sandoval, who comes to read to her.

The "little official" ["oficialito"] is undisputedly the General's subaltern within the rigid hierarchy of the army. However, his relationship to la Generala is necessarily anomalous; first, because she has no seniority in age, second because the authority she assumes is not her own, and third, she is female and so is extraneous to the military hierarchy. To complicate matters the corporal is a feminized dandy; he too is a delicate child in obeyance to the father. La Generala's vulnerable spot, which causes the corporal to slip her control, is her lack of knowledge and her exclusion from a male-oriented cultural and literary tradition. Her inability to differentiate between a novel by Zola and one by López Bago is interpreted by the Corporal as ignorance and lack of taste. Once she is excluded from the culture of the written word and the mind, she is relegated to the world of nature and the body, and is perceived by the corporal as seamstress, animal "female" ["hembra"] or bird-brain.[11] The pretentious dandy, on the other hand, has read Clarín's *Paliques* and, like the narrator, participates in the social and cultural relations between men which "though hierarchical, establish or create interdependence and solidarity among men that enables them to dominate women."[12] The fragile status la Generala had borrowed thus collapses. The girl is aware that the struggle for power is an ongoing process and reestablishes her equality by assuming yet another role, the grandmother who chides the clownish little boy, inverting hierarchies once again through burlesque. The story evidences the absence of a clear locus of authority, reinforced by the ambiguity of the various interpretations suggested by the open-ended narrative. Does the General accept Currita's explanation? If not, does he take the matter seriously and punish the frolicsome but insubordinate couple? Within realist conventions, he probably would, but possibly would not in lighthearted buffoonery.

A first reading suggests that the General, and all he represents, is outmatched by the collusion of the young people (the outsiders; woman and the subaltern). But does la Generala get what she wants by means of a strategy of seduction (she is doctor "in all kinds of winking and flirting" ["en toda suerte de guiños y coqueteos"] [142]), or by complying with acceptable roles of authority, grandmother to child? Either way she seems to enjoy the best of both worlds, gaining social status through her husband and sexual freedom within the limitations of marriage. However, if she were caught and punished she would indeed be enacting the romantic role of the Condesa de Iseult (who sacrifices herself for a man) in Barbey d'Aurevilly's novel, a role which she had rejected but which the Corporal had wished her to comply with.[13] In one sense this is to be expected given the cultural manipulation of the "folletines" [newspaper serials] in the context of a deficient education and sexual repression. Is not the weakened hierarchy simply reconstituted by the Corporal himself who takes advantage of the lapse of authority to catch the rebellious canary and put her back in his own cage? Currita falls captive to the mirror image of the General in this self-perpetuating power structure. Is not the General in control all the time, for without him there would be no transgression? Such ambiguity points to a female protagonist perched in a fine balancing act between fluctuating identities and social positions defined by masculine desire (old and young; masculine and feminine attri-

butes; noble and plebian; cunning and naive; mistress and grandmother; domesticated and wild). Where in the text is the real
Currita Jiménez? A feminist critique would suggest that what the
narrator eludes is precisely the female subject, the irrepresentable
space "other-than-himself" over which he has lost control.[14] A female subject is insinuated between the masks the character dons
and the roles she plays. The narrator is unconcerned; he directs
his comments to a male readership (Currita shows "the impression-
ability of so many women" ["la impresionabilidad de tantas mujeres"] [145]) with an ironic smirk because this is a stock comical
situation, a parody of the old General cuckolded by the flighty
young sympathizer of the budding women's emancipation movement of the 1880s.[15] It is also clear that because the narrator is in
collusion with the Corporal (he might criticize religious education
but he shares the Corporal's tastes in literature) irony is directed
against the voyeuristic narrator himself.

In "Octavia Santino" (1892) the eponymous protagonist and her
lover are neither wealthy nor powerful, but acceptable social
boundaries are transgressed in other ways. Here it is the Church,
rather than the army, which institutionalizes the masculinist
worldview. The dying Octavia is both mistress and mother to the
younger Pedro Pondal, her "little son" ["hijito"] (97). Erotic and
maternal love coalesce in a melodramatic drama of incestuous desire and frustration set in the enclosed space of a bedroom at the
side of the deathbed. The bed itself, dominating the scene, associates unlawful sex and death from the first. In true decadent fashion,
moral degeneracy is reflected in physical deterioration. A first
reading suggests that Octavia wields the upper hand; she is Pondal's senior, has initiated him sexually and at the same time gives
him "parental" permission to marry when she dies. For him, she is
the embodiment of the feminine and in her body the contradictions
experienced by the oedipal male between lover and mother are
resolved. But the story's ending is again ambiguous. Is the idealized Octavia victim or perverse temptress? Was she really unfaithful to Pondal and, if so, does she tell him because she is cruel or
because she wants to repent? If she has remained faithful and lies
so that Pondal will forget her, her gesture is the ultimate romantic
self-sacrifice. In which case, she has died in mortal sin for his
sake and far from representing feminine treachery she stands for
unworldly goodness. The notion of sin originating in sexual behavior which does not conform to the tenets of the Church is introduced in the text through allusions to an absent priest. This textual
presence is a source of tension as it foregrounds the moral code

the characters transgress and their possible punishment, steeped in eschatological connotations. Certainly the Gothic setting in a wintry Galicia reinforces the idea of hell and damnation. It is suggested (e.g., in the reference to the visit of General Rojas's daughters and the sketch of the children playing outside) that Octavia is so upset by her anomalous situation that Pondal feels obliged, at last, to propose a deathbed marriage. In the final analysis, the female protagonist is placed in an impossible situation, her moral and spiritual worth defined according to the Church and to her social status defined by a man. The surrogate mother has no acceptable role to play, no spiritual or moral worth or identity. Bedbound, dependent on Pondal for her physical welfare, spiritual peace, and social position, she is an unlikely temptress. Although both lovers break moral codes, she is more affected than he because one outcome is certain: she dies after an attack of hysteria without confession, convinced she is condemned. It is not difficult to see Pondal as an ironic caricature of the romantic poet-lover. His "Letters to a Mistress/Loved One" [Cartas a una querida"] (rather than to a wife [mujer]) point to a latter-day Bécquer whose magnanimous love founders on narcissism. The writing subject is male; like the implicit author, he has the last word. The female is no more than the reflection of his own complex subjectivity, the object of his poetry. He is devastated by her death, not because of love, but because she leaves him incomplete with nothing to recreate; his hurt pride attests to his inflated ego.

The two early stories, arguably the most realistic of the short fiction presently discussed, reveal a concern for the precarious situation of women in relation to the pillars of the Spanish establishment: the army and the Church. Late romanticism is not taken seriously.[16] Such early indications in Valle-Inclán of an all-encompassing ironic perspective become more evident after 1892. By 1893 he was in Mexico and that year he published three key stories which extend his social and cultural critique from a focus on gender and class, to one involving race, colonialism, and the exotic. The opening paragraphs of "La Condesa de Cela" (["The Countess of Cela"] 1893) show power firmly in the hands of the Countess who enjoys status, seniority, and wealth. She even supports financially the younger Mexico "Criollo," Aquiles Calderón, whom she treats as her "Newfoundland dog" (56). In a reversal of normal gender roles, the male gains his power and sense of self-importance from the female patron. Obviously, however, the Countess's power exists only in as much as it is borrowed from her husband (if her husband is Pedro, son of the elder Countess in "Rosarito," Julia is countess by marriage, not by lineage through her father). Her actions also depend on the will of her brothers. The locus of power then is clearly the Conde who, despite his absence (like the narrator), controls the puppet characters. It is only his benevolence in relaxing the law of the father that makes the Countess's affair possible; the money she passes to the student is his. The Conde controls the compliant female who in turn ensnares the "criollo." Again, a political allegory emerges; the aristocratic elite wields power over the (ex)colonies albeit through bourgeois intermediaries within their direct and contractual control. The Countess condones this arrangement; love for her is a mere "negocio," a commercial exchange. Ending her relations with the student is like breaking the dinner set (63). But within a capitalist patriarchy she too becomes a commodity; she is reified as her husband's property, a marble statue which has to remain in the family. In the market of heterosexual relations she is both commodity and consumer; she purchases her pleasure from her lover whose body she receives and consumes, so inverting the role of the prostitute. Although her affair is an exchange (and therefore based on relations of inequality and domination), from her point of view it is a charitable mission; she gives money and the status it entails in return for nothing of material value. Thus, in debasing the body of the "criollo" and his sexuality she debases her own with regards to her relationship with the Conde. Of the two protagonists, the Countess is the most clearly dehumanized; she is a cat, swan, bird, sculpture, apple, cherry; a fetish to be possessed or devoured. Even when represented as a human being she constantly changes her appearance enacting roles or donning masks: the bored schoolgirl; the "victim in the home" ["víctima del hogar"] (74); a Moor in a fez. The Countess is no more than a hollow shell; "I have no character" ["Yo no tengo carácter"] (72) she admits, and warns Aquiles, "wake up, young man. Appearances deceive" ["desengáñate, rapaz, las apariencias engañan mucho"] (60). Aquiles's weak spot is his social inferiority complex. He is the recipient of money (status and identity), and in this respect he is as much a part of the market system as she; he gives himself in exchange, his body is consumed by her and he too is commodified as the subordinate partner. The figures of this sordid drama fight out their material and sexual exchanges, manipulated by the absent source of capital, the locus of power.

The narrative suggests two strategies for the subversion of capitalist hegemony. The first involves the potential resistance of those outside a capitalist market economy: the primitive savage, repre-

sented by Aquiles. The second involves female sexuality and consciousness, counterkinship patterns based on matriarchy and
mothering, represented by the Countess. Both strategies come into
play briefly when a surge of shared emotions, feelings, and desire
between the female and the "civilized savage" ["salvaje civilizado"]
(69) threaten the materialistic clutches of patriarchy. The law of
the father is threatened for a moment by another Countess
glimpsed behind the masks, not by the mistress or wife but by the
caring mother (she has at least three children) and loving daughter.
This is most obvious when she removes her clothes, the trappings
of the bourgeois life-style and the deceptive exterior she wears for
men. Her naked body, lacking signs of social status, reveals her as
female but for the same reason it makes her vulnerable to the
male "criollo," whose masculine sexual excitement is rooted in the
sadistic desire to take revenge.

For Julia the matrilineal proves stronger than the erotic; she
leaves Aquiles when he questions her own mother's moral decency.
Julia's reaction is one of female solidarity, but it also shows how
caught up she is in the dynamics of capitalist patriarchy. By putting
in doubt her mother's honor Aquiles questions the very identity,
both public and private, of the Countess herself. Her status as
(legitimate) daughter who in turn mothers (legitimate) daughters
within a lawful monogamous relationship is suddenly threatened,
as are the legitimate foundations of her own daughters' future roles.
She gives up her affair for the sake of her daughters, but not before
revealing a possible explanation for the multiple masks she hides
behind; as a woman she needs a shield to protect her against "the
dark sadness of life" ["las negras tristezas de la vida"] (62). The
point is that both Julia and Aquiles are outsiders and are victims
of repression, and both have sources of desire and willpower within
them sufficient to subvert the oppressor: female bonding and natural sentiment. Both, however, are inevitably engulfed by patriarchy
whose rules, if they are to survive, they must obey. The instrument
of domination in this particular story is, again, the Church collud-
ing with the power elite to control women and "salvajes." The
narrative suggests that women are conceded power only as part of
a lawful (condoned and contractual) alliance with men of the dominant class (as mother, wife, or daughter). The legitimacy of their
claim to power depends on obedience to Catholic morality. The
Countess (with "the heart of a brotherhood" ["corazón de co-
fradía"] [58]) collaborates with the establishment to gain protection
for herself and her daughters, while the (post-)colonial male—despite his gender—is abandoned. Unlike the heroine of the romantic

novel la Generala reads, the Countess does not sacrifice herself for love. Her realistic approach, that of a female bourgeois, is what wins the day; she has no other option. The Countess is, in the final instance, no unfeeling "femme fatale" but, paradoxically, the "víctima del hogar."

The focalized narration of "La niña Chole," ["Mistress Chole"], subtitled "del libro *Impresiones de tierra caliente* por Andrés Hidalgo" ["from the book *Impressions from the Hot Land* by Andrés Hidalgo"] (1893), distinguishes it from the other stories of *Femeninas*. It is narrated in the first person by a cynical protagonist recounting, in old age, his tale of disillusion. The narrator doubles up as character, although his discourse differs little from that of the anonymous narrators of the other stories. He presents the story as a journey into the past, into a world of myth and fantasy where several characters parade as animated frieze figures, but hardly speak. The play of focalization, at times internal (the young romantic patriot, associated with the Visigoth and Conquistador) and at times external (the same man years later) creates a disjunction between the present voice of experience and past idealistic action. There is a gap between the sequence of events and the commentary of the narration similar to that of a silent film with voice-over. Such a strategy enables the protagonist to engage in a romantic adventure while at the same time maintaining a distanced cynical perspective of his youthful self. He is conscious not only of his former naive idealism synonymous with a false idealization of woman, but also of misguided concepts of masculine authority when faced with the power of female seduction.

The prime source of disillusion is the realization of the power of money, one of the principal motifs of the story. Social status and control of women is shown to depend not on traditional notions of manhood or noble birth but on material wealth. Hence the sway the Anglo-Americans, Chole's husband and the crass "Jewish yankee" ["judio yankee"] (135) she flirts with, have over her. Material wealth confers status and power on the "criolla," despite her ethnic origins and gender. Yet in exchanging her favors for this, she approximates the position of a whore (suggesting analogies with La Malinche) on the international market. A political reading is: Chole represents Mexico, Spain's South American possessions and area of influence, territory to be explored and ruled. She is wooed away from her traditional master by Anglo-American commercialism. As Clara Luisa Barbeito points out with reference to the later version of the story, the "Sonata de estío," Chole is the archetypal concept of America that seduces the conqueror, and the narrator-protagonist's fear of losing himself in the Aztec Empire suggests the independence of the South American possessions and the end of Spanish power.[17] The correlation between woman and colony subordinated to patriarchal hegemony is evident; both "hot land" ["tierra caliente"] and "lover" ["querida"] are the sources of sensuous desire and appropriation. South American woman, in as much as she is female and colonial, is conceived by the romantic Spaniard as a living myth and her setting a paradisal, rather than historical, reality: a mythical Aztec Mexico-cum-classical Greece. Chole herself is described as an Inca princess, Greek idol, bronze statue, exotic priestess—the embodiment of the arcane, immortal, female Other. She is the vessel of the Spaniard's desire, remote, untouchable, sacred, and universal (Greek, African, Arabic, Jewish, and Hispanic). This ideal feminine is of the narrator's own making, but it is also a symptom of the culture to which he belongs, as suggested by the reference to the long tradition of Spanish love ballads, going back to the *Cancioneros,* and propagated orally by women (117). Not so, of course, for the Anglo-Americans who use the "criolla" in a real world of commerce and whom she uses in turn. Significantly, only female sexuality represents unreality and dreamlike effect. The male Maya is portrayed as slave ["siervo"] and savage in a historical reality. This explains the inclusion of the episode of the Indian thief, who—poor and desperate—needs money. Despite his gender, he is powerless in comparison with the "criolla" whose game of seduction undermines male power. The attempted robbery contrasts, then, two gender-differentiated strategies for the subversion of power: male violence and female seduction. The Spanish narrator foils the first without difficulty but is at a loss of how to react to the second.

The crux of the story is the shattering of man's ideal vision of woman. Chole's superficial attractions hide a cruel and depraved inner reality made all the more obvious when she exercises power. This decadent motif of horror beneath beauty runs throughout the narrative: Chole is described as Salambó (an obvious allusion to Flaubert) and with other decadent images (malevolent flower, strange plant, and snake). Indeed the very repudiation of romantic ideal love is decadent in itself. But, as we have seen, the story has a further political dimension. Despite being a female outsider, the "criolla" dominates the male black—male in the New World but not human—and his ritual sacrifice exemplifies this. A savage monster, created by the Spanish and Anglo-Americans, she asserts her supremacy by subordinating the prostituted black whom she (briefly) seduces and whose life is exchanged for a few coins. She uses similar techniques with the Anglo-Americans while the Spaniard looks on, out of the power game. Her behavior suggests that the "criollo" class destroys the black—but only by means of Anglo-American financial aid.

The ideal female figure steps out of the frieze and becomes all too human. This is what shocks the narrator. Her actions echo the relations of domination and submission of a masculinist society, but as a woman no longer idolized the dualisms informing that society allow her to be represented in no other way than as natural animality. By the end of the story she embodies not so much natural paradise as the law of the jungle and is feared rather than revered. She never occupies domestic space but always the public domain (unlike the other female protagonists of *Femeninas*). Nor is she seen within a family network, other than that of her husband who is himself sexually ambiguous. Described as Herculean, nevertheless he has no facial hair and his eyes are "neutral." Similarly, the yankee's beard is "ox coloured" ["color de buey"] (127). There is no father-figure to control Chole. When the narrator realizes the horror of unconstrained female power he too retreats in fear and reads universal female depravity into this particular incident. The story is the most cosmopolitan and colorful of the collection and functions as an "espejismo" ["mirage"] of timeless beauty, shattered by the inhumanity, racism, and heartlessness of mercenary commercialism. The narrator, shocked out of the dream of idealized woman and the exotic Other, is forced to enter violent, competitive, contemporary reality which reverses traditional roles—both at the level of interpersonal relations and international politics. His anxiety of loss and powerlessness is rooted in the fact that his worldview is irrelevant, indeed contraproductive, in the contemporary order. There is no nostalgia in the ironic perspective of the older cynic who scorns his young self and, at the same time, traditional concepts of the role of women, world power, and the Spanish Empire. And the corporeal representation of all this conflict (within the individual and in the Hispanic world) is the contradictory female figure: repellent/attractive; priestess/temptress; beautiful/horrific.

In "Tula Varona" (1893), another Spanish traditional type—the Duquesito—(son of the Duke of Ordax and related to the Condesa de Cela) is portrayed as inexperienced, inane, and ignorant. He too has his comeuppance. He is hunted, lured, and caught by a "criolla" from the River Plate area, as her taste for "mate" implies. The story is about role reversal. Tula engages in masculine activities (fitting with her second name)—she bets, drinks, smokes, and

inhales, has a gun, is an accomplished fencer, and takes the initia-
tive in seduction. She is also endowed with male attributes, such
as a "manly laugh" ["risa hombruna"] (80) and short hair. On the
other hand, for the effeminate Duquesito, she is voluptuous and
sexually attractive. In addition, part of the story takes place on
the mountainside, in open space, relating Tula to the wild and un-
tamed but part is set in the domestic space of her wealthy home,
her exotic "nest" ["nido"] (84). She is bisexual; cultured and wild;
seductive and hostile. Tula defies all binary gender categories and
in this way asserts her mastery. This is most apparent in her control
of language, her erudition, wit, and irony. Having appropriated the
kind of discourse associated with male seduction, she consistently
preempts the Duke and parodies his words, refusing to take them
seriously and so subverting and ridiculing his patronizing pretensions to control her through language. She uses words as weapons,
jousting with male-centered discourse, then fencing physically with
the lecherous Duke and beating him on both occasions. Tula is
indeed the strongest, most independent female figure in *Femeninas*. The Duke sees her as both Venus and Diana, the huntress who
provokes then punishes male desire while the narrator suggests
she is lesbian having experienced "certain intimacies" ["ciertas
intimidades"] (82) with an English "doncella" ["lady's maid/
maiden"].

Again, there is a political subtext to the story. Tula represents
"las Indias" ["the West Indies/Indian women"] striking back to
conquer and punish the decadent seat of imperial power. She
stands for the rebellion of the oppressed: women and the colonials.
When the Duke offers to share a cigarette (i.e., sexual relations)
with Tula, he makes explicit the political and economic relations
between metropolis and (ex)colony. "Imagine that you have to pay
duty to the State, and that the State in this case is me" ["Figúrese
vd. que ahora se pagan en esa moneda los derechos al Estado, y
que el estado en este caso soy yo"]. He represents overlordship
and she, as woman and South American, owes him duty/sexual
favors. But Tula retorts, "I'm a smuggler" ["soy contrabandista"]
(90) and refuses to pay or acknowledge the law. Later this political
analogy is reinforced when the point of her foil is compared to the
poisonous dart of an Indian. Woman (like Indian) uses her arms
(words, body, and weapons) aggressively and seductively in her
struggle with centralized, patriarchal power. Hierarchies are
threatened as the woman/"indio" refuses to play according to the
rules set by another. This confuses the Duke; which role should
he play? How should the oligarchy react when the tables are

turned? In the story he retreats when faced with a sexual and political revolution. However, there are at least two flaws in what looks like a piece of radical feminist fiction. The first concerns an important detail; the "criolla" owes her wealth and status to a husband, from whom she is now separated. He is absent, as is a controlling father-figure. The second involves the final scene when a naked Tula contemplates herself with satisfaction in the mirror. She enjoys her own sexuality, touching herself with onanistic "sensual langour" ["languidez sensual"] (92). But the scene also implies a centaurlike male gaze, the gaze of the male reader and, above all, of the voyeuristic narrator whose third-person narration is the ultimate authority.

The last of the stories in *Femeninas,* "Rosarito" (1894) is the only one in which an utterly powerless female is deliberately seduced and killed off by the dominant male. The story also reverts to earlier motifs involving not overseas possessions but the family and the Church. There is little ambiguity as regards gender roles although the story leaves a number of questions unanswered. The setting is not the cosmopolitan 1890s but rural Galicia of the 1860s and the genre is the Gothic mystery tale, dealing with romantic themes: religion, nobility, liberalism, and rebellion. Women are identified from the outset with the protective interior of the Pazo. The grandmother, the Condesa de Cela, represents a long noble lineage (reference is made to at least four generations); she is experienced and knowledgeable but her power is limited as she is a near invalid. The only man in the Pazo is a priest. Because the Conde is dead and the son Pedro is absent there is no father/husband figure to protect the adolescent Rosarito from extraneous males. Rosarito, as her name suggests, is portrayed from the start as a saint. "Golden lily" ["lirio de oro"] (164), she represents the Virgin, the Madonna, all that is divine, unblemished, innocent, and good. Her antagonist is the notorious Don Juan Manuel Montenegro, the personification of evil. He enters the Pazo as a malignant, unrestrained force from the shadowy exterior, invading the women's private space and exuding masculine charisma and power, and entrance is afforded because he is a distant relation (the grandmother's cousin). Don Juan Manuel is the epitome of the impious romantic hero, a veritable Marquis de Sade; "heretic" ["hereje"], "freemason" ["masón"], "libertine" ["libertino"], "atheist" ["ateo"], political exile, adventurer, likened to a pirate, "troubadour" ["trovador"], "poetaster" ["coplero"] (155–57) and associated with Espronceda himself, he is a living legend. He has a story to tell, unlike Rosarito who has none, and is adept—according to the narrator—at reading the untold signs of Rosarito's unconscious desires and masochistic fascination with the Other. He seduces her until she falls in his power. As an iconoclast, Don Juan Manuel has no respect for his noble lineage, for the Church, or for traditional concepts of female honor. He rapes Rosarito (as the shouts suggest) in a room dedicated to a saint, kills her with her own hairpin, and escapes through the window. The young female, then, (representing enclosure, passivity, stasis, and lack of experience) has no power and is destroyed by the male (representing experience, action, and liberal freedom). Don Juan Manuel makes a point of asking whether Rosarito holds rights of primogeniture ["mayorazga"]; she does not. Rather, she fulfills her female role with the family by knitting bootees for her baby brother, the heir. The power of Don Juan is not that of the establishment or institutionalized patriarchy. His is uncontrolled, deviant masculinity which is shown to be violent and destructive. As a Spanish liberal in exile he works to subvert the traditional order so that one reading of the story would be to draw an analogy between liberalismo, "licentiousness" ["libertinaje"], and the diabolic.

However, Don Juan's attitude to women is fundamentally conservative. Once he has defiled the girl who is bound to the Catholic binary virgin/whore, he leaves her no other option than death. Rosarito, neither virgin nor heir, would be no great loss to the males of the family; she is not necessary for patrimonial transmission, nor can her sexuality be incorporated into matrimony. She is expendable and as such is sacrificed to masculine desire. Don Juan's masculinist ideology proves stronger than his professed radical ideas and the fleeting glimpse of amoral permissiveness (when Rosarito is described as a Greek caryatid). He represents a deep-seated male supremacy that nineteenth-century liberalism does not even address. As Nancy Hartsock points out, "The gender carried by power [in such a society] associates masculinity and domination and by means of this connection fuses sexuality, violence and death." Don Juan, then, epitomizes capitalist patriarchy and its "one-sided relations of domination and submission . . . the dynamics of hostility, revenge, and fascination with death."[18] In other words, although institutions of the establishment might come under attack from those like Don Juan who wish to subvert a political system, a deep patriarchal structure remains untouched and hence aggression perpetrated against women continues. Indeed, rape and murder could be seen as the outcast's means of revenge on his family and society. In a Freudian reading his failure to repress sexual instincts and his transgression of the

146

CATHERINE DAVIES

incest taboo, implies the collapse of the (Spanish) civilization he represents. Don Juan's apparent flouting of the rule of exogamy and the suggestions of incest, point to the crumbling of the decadent Montenegro line. The story can also be interpreted as a parody of the melodrama and mystery of Zorrillalike romanticism and a wry look at a "real" Don Juan (unrepentant and unabsolved). This would account for the exaggerated Gothic touches: the vampirelike protagonist, the black cat, the strange shadows on the wall, the flickering candles, the clock striking midnight. An ironic perspective thus subverts and dismantles in a different way the ridiculously anachronistic worldview associated with the landed nobility and Spanish romantic excess.

If "Rosarito" is a parody of romanticism, *Epitalamio* (1897) parodies the modernist aesthetic and subsumes a critique of female compliance with a masculinist worldview. Several critics interpret the story as a feminist text.[19] The wealthy, experienced protagonist Augusta (married to an absentee husband, Juan del Alcázar, representative of Spanish power and tradition in Madrid) takes on a younger Italian poet-prince for her lover in her (husband's) Galician country residence. She assumes the role of the absent father and arranges a marriage between the Prince and her daughter, Beatriz, in order to keep her lover within the family. As such she seems to be in complete control—as seductress and mother— redefining the family unit in order to suit her own desire. But this is only one reading. Augusta is obliged to such deviance given existing social, cultural, and moral constraints. Unable to break the marriage sacrament and divorce her husband legally, legally and economically powerless if she left him, yet obliged to live in a monogamy in which extramarital relations are unacceptable, if her desire is to incorporate a sexual partner into the household and legitimize his presence, she must resort to arranging a purely contractual marriage between her lover and a younger female under her authority, in this case her daughter. This way the lover becomes an affine acceptable to patriarchal kinship and sexuality is channeled through a proper matrimonial system. But because the lover is a husband-substitute, the relations between him and Beatriz would border on the incestuous. This potential flaunting of the moral codes of the establishment and threat to ruling-class kinship structures is what makes the story decadent and potentially subversive. The would-be marriage feast is presented as a pagan ritual outside the limits of Catholic control.

However, the narrative subtly suggests grave flaws in this woman-centered arrangement. It is no more than a comedy enacted for the pleasure of the Prince who can afford to be a passive observer because patriarchal culture works in his favor. He is in a position to possess, sexually and otherwise, mother and daughter who, pitted against each other, are the ultimate victims despite Augusta's efforts to the contrary. Augusta herself is inscribed in the text as a mine of contradictions. She seemingly cares for her daughter yet deceives her, and wants her marriage to the Prince to remain unconsummated. Maternal love and sexual desire are mutually exclusive and continually frustrate each other. Augusta is confronted with untenable binaries, such as monogamy/polyandry; philia/eros; self/other; autonomy/dependency. She adopts at least two personae in the story—the mother (manipulating language and defining events to conform to an acceptable mother/daughter relationship) and the seductress (behaving in a way which conforms to an erotic relationship). Jealous rivalry between mother and daughter suggests an incipient Electra complex on the part of Beatriz. Similarly from a psychoanalytical point of view, the girl grows up when she changes her object of desire from the mother to the Prince. All of which suits the Prince. And in the final analysis this untoward arrangement has been deemed necessary because of the imminent return of the husband, who as absent cause, like the omniscient narrator, remains in overall control. Fear, anger, and desperation can be read into Augusta's actions as much as defiance and cool calculation. Above all, the flimsy network of newly defined interpersonal relations construed by Augusta never materializes. The marriage does not take place; Augusta and the Prince are merely acting out a comedy. The unsuspecting object of the joke could be the female child, but then her "Minerva look" ["mirada de Minerva"] (183) implies as much misdirected cunning as her mother. Does this story, then, describe awesome and depraved female power, whether as a warning or as an example of a feminist strategy to undermine kinship patterns, monogamy, and patriarchy? Or does it point to the abuse of female sexuality in Restoration society, revealing the impossible situation in which women (girls and adults) find themselves?

Epitalamio abounds in literary allusion and can be interpreted as an ironic comment on the artificiality of male-centred modernist literary discourse compared to potential and yet unfulfilled female strategies of cultural and social innovation. Catherine Nickel argues that Augusta is verbally as skillful as the Prince: she is a female dramatist extremely proficient in the creation of oral, not written, texts.[20] Augusta "exercises verbal power" and "creates roles and situations" in a comedy she imposes on others; this counterbalances the traditional roles of author as subject and female as object of his creation. Extending this argument, Augusta is an actress improvising a script according to her relationship with others while the Prince, on the other hand, remains aloof, a detached observer. He never actually puts pen to paper in the story and is clearly hoodwinked by previous literary models—notably the French (Dorevilly, Parnasians) and Italian (Pastorela mundana, Divina Comedia, Commedia Dell'Arte).[21] Hence his name Attilio Bonaparte. He consistently attempts to freeze the conflicts and emotions of the raw life experience of women into male modernist literary paradigms; the episode of the milking of the cow is the most obvious. The allusion to Darío's *Prosas profanas* in the Prince's *Salmos profanas* [Profane psalms] and *Letanías galantes* [Gallant litanies] is clear. The whole story alludes to Darío's poem, "Era un aire suave" ["It was a gentle air"] in which the classical setting (a garden, terrace, and large house) and the female protagonists are described similarly. "La marquesa Eulalia" ["La Marchioness Eulalia"], "maligna y bella" (["evil and beautiful"] 89) is as beautiful, perverse, and destructive as Augusta, and also transgresses social hierarchies by privileging a page to suitors of more noble stock. However, the ménage à trois in the poem (one woman and two male rivals) is inverted in the "novella" where it involves one man (a Parnassian Prince) and two female rivals—mother and daughter. Augusta is not in control of the situation as is Eulalia; she does not represent universal female depravity. Despite the Prince, who equates Augusta with poetry as does the poet in the case of Eulalia, the narrator portrays Augusta more as a desperate, pathetic snob.

The Prince himself embodies both modernist author and modernist character, and it is this metafictional perspective which allows for irony; the Prince is far from being indifferent to the politics (power distribution) of real life, despite pretensions of "Art for Art's sake." His opportunism is suggested in analogies with Mephistopheles, Borgia, and Don Juan, and his discourse, inasmuch as it is that of a male-centered culture, necessarily concerns power. Women (Augusta and Beatriz) are the objects of his creation as literary signs not as human subjects: Augusta is the muse of the Bacchantes; "Dalila tentadora" ["tempting Dalila"] Venus, Vestal virgen, and Madonna. Beatriz is Gioconda, Minerva, "the half opened bud of a rose" ["capullo entreabierto de una rosa"] (198). Woman is a sign, and the poet can manipulate her in his own interests. Arguably, then, it is this unattached, extraneous (foreign), powerful (in status and authority) male, apparently apolitical, who constitutes the greatest threat to patriarchal family values. Augusta cannot emerge triumphant from the contest of creation through language and role playing. She cannot step out of the cultural models subsumed by the canon (the above-mentioned genres hardly express female desire) or out of the language of patriarchal culture and its "dualistic teleologies"; "her plot is not her own."[22] Neither is she able to represent herself. Irrepresentable, she is reduced to a series of self-destructive postures, the parody of a caring mother and seductive lover. Her "lush, matronly, ardent love" ["amor de matrona lozana y ardiente" (175) attempts to dissolve false boundaries but cannot live up to the expectations associated with either role. Her attempts to create fictions are only to deceive herself and another woman. Indeed, she forces herself to be the female sign of the Prince's desire. Augusta's compliance with the male centered perspective is evident in a conversation she has with the Prince (180). She likes to see herself in the black and gold (evil and heavenly) eyes of the Prince and to cast herself in his image of her. Conceived by his gaze, she is a reflection of his own dichotomous goodness and evil. She sees herself only as he sees her. But his eyes (like his language) are treacherous and outside her control. She wants to possess his gaze, his image of herself, but cannot because they are his eyes; she cannot control his image-making of her and so neither her own identity. The Prince offers her his eyes; he'll see with her eyes, he says; her eyes—after all—are only a reflection of his own. She is of his making.

Oxymora point to attempts to bypass the limitations of language. In the reciprocal negation of opposing terms such as uncontaminated with scruples" ["impoluto de escrúpulos"] (175), "cynical, luxurious candour" ["candor cínico y lujuriante"] (177), "divine immoralities" ["divinas inmoralidades"] (177), "Venus of the boulevard" ["Venus Bulevardista"] (181), and "candid cynicism" ["cinismo candoroso"] (204), the reader glimpses what the narrator cannot put into words, what is hidden by the superficial female models created by the Prince and the shimmering facade of the narrator's modernist discourse. The undefined term emerging from the dichotomy suggests woman (Augusta) eluding binary discourse. In this story, then, a potentially subversive sexual freedom is shown to be nothing but hollow fiction. Deeply rooted patriarchal morals and family values remain steadfast. A woman tries to demolish untenable categories and fails because she privileges a male-centered approach. Then again, what else could be expected from a representative of the degenerate, bourgeois nouveau riche? As long as women depend on patriarchy—the text implies—noth-

ing will come of their subversive strategies nor will they fulfill
their desires.

Undoubtedly, Valle-Inclán's early short fiction is open to political readings. What is important is the role woman plays in this
potential subversion. Woman is not simply the embodiment of a
male spiritual and aesthetic quest, nor even the debased representation of its failure as in the romantic and modernist aesthetic. The
female is studied rather in the specific historical context of end-of-
century ruling class social and kinship networks. In *Femeninas*
and *Epitalamio* she constitutes the basis of these familial and social
structures and her relations with men, compliant or otherwise,
uphold or undermine patriarchy. Valle-Inclán sees the dynamics of
his contemporary society predicated on sexual relationship and
gender difference rather than on political institutions, on domestic
rather than on public arrangements. But the apparently objective
narrator, who colludes with the male reader, leaves the texts ambiguous. Are women to be considered clandestine subversives or
reformers of the establishment and its hierarchies of racial, age,
religious, and national differences? Does the author, aware that
"women are located on a boundary between kinship relations and
state structures in a way in which men are not," suggest the need
for a revolution in kinship, possibly through seductive strategies?[23]
The stories reinforce the fin-de-siècle ideas of a horrific threat
hidden beneath the delightful female facade, and they also express
female frustration as would Lorca's work later. The women are
clearly more than decorative objects; they constitute an essential
part of the dynamics of community. Yet as fictional characters,
constructed by the male gaze, they hardly possess their own identities. Can they then be considered subjects? Women are certainly
not subjects of written discourse: only the Condesa writes and her
letters are destroyed. Otherwise the authors and narrators are men
who create the female verbally, and as Catherine A. MacKinnon
argues, there is no such thing as objectivity; the "nonsituated distanced standpoint" is that of the male.[24]

Valle-Inclán left a number of testimonies of his abhorrence of
the Spanish status quo of those years.[25] Spain was a monarchy,
that is, in the words of Alice Jardine,

> the determination of alliance and filiation through the father within the
> Judeo-Christian tradition at a very symbolical level. Any disruption of
> the symbolic chain within that tradition involves the law (both human
> and divine) and the very fabric of social structure. It is filiation and

history, through the Divine right of the (Catholic) king which has, for centuries, formed the matrix of substitution[26]

in this culture. This disruption of the very patriarchal foundations of Spanish society, its symbolic traditions and laws is what characterizes *Femeninas* and *Epitalamio*. The striking absence of a father-figure moreover implies a shift from monarchical to democratic symbolic traditions, from patriarchy to matriarchy.[27] Two further points suggest that while Darío's revolutionary project tended toward the subjective and the aesthetic, Valle-Inclán's was pitched toward the aesthetic and the social. First, the interpersonal relationships described in these stories were sufficiently important for Valle-Inclán to return to them again and again in his later work, to the point that in *Femeninas* "there are no stories as such, but themes to develop" ["no existe cuento en sí mismo: existen temas a desarrollar"].[28] Second, in these works he set about creating his own genealogies, in one sense contemporary, but in another classical. The predominance of female Roman names, Julia, Octavia, Tula Varona, and Augusta, connotes the concealed presence of a powerful matriarchal countertradition. Valle-Inclán joins the transnational modernist enterprise, the "new emancipatory project" described as the elimination of "dogmatic residues, colonized mentalities, and ossified cultural patterns" by means of a political revaluation of women in society.[29]

Notes

1. All references are to *Femeninas. Epitalamio* (Madrid: Espasa-Calpe, 1977) which reproduces the original editions of 1895 and 1897 respectively, and *Prosas profanas*, ed. Ignacio M. Zulueta (Madrid: "Clásicos Castalia, 1987), and will be given in parentheses in the text. I do not take into account earlier versions of the stories included in *Femeninas* and *Epitalamio,* for example, "El canario" ["The Canary"] (an earlier version of "La Generala"), nor later variations which appear in *Sonata de estío* (1903), *Corte de amor* (1903), and *Jardín umbrío* (1903). I have also consulted the first edition of *Femeninas* held in the Biblioteca Nacional, Madrid.

2. Catherine Davies, "Woman as image in Darío's *Prosas profanas,*" *Romance Quarterly* 36 (1989): 281–88. Subsequent to the publication of this article I came across A. L. Hammond-Williams, "Visions of Disharmony in *Prosas profanas:* The Woman on the Balcony," *Journal of Latin American Lore* 12 (1986): 181–207. the conclusions of this intelligent study confirm my own, although emphasis is laid on the contradictions in Darío's personality rather than in those inherent in the female sign. See also Michel Foucault, *The History of Sexuality. An Introduction* (Harmondsworth: Penguin, 1978), 57–60.

3. Michael Mann, "A Crisis in Stratification Theory?" in *Gender and Stratifi-*

cation, eds. Rosemary Compton and Michael Mann (Cambridge: Polity Press, 1986), 41–42.

4. L. Ramos-Kuethe, "El concepto del libertinismo en la narrativa temprana de don Ramón del Valle-Inclán," *Hispanic Journal* 4 (1983): 51.

5. Roberta Salper, *Valle-Inclán y su mundo: ideología y forma narrativa* (Amsterdam: Rodopi, 1988), 89.

6. Ibid., 57.

7. Manuel Bermejo Marcos, *Valle-Inclán: Introducción a su obra* (Madrid: Anaya, 1971), 61.

8. Michael P. Predmore, "El modo dominante de las *Sonatas* de Valle-Inclán. ¿Esteticismo, ambigüedad o sátira?" in *Textos y sociedad: Problemas de la historia literaria,* eds. Bridget Aldacara, Edward Baker, and John Beverley (Amsterdam: Rodopi, 1990), 241. Margarita Santos Zas, "Estéticas de Valle-Inclán: Balance crítico," *Insula* 531 (Marzo 1991): 9.

9. César Barja [1935], quoted in *Ramón del Valle-Inclán. An Appraisal of His Life and Works,* ed. Anthony N. Zahareas (New York: Las Americas Publishing Co., 1968), 192.

10. V. N. Volosinov, *Freudianism. A Marxist Critique,* trans. I. R. Titunik (London: Academic Press, 1976), 14. It is interesting to note that Freud and Breuer's seminal essay, "On the Psychic Mechanism of Hysterical Phenomena," expounding the concept of the unconscious, was published in 1893 and in their joint book, *Studien uber Hysterie* in 1895.

11. Catherine Nickel, "Valle-Inclán's 'Generala': Woman as Birdbrain," *Hispania* 71 (1988): 228–34 (essay in this volume). See also L. T. González del Valle, "La parodia del honor castizo en 'La generala,'" *ALEC* 11 (1986): 279–93.

12. Heidi Hartmann, "The Unhappy Marriage of Marxism and Feminism," in *Women and Revolution,* ed. Lydia Sargent (Boston: South End, 1981), 14.

13. This literary allusion introduces incest as a subtheme. See F. Mugnier, "Le complexe d'Oedipe dans la fiction de Barbey D'Aurevilly," *Romance Notes* 31 (1990): 19–23. See also Fernando Lázaro Carreter, "Sobre la prosa modernista de Valle-Inclán," in *Homenaje al Profesor Antonio Vilanova,* eds. Adolfo Sotelo Vázquez and Cristina Carbonell (Barcelona: PPU, 1989), 285–300.

14. Alice Jardine, *Gynesis: Configurations of Woman and Modernity* (Ithaca, N.Y.: Cornell University Press, 1985), 25.

15. Interesting in this respect is Carol Maier, "Toward a Definition of Woman as Reader in Valle-Inclán's Aesthetics," *Museo de Pontevedra* (1986): 123–30.

16. For a different view see Robert Lima, *Valle-Inclán: The Theatre of His Life* (Columbia: Missouri University Press, 1988), 57, who refers to the "purely Romantic channels" of the texts.

17. Clara Luisa Barbeito, *Epica y tragedia en la obra de Valle-Inclán* (Madrid: Fundamentos, 1985), 69.

18. Nancy Hartsock, *Money, Sex, and Power* (New York: Longmans, 1983), 151, 176. M. José Rivas Domínguez, "Valle-Inclán entre el decadente y el nuevo siglo: 'Rosarito,' de la esperpentización al esperpento," *Letras de Deusto* 41 (1988): 127–44, considers the story as "esperpento."

19. See Catherine Nickel, "The Relationship of Gender to Discourse in Valle-Inclán's 'Augusta,'" *Romance Notes* 30 (1990): 141–48.

20. Ibid., 145, 147.

21. Valle-Inclán deplored imitations of the Spanish canon. See his prologue to *Corte de amor* [1908, 1914] quoted by Antonio de Zubiaurre in *Femeninas.*

Epitalamio, 15, and Ramón del Valle-Inclán, *The Lamp of Marvels,* trans. Robert Lima (New York: Lindisfarne, 1986), 46–49.

22. Jardine, *Gynesis,* 231.

23. Henrietta L. Moore, *Feminism and Anthropology* (Cambridge: Polity Press, 1988), 184.

24. Catherine A. MacKinnon, "Desire and Power: A Feminist Perspective," in *Marxism and the Interpretation of Culture,* eds. Cary Nelson and Lawrence Grossberg (Chicago: University of Illinois Press, 1988), 108.

25. See comments such as "I hate . . . the bullfight, religion, and the military" ["Odio . . . los toros, la religión y el militarismo"]; "youth should be iconoclastic" ["la juventud debe ser iconoclasta"]; "this praise for everything hallowed, that admiration of everything with antique dust, are always a sign of intellectual slavishness" ["esta adulación por todo lo consagrado, esa admiración por todo lo que tiene polvo de vejez, son siempre una muestra de servidumbre intelectual"]; and "the modernist is the one who disturbs" ["el modernista es el que inquieta"], in the prologues to *Sombras de vida* and *Corte de amor.* Quoted in Lima, *Valle-Inclán: The Theatre of His Life,* 65, 307, 309.

26. Jardine, *Gynesis,* 231.

27. Jardine, *Gynesis,* 231–32. She adds, "It is not the father as king or priest and the mother as sacred incestuous object that are primary in the democratic symbolic economy, but rather the maternal function as a replacement for the father, as the central locus of (phallic) power within the nuclear family."

28. Eduardo Tijeras, "El cuento en Valle-Inclán," *Cuadernos hispanoamericanos* 199–200 (July-August 1966): 403–4.

29. Iris Zavala, "The Social Imaginary: The Cultural Sign of Hispanic Modernism," *Critical Studies* 1, no. 1 (1989): 24, 25.

Woman Transfixed: Plotting the Fe/Male Gaze in "Rosarito"

MARYELLEN BIEDER

One of Valle-Inclán's most masterful and memorable short stories, "Rosarito," models the author's narrative strategies and gender coding at the turn of the century and prepares the ground for his *Sonatas.* The highly visual nature of the text, which is almost entirely "viewed" by either the narrator or one of the characters, led me a few years ago to examine Valle-Inclán's multiple and shifting narrative focalization to elucidate the relationship between viewing and narration.[1] In my article I traced the changing narrative focalization in "Rosarito" as the undramatized narrator shifts his field of vision to merge with the focalization of first one character and then another.[2] Building on this narratological analysis of "seeing" as it structures the movement of "Rosarito," I now propose to shift my emphasis to the intersection of seeing and gender in this same richly problematic text.

The dynamics of the male gaze in Valle-Inclán's short story lead me away from the more formalistic approach of my earlier study to a consideration of desire, voyeurism, and fetishism. I draw here on theories developed by film critics, especially Laura Mulvey and Teresa de Lauretis, as well as on Bram Dijkstra's study of fin-de-siècle art and narrative.[3] By appropriating these analyses of voyeurism and fetishism, I hope to show how Valle-Inclán implicates his reader in his voyeuristic narrative construction.[4]

In borrowing from cinema criticism its analysis of the "male gaze," the look that encodes the male's desire, I define it as embracing both the narrator's look and the look of the central male character. The dynamics of seeing in Valle-Inclán's narrative positions the reader as voyeur alongside the focalization of the male-gendered narrator and of both male and female characters, manipulating the reader/viewer's response in much the same way as cinema does. It is the male-gendered narrator/focalizer who empowers the male gaze and subjugates the female gaze which "holds the look, and plays to and signifies male desire."[5] My thesis is that the empowered male gaze structures the narrative and determines the closure of "Rosarito." While the female gaze remains subordinate to language, the dominant male gaze silently penetrates and fixes woman as object. Thus woman is both held fast by the look and trapped in the web of language (story). Valle-Inclán's narrative strategies implicate us in the gaze of desire, seduction, and betrayal, that entraps the virginal/complicitous Rosarito.

Mulvey argues in her seminal study of "Visual Pleasure and Narrative Cinema," that "mainstream film coded the erotic into the language of the dominant patriarchal order." This produces a gender hierarchy in which, in Mulvey's words, "pleasure in looking has been split between active/male and passive/female," between "woman as image, man as bearer of the look."[6] The coding of the erotic, I would argue, is precisely what Valle-Inclan's narrative articulation foregrounds. In cinema's "manipulation of visual pleasure," according to Mulvey, woman functions as an erotic object on two levels: "for the characters within the screen story," and "for the spectator within the auditorium." Dru Dougherty makes a similar point in discussing eroticism in Valle-Inclán's theater, when he observes that one character's eroticism not only arouses a response from other characters, but "will (as intended) arouse the audience."[7] I am suggesting that the manipulation of narrative focalization in "Rosarito" produces a similarly dual fetishization of woman seen through the gaze both of the male character and the complicitous reader.[8] In "Rosarito" the narrative focalizes the eponymous female character as icon, "displayed for the gaze and enjoyment of men, the active controllers of the look."[9] What Mulvey helps us see is that the looks of the focalized narrator, the male character and the reader/spectator coalesce in the construction of woman as icon. This iconogaphy employs the representational codes of synechdoche, cliché, and metatrope identified by Helena Michie in her study of the textualization of the female figure in *The Flesh Made Word: Female Figures and Women's Bodies*.[10]

In cinema the spectator reproduces the gaze of male desire both voyeuristically and vicariously. Mulvey contends that "conditions of screening and narrative conventions give the spectator an illusion of looking in on a private world," fostering "the illusion of voyeuristic separation."[11] Valle-Inclan's short story, with its play of light and darkness, maneuvers the reader into a voyeuristically distanced position similar to the spectator in a darkened theater watching "the brilliance of the shifting patterns of light and shade on the screen." At the same time, however, if the woman is the property of the male protagonist, the spectator can possess her too "through participation in his power."[12] Thus the dynamics of the empowering male gaze, the fetishized woman, and voyeuristic pleasure control the spectator/reader response to a "hermetically sealed world."

In their analyses of the look, de Lauretis contends, film theorists such as Mulvey have disregarded the question of "sexual differentiation *in the spectators*" and defined "cinematic identification as masculine, that is to say, as an identification with the gaze, which both historically and theoretically is the representation of the phallus and the figure of the male's desire."[13] This leaves unexplored the *female* spectator's relationship to the male gaze and the male desire it speaks, as well as her relationship to the object of the gaze, woman as icon. It is precisely the question of gendered reading—the response to the dominant male gaze by female as well as male readers—that I am raising in my reading of "Rosarito." If the gaze of the cinema spectator is voyeuristic, as Mulvey shows, is not the reader's experiencing of scopophilia (the pleasure in viewing), fetishization and seduction in "Rosarito" similarly a voyeuristic objectification of woman? Where, to pose the question in terms of visual positionality, does the female reader look when she reads Valle-Inclán's story?

In addition to the conventions of looking Mulvey discusses for mainstream cinema—"woman as image, man as bearer of the look"—woman in Valle-Inclán's narrative may also bear the look focalized by the narrator. Female focalization dominates the last section of "Rosarito," when the narrative adopts the grandmother's angle of vision, but female desire is absent from this look of sorrow. In the opening scene and at various points throughout the story, however, Rosarito's nascent scopophilia focalizes the narrative and speaks her desire. The active/passive nature of her look and her simultaneous objectification/desire for subjectivity give ambiguity to Valle-Inclan's articulation of the gaze. This raises the question of whether in "Rosarito" the female gaze passively mirrors the male gaze, in narcissistic confirmation of it, or whether it also, to regender Mulvey's words, recognizes the *male's* "perfect to-be-looked-at image" (24) and subjects him "to a controlling and curious gaze"?[14] If the male character, and with him the focalizer and reader, are obsessive voyeurs "whose only sexual satisfaction can come from watching, in an active controlling sense, an objectified other,"[15] is Rosarito in the same sense a voyeuse whose pleasure lies in a devouring look?

The female icon represents both pleasure and anxiety, according to the psychoanalytical categories of Mulvey's analysis: "the woman icon, displayed for the gaze and enjoyment of men, the active controllers of the look, always threatens to evoke the anxiety [a threat of castration and hence unpleasure] it originally signified."[16] She posits two avenues of escape for the male from the threat of sexual difference: voyeurism, which she associates with "subjugation through punishment or forgiveness" and fetishistic scopophilia, which "builds up the physical beauty of the object, transforming it into something satisfying in itself" (21–22). It is in the interplay between these two responses to the desire for/fear of woman that Valle-Inclán shapes the ambiguity of his ending and withholds from his reader the pleasure of experiencing its climax. If the reader is positioned as voyeur/se in "Rosarito," what precisely has s/he (not) seen: a rape, a murder, a suicide?[17]

In my reading of Valle-Inclán's "Rosarito," the manor house [pazo] inhabited by the female-headed household of the Condesa de Cela, her granddaughter Rosarito, and the family chaplin [capellán] Don Benicio, is a world outside history, the repository of the patriarchal practices of a culture that defies time.[18] Like the world of the narrative itself, the two principal characters—the "household nun," virginal Rosarito,[19] and the libertine émigré, the aging Don Miguel Montenegro—are ambiguously coded. Rosarito is at once a maiden domestic angel and a nascent woman awakening to desire through the language of female experience. She is associated with the Virgin Mary and with the martyrdom of Christian saints as well as with the pagan moon. The intruding Montenegro, prodigal cousin of the Condesa's husband, stands in opposition to inherited cultural practices and values embodied in the manor and plays the role of a romantic seducer [seductor romántico] who renews himself through repeated conquest. If in Rosarito culture ultimately succumbs to nature, in Don Miguel, the individual brutishly and brutally overrides tradition. Only the ageless Condesa remains, at the end of the story, to observe the eruption of the anarchic forces of nature and sexual desire in a closed world ruled by the rituals of repressive social institutions.

It can be argued that, in terms of genre, the narrative of "Rosarito" is structured on the conventions of the gothic novel: "[t]he image of woman-plus-habitation and the plot of mysterious sexual and supernatural threats in an atmosphere of dynastic mysteries within the habitation."[20] The tradition in which Valle-Inclán inserts his story is not, however, the female gothic of Ann Radcliffe, but the regendered gothic of Byron and Sade in which male desire is

neither tamed nor controlled. In Don Miguel Montenegro the roles
of villain and hero fuse, following the model of the Byronic lover
(216) and "the sexual and sadistic games" and "satanic imaginings"
of his successor, the Marquis de Sade (219).[21] Through his "piercing
and controlling glances" (222), the gothic villain awakens in the
female a gaze that mirrors his own desire.[22] This shift from a fe-
male-centered to a male-centered gothic, repositions the reader
from gazing with the vulnerable maiden, to accompanying the controlling male gaze. In "Rosarito" only at the climactic moment of
the story, when sexual desire translates into violation and violence,
does Valle-Inclán abandon the shifting focalization of maiden and
seducer and the visual interplay of dominant and subordinate
gazes.

The *pazo* in "Rosarito" is an idealized space that, like the castle
of Gothic fiction, suggests "a nostalgia for romance, chivalry,
Christian goodness, and divine order,"[23] a nostalgia subverted in
turn by Valle-Inclán on a cosmic scale. The power of gazing corre-
lates in the story with the interplay of light and darkness, of sight
and blindness, of presence and absence. Within the darkened
manor, a circle of light encompasses the Condesa, Rosarito, and
the *capellán,* who reads from the lives of the saints [*santoral*]. The
young woman seems to conjure up her cousin, Miguel Montenegro,
from out of the undifferentiated darkness that suffuses and surrounds the mansion [*palacio*]. Her gaze looks inward with "los
ojos de la imaginación" ["the eyes of her imagination"] (182) at the
same time that it looks into the world outside the conventlike *pazo*
and brings forth the man who arouses and incarnates female desire.
From the moment she first senses his materialization, Rosarito
associates him with the devil, asking the chaplain whether he might
be "a sign from the other world" ["algún aviso del otro mundo"]
(174).

Against the stasis of the opening scene and the iconic character
of the narrative, Rosarito moves toward a subject position. Hearing
a sound inaudible to other ears, a sound that comes as much from
within her own desire as from the world beyond the manor house,
she looks outside herself into the chaos of nature. Blocking out the
chaplain's voice, her attention riveted on the sound emanating from
within and without, she belies the narrator's assertion of her piety.
Shifting her gaze from the ordered, familiar domestic world, Rosarito attempts to penetrate with her eyes the confusion of dark, tan-
gled foliage. Her auditory perception disassociates her from
culture and links her to the disruptive forces of nature and the
intruding moonlight. The *pazo* constitutes an "inviolable space of

erotic reverie," as Naomi Schor has termed the convent,[24] and this overlay of the spiritual and the erotic shapes and anticipates Rosarito's expectations and response. Like the Princesse de Clèves gazing at the portrait of the Duke, Rosarito's erotic reverie of Don Miguel de Montenegro is interrupted by the discovery of her cousin gazing at her.[25]

Rosarito breaks into the reading of the Chaplain's exemplary narrative to announce Don Miguel Montenegro's irruption into their hermetic and tradition-bound world. With his arrival the timeless routine within the ancestral home is violated by change and conflict, transgression and nature, power and pleasure. Rosarito's gaze seems to impel Montenegro into a female world bound by the very institutions and traditions that he violently subverts and subordinates to his personal control and authority. Like Pandora opening her box, Rosarito wills the forbidden world of temptation and desire to invade her world through her identification with collective female memory. Thus Don Miguel enters the narrative as the subject of Rosarito's life-giving gaze and female oral tradition.

Awakening to womanhood, Rosarito simultaneously remembers and projects the collective desire of the women of her class and culture. Two texts compete in her scripting of herself: the words of the chaplain's reading from the *santoral* within the feeble encompassing light, and the remembered words of the stories women tell other women about the love of their life, Miguel Montenegro. One is a written text, encoding the dominant patriarchal tradition; the other is the female oral tradition, the collective voice of silenced and subordinate woman. At the same time, the power of her cousin's gaze provokes in Rosarito a masochistic fascination: "Don Miguel infused her with fear, but a suggestive and fascinating fear" ["Don Miguel la infundía miedo pero un miedo sugestivo y fascinador"] (192). The narrator naturalizes these contradictory responses to the visual in auditory terms, as the response to a "frightening and beautiful story" that holds the listener in thrall: "He appeared to her like the hero of a frightening and beautiful story to which one listens shivering, and which, nevertheless, holds the listener captive to the end, as though spellbound" ["Aparecíasele como el héroe de un cuento medroso y bello cuyo relato se escucha temblando, y, sin embargo, cautiva el ánimo hasta el final, con la fuerza de un sortilegio"] (192). The figure of the passive, listening Rosarito bewitched by storytelling anticipates her dual subordination to the male gaze and to a story come to life.

The textualized Montenegro mediates between Rosarito and the figure of her cousin on whom she gazes: she sees the legend, the stimulus of female desire, the incarnation of the remembered words spoken by other women. That is, the Montenegro standing before her is the word made flesh. She bears a doubled memory of her cousin: encoded in different languages and gender experiences. As a child she vicariously shared both the male-world interaction of her grandfather's visit to his imprisoned cousin—the demythified rebel tamed and controlled by the forces of the patriarchy—and the female-world oral narrative of her aunt's passion and promise— the mythified male who embodies the promise of romantic desire. Montenegro is thus mythified both by/for women, as the emblem of the erotic, and for men, as the emblem of passionate action. This situates the model for Don Miguel doubly within the text of romanticism, as the dual tropes of the imprisoned outcast and the absent lover.

Rosarito's naming of Montenegro stimulates her and the chaplain to vie in repeating their memories of Don Miguel and recounting tales from the collective oral tradition, thus bringing his mythical figure, evoked through language, into their circle before he physically appears in their midst. From their positions of dependence, they exhibit an admiration for his freedom and for his uncontrolled exercise of power. The narrator contributes to this mythification of Montenegro with a long section of nonfocalized discourse (sec. 3, 178–81). Patient and passive listeners of the chaplain's narratives, Rosarito and the Condesa textualize life and project the model of the *santoral* onto the unfinished story of Montenegro's life. Desiring to empower herself through narrative, Rosarito projects herself as the mediator of her cousin's redemption and his reinscription into the religion and the static world of his birth. But she conflates two traditions, the written one that empowers her as mediator, and the oral one that casts her as object. In her desire to write the ending of his story, she overlays the lives of saints with sinners. The Condesa's memories, on the other hand, are embedded in social codes; she subordinates history and legend to the conventions governing relationships between cousins. While she grants him the equality due a cousin in the patriarchal order, he claims his dominant position in the gender hierarchy and his authority as a primogenitor [*mayorazgo*]. Disregarding the Condesa's status in the de facto matriarchy, he assumes the authority of male head of household in the absence of any other male claimant and enacts the ancient droit de seigneur.

Through the power of the gaze, the conflict between Don Miguel and the convent/manor is coded not only in erotic terms, but in terms of history versus tradition, nature versus culture, male versus female, demonology versus Christianity, language versus silence, transgression versus conformity. These overdetermined dualistic pairings are grounded in the opposing textual traditions and multiple cultural and literary codes that Rosarito and Don Miguel activate. Mythologized both by the narrator and by Rosarito even before he makes his appearance, Montenegro is coded as the prodigal cousin, the incarnation of childhood memories, the subject of inherited female fantasies, the rescuer of the damsel trapped in oblivion and routine, and a beleaguered relative in need of female solace and salvation. The chaplain and the Condesa see him as the embodiment of anarchy and change, a threat to the order and traditions of their world. In the narrator's gendered focalization and in Don Miguel's (male) gaze, woman is coded in the chivalric tradition as an orphan to be rescued (189); in the courtly love tradition as an object of chaste admiration (195); in the sentimental tradition as the reincarnation of a former love (195–96); in the romantic tradition as the sacrificial figure who expiates man's sins to assure his salvation (197); and in the erotic tradition as the object of male desire.

Rosarito sees herself as the agent both of Montenegro's spiritual (as in hagiography) and bodily (as in sentimental fiction) salvation. She is the mediator who, by naming the horse that provides him with a means of escape, restores to him the sexual dominance and invincibility that define his masculinity. At the same time that she assures his escape, she becomes the agent of her own subjection. By invoking the dual male/female transmission of the mythified Montenegro, she implicitly challenges her cousin to prove himself irresistible to a woman and untamable by the authorities of the patriarchy. Only the chaplain, not blinded by woman's mythification of the male or by her desire to script Montenegro into her narrative models, identifies him with the devil and tries to banish him from the manor house.[26]

First anticipating and then collaborating in the demonization of Montenegro, the narrator labels him an iconoclast and a heretic, a threat to the inviolability of the hermetic world of the *pazo*/convent (179–80). One trope in particular sets the parameters of the clash between convention and libertinism: Don Miguel as "haughty and cruel like a noble Arab" ["altivo y cruel como un árabe noble"] (180). Like the historical enemies of the Catholic religion and culture in Spain, he will disregard female virginity, the sanctity of home, and respect for women and family. Don Miguel's own textualized self is modeled on Lord Byron: "In his youth he had met Lord Byron and the poet's influence on him had been decisive"

["En su juventud había conocido a lord Byron y la influencia del poeta inglés fuera en él decisiva"] (196). He ignites the flame of Rosarito's passion within the protective walls of her convent/home, much as Don Juan Tenorio's letter and subsequent presence seduce convent-bound Doña Inés in José Zorrilla's play. Montenegro's violations accumulate across the narrative sequence: the space of the manor house, the Condesa's hospitality to a cousin, matriarchal authority, Rosarito's innocence, and finally Rosarito herself.

If Rosarito's meditative gaze anticipates/announces the appearance of her cousin, the male gaze performs two opposing operations, at once objectifying and penetrating her. The "virile subjectivities"[27] of both the narrator-as-focalizer and Montenegro-as-focalizer see Rosarito as an iconic surface. The focalization of the narrator, exclusive focalizer of sections 1 and 3, and Don Miguel dominate the narrative, punctuated only by Rosarito's gaze and by the Condesa's partial focalization of the last section. The reader thus sees Rosarito first and predominantly through male eyes. The narrator enhances her viewed nature by projecting her as "pious" and by conflating her surface and her essence in a unified sublimated whole. She is thus not seen as an individual but as the embodiment of a gendered response, a sign in a system of belief.

The nakedness of Rosarito's unguarded gaze as she anticipates/responds to the incarnation of her desire generates the sequence of narrative action. She becomes vulnerable to the narrative voyeurism that transforms her into the flat surface of a canvas. The focalization of Rosarito as the model for a painting mediates her textual representation: "Seen in the faint light from the lamp, with her blond head divinely foreshortened; the shadow of her eyelashes trembling against the marble of her cheek. . . ." ["Vista a la tenue claridad de la lámpara, con la rubia cabeza en divino escorzo; la sombra de las pestañas temblando en el marfil de la mejilla. . . ."] (172). This figural representation, what Helena Michie calls a metatrope or doubled metaphor, places another representation—a painting or a written text—between the viewer and the woman's body.[28]

The nature of woman is doubly distanced, hidden beneath a surface made familiar and conventional. The male gaze of narrator and Montenegro dismembers Rosarito, textualizing her body. In the fragmentation and fetishization of the coded female body, hair, eyes, hands, and arms figure most prominently. Through metonymic displacement, these visible parts carry the erotic charge of unnameable, private parts in what Michie calls "the sexual/rhetorical act of intrusion, unveiling, and reveiling."[29] Rosarito's hands—"pale hands, as transparent as a saint's; hands both mystic and impassioned" ["manos pálidas, transparentes como las de una santa; manos místicas y ardientes"] (173)—with their deathlike transparency suggest an autoerotic ecstasy, passion, and violence. A conventionally iconic surface, her image repeats a familiar representation: "Rosarito brought to mind those naive Madonnas painted against a field of stars" ["Rosarito recordaba esas ingenuas madonas pintadas sobre fondo de estrellas y luceros"] (172). Viewing Rosarito as a work of art "immobilizes her" and "gives her the sort of permanence all art objects possess" when well displayed, as Noël M. Valis observes of Concha in Valle-Inclán's *Sonata of Autumn* [*Sonata de otoño*].[30] The encoding of sexuality through the Pre-Rafaelite fetishization of hair also mediates the narrator's view of Rosarito: "that sadly bowed head which, with its golden tresses divided by a straight part, had a certain Pre-Rafaelite chastity" ["aquella cabeza melancólicamente inclinada que con su crencha de oro, partida por estrecha raya, tenía cierta castidad prerrafaélica"] (186).

The iterative power of such descriptions implicitly inscribes Rosarito within the proposition that "all women are alike, all replaceable." This practice of representing woman's body in terms of the familiar, the already seen and read, Michie argues, serves to restrain "sexual and intellectual arousal."[31] In Valle-Inclán's narrative woman is the object of the male gaze through repetition of the familiar and the attraction/threat of sexual difference. If Rosarito arouses desire in Montenegro, it is not a desire for her as individual, but a response to her generative gaze and the need to see himself at its center. His desire to possess her is the desire to control not *one* woman but *all* women. She is, as Michie writes of another protagonist, "a cipher of *male* lust," "a reflection of [his desire]," "a blank page on which [he writes his narrative] of her significance."[32] For the narrator she is a visual icon—untouchable, surface, and not flesh; for the scopophilic Don Miguel, a fetishized object. Montenegro's gaze transforms his cousin into an iconic surface, the visual repetition of his desire for woman, and penetrates—violates her body.

It is the male, in Mulvey's words, who "articulates the look and creates the action."[33] In Valle-Inclán's narrative, the male gaze returns and replaces Rosarito's originating gaze, becoming both origin and recipient of his own look. That is, the reader assumes the desire embodied in the male gaze for the female object. Through focalization we see Rosarito first as the male-voiced narrator and then as the male protagonist sees her: as an object in their field of vision, fetishized and metaphorized by the male gaze. The viewer/ reader is complicitous in a voyeuristic exercise of power that objectifies and subordinates the viewed object (woman) to the viewer's gaze, thus diffusing her threat to the power of the male.

For Montenegro, Rosarito embodies a triple enclosure within herself, within the convent/*pazo,* and within the tradition that threatens to confine him. Her female sexuality entraps his male autonomy. As the embodiment of culture, patriarchal values, and domesticity, Rosarito stands in the way of his escape, his freedom, and his unfettered future. Like Ulysses confronting Circe, he kills the woman whose presence in his path reduces him to nature and diminishes his power. To violate Rosarito is to violate taboo, to repeat the pattern of violations—symbolic, verbal, transactional— that defines his relationship to the patriarchy that he both exploits and rejects. His dominance in a hierarchical world comes from transgressing its norms and from asserting his authority over them. To kill Rosarito is to reenact the destruction of that part of himself bound to culture and to liberate once again his anarchic, lawless self.

The story's opening scene prefigures its denouement as Rosarito's hidden passion and fear of the unknown (death?), belied by her saint's hands and the domestic dexterity represented metonymically by her embroidery needles, provoke the single violent physical response we witness: "Deeply distracted, she jabbed her needles into the arm of the sofa" ["Profundamente abstraída, clavó las agujas en el brazo del canapé"] (173). The narrative thus encodes both the conformity to gender conventions of Rosarito's static iconic surface, and the disruptive potential of her sublimated passion as she gazes inward at the figure of her cousin transmitted through collective female memory.

Rosarito's desire, intensified by Montenegro's gaze, is mediated through the language of other women's desire; her timid and discontinuous gaze reenacts their desire. As he fetishizes her as the object of his gaze, she textualizes him, writing the aging émigré into the plot of unfulfilled female longing, as well as into the plot that makes the female the agent of male salvation. The narrator stands apart from her focalization, pulling the reader with him as he expresses admiration for Montenegro: "You should have seen, . . ." ["Era cosa de ver, . . ."] (180). On the threshold between the innocence of virginity—the martyred virgin of the *santoral*—and a woman's desire—the repetition of generations of unsatisfied female desire—Rosarito subordinates her individual experience to oral tradition. Her gaze challenges Montenegro to repeat and thus reaffirm the legend that is the collective memory of women, transmitted to Rosarito by her aunt, Amanda de Camarasa, whose name anticipates both the passion (*amanda* ["loving"]) and the deathbed (*camarasa* ["blank—empty—bed"]) that await Rosarito.

In textualizing her cousin, Rosarito misreads him, scripting his repentence and salvation through her agency, against his counterplot of the seduction and destruction of iconic woman. Thus she brings male/writing and female/orality into deadly conflict. Although Rosarito is consistently represented as a viewed object rather than a text by the narrator and the characters, she also functions as a textual construct in Montenegro's script, as he does in hers. His seduction plot repeats both a male textual tradition and his own previous experience, whereas Rosarito is a novice whose scripts derive exclusively from (female) oral and (male) textual transmission. Once his role is identified by the narrator, Montenegro's familiar seducer script requires no further preparation for the reader, who anticipates the unfolding of a plot that lies outside Rosarito's textual knowledge. In contrast, her memory of Amanda de Camarasa's story invokes a plot based on female experience that must be elaborated for the reader because literary competence does not encompass it. From the outside, Rosarito's erotic projection of Montenegro is consistently mediated by the language of others, while his erotization of her is more immediately visual. She is the visual icon, the object that catalyzes his seduction plot, whereas both her (male) repentence script and her (female) romance script place him in the subject position.

An underlying threat of gender role reversal destablizes the facade of gothic conventions and unmasks the ambivalence of the male gaze. Miguel Montenegro enters the narrative in a position of weakness: vulnerable, pursued, unmanned without his horse. Nina Auerbach reminds us that the horse, a "celebration of sexual power," has also been associated with the animal nature of fallen women.[34] By identifying a Bucephalus that only Don Miguel's mastery can control, Rosarito offers a corrective to the renegade's immobility and vulnerability—his presence in a female household without a horse—and restores his masculinity. Facilitator of the animal that will allow her cousin to make his escape, she embodies a hidden passion and a recognition of male sexual power. Like her grandmother, she gives expression to a desire to tame and redirect the male animal through the authority of saintly models. If the Condesa tries to invoke the power of Fray Diego de Cádiz by putting her cousin in the room where the Saint once slept, Rosarito more actively seeks to bring Don Miguel spiritual as well as physi-

cal salvation. Although she takes her models from the lives of
saints, she writes a role for herself that is reminiscent of a Doña
Inés to Montenegro's Don Juan Tenorio, projecting her cloistered,
virginal hand as the agent of his salvation. But in Zorrilla's play it
is not Inés but her reincarnated memory that stretches out a hand
to redeem her lover. Rosarito, like Amanda de Camarasa and the
endless succession of identically iconic women, sacrifices herself
for a lover who accepts temporal but not eternal salvation at her
hand and then abandons her.

Upon entering the manor house, Montenegro responds to Rosarito's gaze, first perceiving her awakening desire, then penetrating
her eyes with his own gaze, and ultimately destroying her power
to gaze (unman him). This visual penetration/violation anticipates
his (unseen) possession/violation of her. In subordinating Rosarito
to a gaze that articulates his desire, Don Miguel not only makes
her an erotic object but, more significantly, conveys the autoerotic
nature of his scopophilia.[35] His narcissistic gaze transforms Rosarito into a surface onto which to project and read his own desire
reflected in the eyes of the other. She is a mirror in which he
confirms his own image; his sense of self depends on a woman's
affirmation of his desirability. With his gaze fixed on Rosarito, he
sees only the reflection of himself. Similarly, Carlos Feal observes
that Concha in *Sonata de otoño* serves as "the mirror in which
Bradomín is narcissistically reflected" ["el espejo donde Bradomín
narcisistamente se refleja"].[36] The voyeuristic Nemours in the *Princesse de Clèves,* as Schor writes, "holds the object of his desire
prisoner of his gaze" and "violates her most intimate secret," be-
holding "his own likeness as viewed through the eyes of an adoring
woman."[37] Montenegro is likewise riveted by Rosarito's gaze and
by the specularity of male and female desire. "Jouissance," for
Montenegro as for Nemours, "is being the spectator of his own
desirability." But what Schor reads in Mme. de Lafayette's text as
a "devastating exposure of the male subject's fascination with the
evidence of phallic power," in Valle-Inclán's narrative is the confirmation and fulfillment of that fascination.

The emblem of the domestic angel, the embroidery needles in
Rosarito's hand as the narrative opens, figure again in its closure
in the form of an ornamental hairpin [*alfilerón*]. Both needles and
pin become disruptive signs in the static representation of woman.
The urgency with which Rosarito jabs her needles into the sofa as
she fantasizes the figure of her cousin metaphorically communicates the intensity of her latent passion and the destructive potential of the hairpin. The force of these subconscious emotions belies

her surface tranquillity and anticipates the unseen thrusting violence of the narrative closure. The focalizer's gaze captures the hidden nature of woman and lays bare the dissonance between the iconic coding of her surface and her hidden passion. In the overarching structure of reversal, the sacrificial death of a woman assures Montenegro's life and privileges memory over emotion. Rosarito's golden hairpin is, in Dijkstra's phrase, a "flèche phallique"[38] that fixes her passivity in death. As an arrow of love in a woman's hand, the pin is as ambiguously gendered as it is in Dijkstra's context: a painting of a woman pointing her arrow at an exhausted king of beasts. In Valle-Inclán's story the beast turns on Rosarito, using her appropriation of his phallic power to annihilate her threat to himself. Once the sign of her virginal containment, the hairpin "thrust into her breast, over her heart" ["clavado en su pecho, sobre el corazón"] (206) repeats and reverses her own earlier action with the needles and violates her heart in a double physical/spiritual rape. That Don Miguel (read: rape) and not Rosarito herself (read: suicide) impales her body with the golden spike is suggested by the adverb "barbarously" [*bárbaramente*], which echoes the "haughtiness" and "cruelty" of the "noble Arab" (180) in Montenegro.

The narrative is framed by Rosarito's response to the penetration of her world by the power of the male gaze. Her three inarticulate cries [*gritos*] record a triple penetration, the first, her penetration by Montenegro's gaze in the opening scene, anticipating and prefiguring the latter two. Don Miguel's green eyes, the displaced site of his diabolic fascination for women, metonymically enact his multiple violations: "they infiltrated love like a poison, they violated souls and . . . robbed kisses from the purest mouths" ["infiltraban el amor como un veneno, que violaban las almas y . . . robaban los besos a las bocas más puras"] (196–97). Two further violations—by Montenegro and by Rosarito's own ornamental hairpin—penetrate her body and give closure to the narrative. Piercing the stillness of the night and the silence of the manor house, the three cries are the only traces of her experience. When she first perceives the materialized presence of her erotic fantasies, her cry externalizes her recognition of her flesh-and-blood cousin. In the language of female eroticism, her inward reveries of female fantasy surface throughout the narrative as "sighs" [*suspiros*], while the intersection of these fantasies with the external world provokes a cry of exposure and violation. The two cries that toward the end of the story pierce the silent darkness of the *palacio,* in which only the offstage Rosarito and Montenegro remain active, suggest a further penetration/violation of Rosarito (202). Strikingly, only the somnolent Condesa hears these disembodied sounds, but, awakened from sleep, she lacks the capacity to locate or interpret them.

Thus the two cries becomes signs with no referent, suspended outside the space and time inhabited by the grandmother and thus resistant to decoding by narrator or reader. Similarly, neither recipient or narrator decodes Rosarito's first *grito,* although the subsequent appearance of Montenegro imposes after the fact a causal link between the man and the sound. The absence of Don Miguel from the closing scene, in which the Condesa recovers her position as focalizer, robs it of a clear causality and leaves only the visual sign of Rosarito's dead body. As before, the question remains open of whether the sounds communicate pain, pleasure or both. Only the pattern of female fear and fascination and woman's inarticulateness in the presence of male sexuality link all three cries to Rosarito. Nevertheless, the doubling of the closing *gritos* suggests a dual penetration: Montenegro's possession of his cousin and the further penetration of her body by the "golden hairpin" ["alfilerón de oro"] that "just moments earlier secured the young girl's braid" ["momentos antes aún sujetaba la trenza de la niña"] (206). Confirming the victory of the forces of darkness over light, the hairpin reenacts Rosarito's "undoing," represented visually by her loosened hair, as it pierces her heart. Dijkstra observes that in late nineteenth-century art a woman's fetishized golden tresses came to signify "the dangers of the clinging vine" entwining the male.[39] This interpretation reinforces the metonymic association of Rosarito's hair with her body, both as the object of male desire and as the emblem of his entrapment. Valis reminds us that in *Sonata de otoño* Concha's tresses are a metaphoric and "a literal snare for Bradomín" that figures the text's "web of sexual entanglement."[40] We might read one act of penetration as the reversal of the other, as the freeing of Montenegro from cultural, sexual, and textual bondage. Disappearing in silence from the narrator's field of vision, he vanishes into the dark from which he emerged. The bonds of kinship and honor broken, he regains his phallic power, expressed in its double, the horse made possible by Rosarito's prior mediation, and the recovers his anarchic autonomy.

The death of Rosarito inverts the order of the manor house: the diabolic presence of Don Miguel displaces the word of God, shapes and shadows move freely through the darkness of the room, and the Condesa takes fright at her own world transfused by the forces of evil. At midnight order turns to chaos, life subsides into death, and inanimate objects come to life. The rape/death of Rosarito reverberates through the cosmos: female desire is punished, freeing nature from bondage to culture. Even death is represented visually, seen through the shocked eyes of the Condesa, in the blood—the sign of (absent) life—that stains the purity of Rosarito's bodice: "Down her white bodice flows a trickle of blood!" ["¡Por su corpiño blanco corre un hilo de sangre!"] (206) Like a butterfly mounted in a lepidopterist's showcase, she is penetrated, fixed to the bed, and displayed.

The death of Rosarito is prefigured not only by her embroidery needles but by Montenegro's evocation of death, when he asserts that "if they came to arrest me, I would get myself killed" ["Si viniesen a prenderme, yo me haría matar"] (197). Romantic hero that he is, he prefers death to captivity, a death in which Rosarito would un/cover his body: "your devout hands would cover me with a shroud" ["tus manos piadosas me amortajarían"]. In the reversal of darkness and light and in the dominance of death over life, it is Don Miguel who un/covers Rosarito and chooses death for her. As Dijkstra has shown for painting, the Dead Lady, the ultimate representation of the passive woman, is an object of erotic desire.[41] Rosarito's total submission in death affirms male dominance and power, and eroticizes the pleasure of power in "the iconic representation of a beautiful woman safely dead."[42] While death awaits the female who threatens the freedom of the Romantic seducer and crosses the boundaries that separate culture from nature, virgin from woman, icon from body, freedom in nature awaits the now resuscitated Montenegro. Read as a fantasy of the recuperation of male power, "Rosarito" writes a turn-of-the-century alternative to the Romantic myth of heroic individualism and a response to the redefinition of female sexuality and autonomy.[43] And yet both Montenegro and Rosarito inhabit anachronistic and sterile worlds that actively, on the one hand, and passively, on the other, resist history.

The story of a second young woman, the orphaned daughter of one of Don Miguel's fellow émigrés, functions as a counternarrative to that of the eponymous, parentless protagonist. In Montenegro's self-textualization, his return to Galicia is motivated by a chivalric duty: "to bring aid to the orphan girl. . . . This mission fulfilled, I will return to Portugal" ["traer socorros a la huérfana. . . . Cumplido este deber, me vuelvo a Portugal"] (189). With this script he writes himself into the tradition of Amadís and Don Quijote, the succorer of widows and orphans, an antithetical narrative to the Byronic model, Like other romantic seducers, he brings deflowering and death to virgins rather than succor. Rosarito doubles for the orphan girl whose story anticipates her own and is in turn interrupted and reversed by Rosarito's death.

As the serpent who first invades the manor garden and then the body of Rosarito, Don Miguel provokes Eve/Rosarito's expulsion from innocent/virginity/life. In the textual model that informs her world, martyred women die to avoid commerce with the devil or disbelievers. The rosary, whose name Rosarito bears, is an icon that embodies language and memory; its text is the passion of Christ and the miraculous power of the Virgin. Through the repetition of language Rosarito enacts a female (profane) version of both the constancy of Mary's love and the sacrificial nature of Christ's passion. She is sacrificed on the alter/bed of love/power for her cousin's salvation. Martyred to her passion, she is reclaimed by nature for the world of darkness and chaos through the agency of the moon whose light amid the dark vegetation is, to borrow Lily Litvak's metaphor, like a window onto infinity.[44] Likewise everything else in this narrative, the visual coding of death as salvation or damnation, grace or chaos, is overdetermined.

Conversely, from the "household nun" suffused with a desire to transform language into experience, Rosarito becomes through her gaze a temptress. Initially the product and embodiment of culture, suspended in the stasis of the *pazo,* she merges with the world of nature and its uncontrolled growth and reproduction. Her aroused sexuality unleashes the unseen forces that inhabit the darkness of the human body and the night. Through these associations the narrative locates in her gaze the transgressive force that disrupts the manor and provokes her death. Time, space, and history seem suspended when she and her cousin pass from the circle of light into the dark passages of the manor to reenact on the chaste bed of Fray Cádiz the saint's struggle against heresy.

The narrator abandons the controlling male-gendered gaze at the climactic moment when desire translates into penetration. By silencing the narrative and obscuring Montenegro and Rosarito from view in the Fray Diego bedroom, Valle-Inclán moves violation and death outside time and the circle of light. Depriving his readers of their own visual penetration of the darkness and their own voyeuristic satisfaction, he forces each reader to project his/her own fantasy of desire on the events of the narrative, to "see what happens." By positioning the reader in the closing scene alongside the Condesa de Cela, the narrative restores the angle of vision of the hereditary values and institutions implicit in the opening scene and now rendered powerless and deprived of continuity by death. The movement from silence to silence thus encircles the narrative. In the closing section of the story, the Condesa de Cela's focalized gaze replaces that of the absent Montenegro as she stands beside the deathbed to which her pious plot to reform a sinner has led her granddaughter. Seeing through the Condesa's eyes, the reader as spectator shares a doubly gendered horror/pleasure in gazing at the "life in death" body. The focalization shifts for the last time from viewing subject to viewed object. Although the grandmother alone gazes at Rosarito's body, the iconic representation of woman usurps her look and reinstates the male gaze of the departed Montenegro.

Closure comes with a death that writes female beauty, vulnerability, and passivity suspended outside time, thus enclosing the narrative in the fetishized representation of woman. Dijkstra locates male pleasure in the "literal equation . . . between virtuous passivity, sacrificial ecstasy, and erotic death as indicative of female fulfillment."[45] Contrasting the viewer's place in the narratives of two paintings, the critic writes:

> One can take the male's position and experience the aggressive-sadistic sentimentality of the dominator for whose sake the woman has died, or one can opt for the passive-masochistic pleasure of self-sacrifice centered in the figure of the dead lady.[46]

I suggest that these two positions similarly exist for the reader of "Rosarito" who may experience either the male's position of dominance or the female's position of passive pleasure in being dominated. Through the narrator's gaze, nevertheless, the reader experiences the "aggressive-sadistic sentimentality of the dominator."[47]

The eroticization of silence and death represents the canceling out of two conflicting literary traditions on which Valle-Inclán draws. The closing iconic representation of the dead Rosarito— "Her blond hair covers the pillow, tragically, like a Mary Magdalene" ["La rubia cabellera extiéndese por la almohada, trágica, magdalénica"] (206)—can be viewed in two ways, either as female martyrdom (suicide), or as Montenegro's response to woman as sexual threat (rape and/or murder). The focalized narrator, ostensibly viewing the deathbed scene through the eyes of her grandmother, reinstates Rosarito as visual icon through "the cult of the woman as corpse."[48] The link between the seductive woman and the dead woman is articulated through the figure of the redeemed prostitute. In a doubled metaphor or metatrope, Rosarito is doubly figured as Mary Magdalene and as a painting of the repent Mag-

dalene, an image sustained beyond the confines of the *pazo* and
the text by the use of suspension points. The last word/image of
the text, "Magdalenic . . ." ["magdalénica . . ."], reverses the image of Rosarito as Madonna in the opening section and inscribes
her into the position of the fallen woman corrupted by desire.
Eroticizing death, the narrative gaze restores both the power of
the male gaze and the female body as icon of desire even as it
records the absence of Miguel Montenegro.

It is also possible to read the story's plot of seduction and death
as Don Miguel's attempt to spend male energy to affirm the life of
his myth and at the same time to free himself from the death-in-
culture that this myth represents. His fear of woman is, read this
way, a fear of death, of entrapment in his own story. As the woman
who provokes his textual reeanctment of his narcissistic narrative,
Rosarito can only liberate him through her own death. Seen either
as repentent suicide or violated victim, Rosarito dies a martyr's
death. To kill his textualized self, he must kill the reflection of that
self in Rosarito's eyes. Read in this way, Rosarito's death both
restores him to life and denies his survival in female memory by
breaking the chain of transmission. In the Christian tradition, death
represents triumph, like the triumph of the repentent Mary Magdalene over sin or a martyred saint over her tormentors.[49] Conversely,
Montenegro's triumph over mortality by killing Rosarito ironically
confirms his own mortality. In contrast, Rosarito, transformed in
death as in life into art, transcends the temporal plane and retains
the immortality of an object displayed for others.

The narrative thus offers readers a double pleasure: the female
pleasure of self-sacrifice in martyrdom and the male pleasure of
fetishized female passivity/death. The refraction of this morbid
eroticism through the gaze of the grieving grandmother marks the
forbidden nature of this vicarious (for both character and reader)
visual pleasure and, ironically, heightens its erotic force. The female reader is caught between the Condesa's gaze of powerlessness
and sterility in a truncated, futureless world, and the dominant
male gaze allied with the forces of unconscious desire, sexuality,
and nature unleashed and nourished by Rosarito's death. For the
female reader, to experience the eroticism of Rosarito's death is
to become the object and not the viewing subject whose look controls the narrative. The fetishization of female passivity offers a
mirror to the female viewer rather than the satisfaction of a threat
subdued. Trapped like Rosarito in the male gaze, the female reader
may experience with her the fascination Montenegro exerts, and

find herself an object trapped in the dominant (male) gaze rather than an empowered subject who inhabits history.

Overcoded and overdetermined as is the rest of the narrative, the ending of "Rosarito" allows for its inscription within the multiple and mutually incompatible conventions of gothic, hagiographic, erotic, and sentimental plotting. If, as Mulvey posits, in cinema the male spectator's gaze merges with the look of the male protagonist conveyed by the camera, the reader shares the gendered desire of the narrator's look at the narrative's close, suspended in the act of gazing at the icon of eroticized death. In narrative the female reader finds herself occupying not only the positionality of focalization, but simultaneously the positionality of the focalized image. In cinema the female spectator, de Lauretis writes, engages in a "double identification with the figure of narrative movement, the mythical subject, and with the figure of narrative closure, the narrative image."[50] She escapes being stranded between the male gaze and the female image by experiencing "both positionalities of desire, both active and passive aims: desire for the other and desire to be desired by the other."[51] This translates in "Rosarito" into the dual if irreconcilable positionalities of pleasure in looking at woman as icon and complicity in the victimization of woman as passive object. In other words, in de Lauretis's terms, the female reader sees with both the bearer and the recipient of the look, both Montenegro and Rosarito, both voyeur and female body. The duality is ultimately as unstable and unsatisfying, as resistent to reduction, as are the competing texts and codes out of which Montenegro and Rosarito construct the plots of their mutual gazing. "Rosarito" leaves the female reader not only with the irreducible ambiguity of the silenced and obscured climax, but with the unresolvable tension of mutually untenable positionalities for the female gaze.

Notes

1. Maryellen Bieder, "La narración como arte visual: Focalización en 'Rosarito,'" in *Genio y virtuosismo de Valle-Inclán,* ed. John P. Gabriele (Madrid: Editorial Orígenes, 1987), 89–100. In that article I draw on Seymour Chatman (*Story and Discourse: Narrative Structure in Fiction and Film* [Ithaca, N.Y.: Cornell University Press, 1978], 151–58); and Mieke Bal (*Teoría de la narrativa: Una introducción a la narratología,* trans. Javier Franco [Madrid: Cátedra, 1985], 110 ff) in defining the focalization in "Rosarito" as alternating between "external focalization" and "variable internal focalization." See also Gerald Prince, *Dictionary of Narratology* (Lincoln: University of Nebraska Press, 1987), 32.

In a recent book, Seymour Chatman argues that only characters can "see," while narrators who do not occupy the story world only report events (*Coming to Terms: The Rhetoric of Narrative in Fiction and Film* [Ithaca, N.Y.: Cornell University Press, 1990], 144). While Chatman rejects the premise, held by continental narratologists, that "*somebody* always 'sees' or 'focalizes' the story" (145), it seems to me that a focalizing narrator best accounts for the "seen" nature of a narrative like "Rosarito" that shifts in and out of the visual range of individual characters. For an excellent analysis of theories of focalization from Genette on, see William Nelles, "Getting Focalization into Focus," *Poetics Today* 11, no. 2 (Summer 1990): 365–82.

2. The narrator of "Rosarito" is not a character in the story world and has no personality; he is thus an effaced or "covert" narrator, to use Chatman's terminology (*Story and Discourse,* 197–211); or an "undramatized" narrator, as first defined by Wayne C. Booth in *The Rhetoric of Fiction* (Chicago: University of Chicago Press, 1961), 151–52. Nevertheless, I find that the narrator, both when nonfocalized and when narrating his own focalized standpoint, shares the attitudes, assumptions, and male-gendered gaze of the dominant patriarchal order within the story world. I therefore consider the narrative voice and vision to be implicitly gendered, despite the absence of any overt gender marking. In my reading, the narrator of "Rosarito" is indisputably marked as male-gendered.

3. Laura Mulvey's 1975 article on "Visual Pleasure and Narrative Cinema" is reprinted in her collection, *Visual and Other Pleasures* (Bloomington: Indiana University Press, 1989), 14–26. Mulvey's theory derives from Freud's analysis of scopophilia (the pleasure in looking at another person as an erotic object) and his recognition of the voyeuristic nature of narrative. My study appropriates some of her conclusions, as well as Teresa de Lauretis's commentary on it in *Alice Doesn't: Feminism, Semiotics, Cinema* (Bloomington: Indiana University Press, 1984). Bram Dijkstra, *Idols of Perversity: Fantasies of Feminine Evil in Fin-de-Siècle Culture* (Oxford: Oxford University Press, 1986).

4. Lou Charnon-Deutsch has studied the connection between narrative art and voyeurism in Leopoldo Alas's *La Regenta* in "Voyeurism, Pornography and *La Regenta,*" *Modern Language Studies* 20 (1990): 94.

5. Mulvey, "Visual Pleasure," 19.

6. Ibid., 16, 19.

7. Dru Dougherty, "Theater and Eroticism: Valle-Inclán's *Farsa y licencia de la Reina castiza,*" *Hispanic Review* 55 (1987): 18.

8. Mulvey cites the device of the showgirl to illustrate the overlay of the characters' and the audience's looks. The device "allows the two looks to be unified technically without any apparent break in the diegesis. A woman performs within the narrative; the gaze of the spectator and that of the male characters in the film are neatly combined without breaking narrative verisimilitude. For a moment the sexual impact of the performing woman takes the film into a no man's land outside its own time and space" ("Visual Pleasure," 21).

9. Ibid.

10. Helena Michie, *The Flesh Made Word: Female Figures and Women's Bodies* (Oxford: Oxford University Press, 1987), 10.

11. Mulvey, "Visual Pleasure," 17.

12. Ibid., 21.

13. de Lauretis, *Alice Doesn't,* 143.

14. Mulvey, "Visual Pleasure," 24, 16.

15. Ibid., 17.

16. Ibid., 21–22.

17. In his recent study of the story, "'Rosarito' y la hermenéutica narrativa," Luis T. González-del-Valle discusses interpretations of Rosarito's death (*La ficción breve de Valle-Inclán: Hermenéutica y estrategias narrativas* [Barcelona: Anthropos, 1990], 139–57). He concludes that Montenegro, unable to seduce Rosarito, takes his vengence by killing her (145). In contrast, Will Risley, in "Hacia el simbolismo en la prosa de Valle-Inclán," affirms that sexual intercourse takes place (*Anales de la Narrativa Española Contemporánea* 4 [1979], cited by González-del-Valle, 154). Gerald Gillespie and A. N. Zahareas, on the other hand, judiciously refer only to "seeming sexual violence" (*Ramón del Valle-Inclán: An Appraisal of His Life and Works,* ed. Zahareas [New York: Las Américas, 1968], 285).

18. First published in 1895 in *Femeninas,* a collection of short fiction, the story underwent numerous transformations in subsequent editions, including changes of title, format, and the name of the male protagonist. For a publication history of "Rosarito," see Eliane Lavaud, *Valle-Inclán: Du journal au roman (1888–1915)* (Dijon: Université de Dijon, 1979), 599–616. I cite from the last edition of the story revised by the author for the collection *Jardín umbrío: Historias de santos, de almas en pena, de duendes y ladrones* (Madrid, 1920), 171–206. In this version the name of the male protagonist appears as both "Miguel Montenegro" and "Miguel de Montenegro." I give all page references in the text.

19. I adapt the phrase from Dijkstra who uses it to characterize the married woman; my emphasis falls equally on the house as convent and the (un)married woman as nun (*Idols of Perversity,* 13–24).

20. I borrow here from Norman N. Holland's and Leona F. Sherman's gendered readings in "Gothic Possibilities" (*Gender and Reading: Essays on Readers, Texts, and Contexts,* eds. Elizabeth A. Flynn and Patrocinio P. Schweickart [Baltimore, Md.: Johns Hopkins University Press, 1986], 215).

21. Holland "Gothic Possibilities," 216, 219.

22. Ibid., 222.

23. Holland and Sherman, "Gothic Possibilities," 219.

24. Naomi Schor, "The Portrait of a Gentleman," *Representations* 20 (1987): 118.

25. A recent study classifies Rosarito as an "innocent victim with no decisive role in the development of events" ["víctima inocente, sin un papel decisivo en el transcurso de los acontecimientos"]; Ma. José Rivas Domínguez, "Valle Inclán entre el decadente y el nuevo siglo: 'Rosarito," de la esperpentización al esperpento," *Letras de Deusto* 18, no. 42 (September–December 1988): 143.

26. Note the opposition of good and evil in the two names: Benicio (from "goodness") and Montenegro ("black mountain").

27. Nancy K. Miller, "Men's Reading, Women's Writing: Gender and the Rise of the Novel," *Yale French Studies* 75 (1988): 44.

28. Michie, *Flesh Made Word,* 102–3.

29. Ibid., 83.

30. Noël M. Valis, "The Novel as Feminine Entrapment: Valle-Inclán's *Sonata de otoño,"* in this volume, 63.

31. Michie, *Flesh Made Word,* 89.

32. Ibid., 61.

33. Mulvey, "Visual Pleasure," 17.

34. Nina Auerbach, *Woman and the Demon: The Life of a Victorian Myth* (Cambridge: Harvard University Press, 1982), 178–79.

35. Stephen Heath, "Difference," *Screen* 19, no. 3 (Autumn 1978): 87.

36. Carlos Feal, "La realidad psicológica en *La sonata de otoño,*" *España Contemporánea* 2, no. 4 (Spring 1989): 51.

37. Schor, "Portrait of a Gentleman," 118.

38. Dijkstra, *Idols of Perversity,* 293.

39. Ibid., 229–31.

40. Valis, "Novel as Feminine Entrapment," in this volume, 64.

41. Dijkstra, *Idols of Perversity,* 49–60.

42. Ibid., 63.

43. I find relevant here Susan Gubar's recognition of "a modernist crisis in masculinity" and the possibility of "establishing the socially shaped anxieties that attend masculinity in a given period" (Gubar, "Representing Pornography: Feminism, Criticism, and Depictions of Female Violation," *Critical Inquiry* 13 [1987]: 737 and 739).

44. Lily Litvak, *El sendero del tigre: Exotismo en la literatura española de finales del siglo XIX, 1880–1913* (Madrid: Taurus, 1986), 183. Rosarito lacks the warning that Concha's old nursemaid gives her in *Soñata de otoño:* "It's very dangerous to sit in the moonlight" ["Miren que es malo tomar la luna"]; cited by Emma Susana Speratti-Piñero, *El ocultismo en Valle-Inclán* (London: Tamesis, 1974), 101.

45. Dijkstra, *Idols of Perversity,* 54.

46. Ibid., 51.

47. I am limiting my analysis to the role of the reader inside the text and the difficulty the real female reader encounters in adopting the position of the implied reader. From outside the text we recognize and take pleasure in Valle-Inclán's conscious manipulation of literary codes and conventions, including iconic representation, and the interplay of strategies of dominance and subordination. That is, we identify the artifice of the literary construct and its intertextuality. It is at the level of the implied reader that I find the closest parallel with the visual experience and gendered response of the movie spectator.

48. Dijkstra, *Idols of Perversity,* 46.

49. Catherine Nickel, "Recasting the Image of the Fallen Woman in Valle-Inclán's 'Eulalia,'" *Studies in Short Fiction* 24 (1987): 289.

50. de Lauretis, *Alice Doesn't,* 144.

51. Ibid., 143.

The Central Role of Sabelita in *Aguila de blasón:* Toward the Emergence of a Radical Vision of Women in the Later Art of the *Esperpento*

MICHAEL P. PREDMORE

Despite the ever-growing bibliography of Valle-Inclán studies, there are still many areas of his best work that remain either neglected or poorly or only partially understood. One such area is the famous trilogy of the *Comedias bárbaras* [*Barbaric Comedies*], which portray the decline and decay of a feudal order in nineteenth-century Galicia. As is well known, the plays revolve around the ancestral home of a nobleman, Don Juan Manuel Montenegro, the firstborn lord of an entailed estate that has belonged to his illustrious family for over three hundred years. It is not difficult to understand why readers and critics concentrate on the imposing figure of Don Juan Manuel, and insist on seeing him alone at the center of each one of these plays.[1] He is, indeed, throughout the trilogy, a dominant presence, tyrannical and despotic, generous and hospitable, and possessed with a tremendous sense of family pride. His word is law, he is king of his territory, and he is responsible (his will and his conduct) for the chain of events that lead to his downfall and to the disintegration of his family estate.

In *Aguila de blasón* [*Heraldic Eagle*], however, the centerpiece of the trilogy,[2] the downfall and the disintegration of which critics have spoken, is only one movement and one pattern. There are other patterns and other expressive elements that cannot be accounted for by this exclusive concentration on the character of the feudal lord. In this essay I want to challenge the idea of Don Juan Manuel's centrality to the meaning and development of the drama. There is a sustained moral allegory, for example, in which the dominant women in the Montenegro household (Sabelita, Doña María, and Micaela la Roja) play key roles. The action of these women and, in particular, the drama of the goddaughter, Sabelita, provide special insight into the complex organization, structure, and symmetry of this brilliant work. What I will suggest as well during the first stages of this study, is that the disobedience and courage of Sabelita, the open defiance and moral authority of Doña María, and the strength and wisdom of Micaela la Roja, place limits on the despotic ways of the old Montenegro, and constitute the beginnings of a significant challenge to the patriarchal feudal order.

These are key aspects of the argument, then, that I want to pursue and develop, and follow at the end with some concluding reflections on Valle-Inclán's treatment of women throughout his literary and dramatic production. We will see, I think, that the emergence of strong feminine characters and voices in the *Comedias bárbaras* signals the first isolated stirrings of social rebellion, and points the way to a more radical vision of women in the later art of the *esperpento*. Indeed, the victimization of women and children in a patriarchal order reaches such alarming proportions in the *esperpento* that protest is directed with increasing vigor toward the injustices of an entire social system, now more bourgeois in nature than feudal. Consequently, the actions and visions of the later dramas project the beginnings of more enlightened attitudes and practices, and, in one particular case, dramatic movement toward a more liberated world.

In order to establish the proper context, let us begin by reviewing briefly the ruinous behavior of the old nobleman, and its effect particularly upon the women of his household. His historic role as *hidalgo* and warrior is almost totally irrelevant in mid-nineteenth-century Galicia. What is most striking almost immediately is the discrepancy between his noble bearing, his pride of family, and his imperial gestures, and his absolutely frivolous and nonproductive way of life. His daily activities include tasting and drinking wine, hunting, and gambling. But his most salient characteristic is his insatiable appetite for women, and his diabolic powers over them endow him with something of the aura of the legendary Don Juan.[3] So self-indulgent and abusive has Don Juan Manuel become, that all the closest members of his family leave him or turn upon him in one way or another. Because of his many infidelities over the years, his devoted and long-suffering wife, Doña María, has left the family manor to live in another house on the family properties. In this regard, Lourdes Ramos-Kuethe has commented well upon Doña María's "renunciation of the traditional role of keeping up with appearances," and "her defiant attitude toward the matrimonial farce."[4] Her goddaughter, Sabelita, whom the old Montenegro has forced to become his mistress, very soon leaves the noble manor, guilt-ridden over the grief she has caused Doña María, whose rightful place she has unwittingly usurped. Sabelita is also driven to leave because of jealousy toward the Miller's wife, Liberata, who has become Don Juan Manuel's newest mistress. It is important to note that Sabelita, despite the qualities of meekness and gentleness which are seen to characterize her ("paloma" ["dove"] and "cordera" ["lamb"] are the words used most often to describe her), has considerably more mettle than critics give her credit for. Early in the play, in the third scene of act 2, she commits two acts of disobedience toward the old Montenegro. She gives the honey, a calculated gift from the Miller's wife for Don Juan Manuel, to the dogs, and stands up to the feudal lord's rage by answering back "con celosa entereza" ["with jealous integrity"].[5] Immediately following this exchange, she refuses to obey her master's order to serve him wine. Such behavior reveals that Sabelita is a more complex and multifaceted personality than is generally recognized, and that there are limits to the cruelty she will endure. Her desperate flight in act 3, driven by rebelliousness[6] as well as by shame, requires a tremendous act of courage and is consistent with this earlier defiant behavior.

The interest of this third scene of act 2 for our purposes is twofold. Not only does it provide insight into the inner strength and grief of Sabelita, but it reveals clearly the special role and place of Micaela la Roja in this family household.[7] La Roja is the ancient and most trusted family servant who moves through the household with authority over the other servants, and enjoys a respectful familiarity with her master and mistress, Don Juan Manuel and Doña María. When Sabelita refuses to serve the nobleman his wine, La Roja serves him instead and quiets the old man with profound words of wisdom and warning. She defends Sabelita, who, in the absence of the saintly Doña María, is to be valued for her true love and honesty, and La Roja further warns her master against the treachery and deception of the Miller and his wife. When the Miller leaves, the old Montenegro confides in her his suspicions about the treachery of his own sons. La Roja does her best to put his fears and suspicions to rest, even though she knows that one of his sons, the eldest, took part in the attempted robbery of his household. The function of La Roja here and throughout the play is to advise, comfort, and scold her master, to act at least as a brake on his uncontrollable behavior, and to maintain as much as possible a semblance of harmony within the family unit.

But despite her efforts to keep peace within the household, she has no influence over the young men of the manor, who by now are out of control. Five of the six sons are beside themselves with bitterness and anger, as they observe their father squander away the family estate through his reckless living and by his bestowing gifts and favors to the tenants under his feudal dominion. The sons have been expelled from the seignorial manor and they respond by plundering the estate, particularly by stealing the rents and seasonal harvest of crops from their mother's property. The eldest son, as we have just mentioned, disguises himself, joins a gang of bandits, and makes an unsuccessful attempt to rob the family manor at the outset of the play. The youngest and handsomest son, Cara de Plata, still respectful of his parents and still, at times, chivalrous in his dealings with others, decides that the only way to avoid becoming a bandit is to go off to war in defense of the Carlist cause. Carlism, from the perspective of the Galician nobility, would primarily involve the defense of their ancient feudal rights and privileges, which, in the very imagery and commentary of the play, is shown to be an absurd anachronism.[8] Little by little the play portrays the progressive alienation of all the members of the Montenegro family from the husband, father, and lord of the estate. He stands nearly alone at the end, with a loyal servant or two and the conniving mistress, Liberata, who seeks to enrich herself and her husband at the expense of the nobleman's weaknesses and dissoluteness.

The play's final scene and its imagery deserve special commentary. Sabelita, the goddaughter, in her anguish and guilt, has very nearly taken her own life by attempting to drown herself in a nearby river. But she was miraculously rescued, and then found and brought back to the family manor by Doña María, who will care for her there during her convalescence. In fact, during these dramatic moments, La Roja goes to announce to her master that Sabelita, in a state of extreme weakness after her near encounter with death, is being carried through the door of his house. She finds her master seated at the dining table eating and drinking with the unscrupulous Liberata. The old servant can scarcely contain her indignation. "Señor amo: ¿qué hace sentado a la mesa con esa mala mujer, cuando la muerte está entrando por sus puertas?" ["My lord master: what are you doing seated at the table with that bad woman, when death is entering through your door?"] (V. vi. 150).[9] This severe reproach, provoked by the intolerable behavior of the old nobleman, prepares the scene for the open rebellion of Doña María a few moments later. Newly reunited with her goddaughter and strengthened by the resolve to protect the young woman this time at all costs from her lecherous husband, Doña María forbids him to see Sabelita and orders him out of their seignorial home. In this dramatic and final confrontation between husband and wife, Don Juan Manuel is soon forced to yield to the moral authority of his rebellious wife. Indeed, the defiant and unshakable resolve of Doña María never to see her husband again is expressed in her last words to him. "¡Adiós, para siempre!" ["Goodbye, forever!"] (V. vi. 152). Ramos-Kuethe has well seen, I think, the social significance of this final parting.

> En esta respuesta no sólo se muestra el resquebrajamiento del matrimonio como base de la estructura social, sino también una nueva actitud en la mujer como componente de la sociedad. Rebelándose, Doña María se niega a seguir en su papel de esposa sufrida. . . .[10]

> [This response shows not only the breakdown of marriage as the foundation of the social structure, but also a new attitude in woman as a constituent part of society. By rebelling, Doña María refuses to continue in her role as the long-suffering wife. . . .]

One of the final images of the play depicts the old Montenegro standing in the doorway of the feudal manor, sobbing under the family's coat of arms, emblazoned with spurs of chivalry and eagles of victory.[11] We are vividly reminded of this ancient family of three hundred years, a noble family whose coat of arms bears the emblem of the proud imperial eagle, evoking the glorious feats of arms of an illustrious lineage. But what has become of this once distinguished family? Who represents it now? A lecherous old man, who has just been vigorously scolded by his ancient servant and ordered out of his own house by his wife, a nobleman who in shame and humility repeats over and over to himself that he is nothing more than a wolf in heat, and who then flees into the darkness of the night. There can be no more dramatic commentary on the downfall and moral corruption of this once illustrious lineage than the grotesque juxtaposition of the imperial eagle on the family coat of arms and this degraded image of one of its last representatives.[12]

Surely it is the case, then, that Don Juan Manuel Montenegro is the dominant figure in one major action and pattern of *Aguila de blasón*. But in this long five-act play, the feudal lord appears only once in act 3, in less than half the eight scenes of act 4, and only once in the final scene of act 5. To concentrate exclusively on him, therefore, is to miss the significance of the drama in the lives of other people. Let us turn, then, to other actions and other expressive patterns that have been for the most part overlooked and unexamined.

One sequence of actions and symbolic imagery involves mother/daughter relationships. We have already alluded to Doña María's forgiving and compassionate attitude toward her goddaughter, whose sense of guilt and shame compelled her to leave the family manor and seek refuge in the countryside.[13] Doña María is at first deeply hurt and reluctant to have further dealings with Sabelita, but her eventual resolve to seek out, forgive, and be reunited with her lost goddaughter gives rise to the most important dramatic action in the second half of the play.[14] This resolve is given an added symbolic dimension by a dream sequence in act 4 in which Doña María converses with the Christ child, who scolds her for allowing Sabelita to leave home, alone and unprotected. The two, Doña María and the Christ child, eventually decide to go out in search of her goddaughter, and as they walk along the road at night, the baby Jesus falls into a deep cave. But the holy child is quickly saved by the intervention of his holy mother. This vision provides us, then, with a Christian allegory of the Virgin Mary rescuing her child and prefigures symbolically what Doña María will do with her child, Sabelita, by the end of the play.

Very closely related to this dream sequence is an important earlier episode in the last scene of act 3. Sabelita is fleeing in the dark of night from the ancestral home of the Montenegro family when she encounters a family of humble peasants. They earnestly request her help. The father (called, in the text, "el abuelo" [the grandfather]) of the pregnant woman in their group explains that, because witchcraft was practiced on his daughter when she was young, she has thus far been unable to have children. The family wants to undo this evil spell and asks Sabelita to help baptize the pregnant mother with water from the river.[15] Sabelita timidly agrees and the ceremony is performed in the middle of the bridge, with water taken from the river. Thus, Sabelita becomes the godmother to the unborn child of the expectant mother, just as she herself is the godchild of Doña María. The religious imagery and aura with which the peasant family is treated, anticipates the Christian allegory that later further defines Sabelita's relationship to her godmother. In the present case Sabelita fulfills the function of John the Baptist to the expectant mother,[16] just as she herself will undergo a baptism in the river where she nearly drowns. And as Sabelita helps cleanse and liberate this peasant family from the diabolic spell of witchcraft, so Doña María helps liberate her later from the diabolic spell of Don Juan Manuel, after she emerges nearly drowned but also cleansed from the river waters.

This mysterious episode with the peasant family contains an important social as well as religious meaning. Sabelita herself is of mysterious origins.[17] She has been adopted and raised in the house of a noble family but is in the constant company of the servants. Her position in the Montenegro manor has been both confused and problematic as a result of the multiple roles of daughter, servant, and mistress imposed upon her. Like the bridge upon which she performed the rite of baptism, she herself serves as a bridge between two social worlds. She has fallen from the noble world, an innocent victim of the moral corruption of her despotic godfather. But at the same time, she contributes to the welfare of the peasant family,[18] and we note with what special care and sacred significance the condition of the expectant mother is described in the play. Sabelita bridges the gap between the decline and fall of one social group, and the renewal and continued vitality of another. The dramatic action and imagery here suggests that the nonproductive, violent, and frivolous lives of the nobility will give way to the hardworking, peaceful, and productive lives of the peasants in a hopeful transition toward some future and better postfeudal society.

To conclude this treatment of mother/daughter relationships, we should note toward the end of the play, the reconstitution of close female bonds that go beyond and deeper than blood relations. As she ponders the meaning of the dream she had the night before, in the presence of Micaela La Roja, Doña María suddenly makes the decision to go in search of Sabelita and she remarks that she will tell Sabelita to return home as her "daughter" again. We note the significant use of the word *daughter* here instead of the word *goddaughter* normally used by Doña María to refer to their relationship. The old servant, Micaela La Roja, fond as she is of Sabelita and overjoyed at this prospect of a reconciliation between mother and adopted daughter, exclaims with emotion, "¡Dama María, mi señora, mi gran señora, hija de mis entrañas!" ["Lady María, my noble lady, my great lady, my precious daughter"] (IV, viii, 132). Here the most expressive use of the word *daughter* occurs again, applied by the old servant to her noble mistress with the deepest of feeling. This is the most dramatic example of the reconstitution of close ties between the principal women of the Montenegro household. All three of these women are devout Christian women. Because of their virtue and because of their shared suffering, they have drawn closer together toward the end of the drama, unified by the strongest of maternal and daughterly bonds.

Consequently, two contrasting patterns in the dynamics of human relationships begin to stand out at the end of *Aguila de blasón*. The disintegration of family relationships within the Montenegro household involves, in particular, the total alienation of Don Juan Manuel from his rebellious sons and the progressive corruption of his relationship to women. Conversely, the reconstitution of close spiritual bonds among the three women we have just treated, as well as the adoptive relationship between Sabelita and the peasant family, reveals the forming of new ties that are certainly superior to blood relations in the Montenegro family. We can further observe that as the men of this family fall into disgrace and degradation, the women rise in their moral stature and Christian virtues. There is a balance of opposing movements that presides over this play, whereby the men fall into spiritual ruin, and certain women, at least, rise in their spiritual worth. The moral superiority of Doña María, as we have seen, is most evident when she orders Don Juan Manuel out of the family manor at the end of the play in order to protect her godchild.

These last observations prepare us, finally, to consider the literary structure of the play, that is, its expressive organization and its overall design. On the basis of the evidence thus far put forth, I would argue, against the critics who assign the role of protagonist to Don Juan Manuel, that *Aguila de blasón* is constructed and shaped around the character of Sabelita. She stands at the dynamic center of the play; she is the hub of the wheel from which radiate all the other spokes of this wheel of humanity. Sabelita is both liked and disliked, loved and hated; she brings out the best and the worst in people. She is loved or inspires the affectionate feelings or passions of Don Juan Manuel, Cara de Plata, and the most loyal servants of the household. She is hated by the other five sons, who are enraged at the privileged place that this adopted daughter has acquired in the affections of their parents. Sabelita is begrudged by the scheming Liberata, who usurps her place as the new mistress of the feudal lord and who plots malice against her. Sabelita is also the object of the more complex emotions of Doña María who experiences love, jealousy, resentment, guilt, remorse, and renewed maternal love for her.

Especially noteworthy is the ability of Sabelita to bring out the humanity and tenderness in Don Galán, a buffoonlike character, who serves as court jester and conscience to Don Juan Manuel. Sabelita is the only one whose plight toward the end is able to penetrate the masks and grotesque behavior of the jester and elicit from him the deepest feelings of sorrow and compassion. Furthermore, as we have already observed, Sabelita serves as a link between the humble and the noble, between the world of peasants and the world of feudal lords. As she contributes, though more as an innocent victim, to the dissension in the household of the Montenegros, she also contributes to the welfare of the family of country people, by her baptism of the unborn child. She is involved in both patterns and both rhythms of the play, in both the fall and the rise, in the sinfulness and the redemption, of different social groups.

Finally, in terms of her own destiny, we can best see her as the main vehicle of the moral allegory of the play. She is the adopted daughter of Don Juan Manuel and Doña María. She stands halfway between them, halfway between the devil of Don Juan Manuel and the saint of Doña María. The pattern of her life, which is the pattern of the play, is her fall into the clutches of the devil and her rescue through the forgiveness of the saint. Most significantly, she both begins and ends the moral drama of *Aguila de blasón*. In the very first scene of the play, she faints in Church, overwhelmed by the power of the sermon, guilt-ridden and trapped in the dark prisons of sin. In the final scene of the play, off-stage but present in the minds of all, still in a weakened condition because of her near drowning, she is nevertheless the mainspring that unleashes the moral force and authority of Doña María, who expels the diabolic Don Juan Manuel from his own ancestral home. The play begins with her trapped in the prison of sin, and it ends with her liberation from the bonds of sin and damnation, and her rescue and redemption through the forgiveness and mercy of her saintly godmother. In all of these many ways, therefore, Sabelita is the dynamic center of the moral and social drama, around which all the other characters, actions, and expressive elements revolve.

As we have indicated at the outset, the victimization and suffering of women and their challenge to male authority in *Aguila de blasón* bring to our attention an emerging pattern in the works of Valle-Inclán. From his earliest short stories and short novels, through his symbolist theater to the later *esperpentos,* from approximately 1895 to 1930, there is the recurring drama of women as innocent victims. In the early work, the young girls and women tend to be submissive and innocent, extremely vulnerable to the encroachments and dangers of a patriarchal society. We recall the savage rape and murder of the adolescent Rosarito by her demented uncle, Don Miguel Montenegro; or the accidental and fatal fall from a window of the child María Nieves in the *Sonata de primavera* [*Sonata of Spring*]; or the cynical deception and seduction of the innocent shepherd girl Adega by a roguish pilgrim in *Flor de santidad* [Flower of holiness]. All of these examples occur in an older seignorial or peasant society, and the meaning of the death and violence experienced by these helpless victims possesses a kind of allegorical significance, historical or religious in nature.

Later in the *Comedias bárbaras,* though the moral allegory impresses a strong design upon these dramas, as we have seen in the case of *Aguila de blasón,* the inner life of women—their suffering, their struggle, and their endurance—is given much greater prominence. Their feelings are complex and at times contradictory, but they matter and they are important. These women dare to break out of the passivity and submissiveness required of them by tradition and convention and make their actions felt and their voices heard—whether it be Sabelita's desperate break from the manorial home and terrifying flight into the darkness of night, or Doña María's resolve to protect her goddaughter at all costs by ordering her degenerate husband out of his own home, or the desperate widow in the play, *Romance de lobos* [*Wolves! Wolves!*], who, in her grief and rage over the death of her husband and the father of her children, hurls oaths and imprecations upon the name of the old Montenegro who is responsible for her tragedy. In all of these ways, women's actions and voices reflect the first stirrings of social rebellion against an oppressive and unjust feudal order.

In the later theater of Valle-Inclán, in his famous *esperpentos* of the 1920s, the victimization of women and children reaches the most alarming proportions, as we have noted in the introduction. His theater is full of the most grotesque spectacles of a degraded and debased humanity. In *Las galas del difunto* [The dead man's finery], the father drives his unmarried and pregnant daughter out of the house and into the profession of prostitution. In *Los cuernos de don Friolera* [*The Grotesque Farce of Mr. Punch the Cuckhold*], the husband, while intending to shoot his unfaithful wife, mistakenly kills his beloved daughter instead. In *La hija del capitán* [The captain's daughter], the father who is a military man, gives his daughter to the General in exchange for protection in a lawsuit, and thus condemns her to a life of sexual bondage.

Yet in these plays and others of the period, there is a higher degree of political awareness and a deeper understanding of social injustice, projected often in the words of the fictional characters and always in the vision of the play. Most importantly, the destiny of women is intimately interwoven into the political, social, and national life of Spain. It is no longer the case that a woman is solely the victim of a decadent marquis, or a wandering vagabond, or a feudal lord of rural Galicia. The unwed mother of *Las galas del difunto* is very eloquent about the fact that the father of her child was taken from her by the Cuban wars, where he was killed in action. The tragedy of her family is the result of the damage done to Spanish society by colonial wars. The grief-stricken mother in *Luces de Bohemia* [*Bohemian Lights*], who carries her dead child in her arms and shouts her grief to the world, knows that her child is the victim of "assassins." Her child has been killed accidently during street fighting in Madrid between workers and the police. The mother's elemental sense of a deep injustice characterizes accurately the criminal character of a terribly corrupted bourgeois order.

The women's voices in the *esperpentos* are stronger, more vigorous, and more significant because the protest is directed now not so much against the actions of a corrupted individual, or against the abuses of a local authority, but, as we have earlier suggested, against the injustices of an entire social system, increasingly bourgeois in nature rather than feudal. Also infusing the actions and visions of these later dramas are the beginnings of more enlightened attitudes and practices: an adulteress in *Divinas palabras* [*Divine Words*] is pardoned rather than stoned to death in a remote village of rural Galicia, and, in *Los cuernos de don Friolera,* the subject of divorce is actually mentioned as a more civilized way to deal with a marriage that does not work. Perhaps the most striking example of a dramatic movement toward a more liberated world is provided by Valle-Inclán's very last *esperpento, La hija del capitán,* published in 1930. The protagonist, called by her nickname "La Sini," is the daughter of an army sergeant and is sexually exploited by her father in the most degrading way. In her relations to her depraved father, and to her exceptionally loyal boyfriend, and to the incredibly corrupt social and political world around her, she radically breaks with the conventions and stereotypes that traditionally govern the conduct of a young Spanish woman. She is not obedient to her father, not concerned about honor, and, though fond of her boyfriend, not interested in marriage. She is unmoved by death and absolutely irreverent with respect to the hallowed institutions (army, Church, and monarchy) of official Spain. Through an incredible act of luck (the wrong man was murdered at the gates of her house), she is presented with an opportunity to exercise her ingenuity and courage to use a corrupt system against itself and to break out of her bondage.

The final scene of the play takes place in a train station in Madrid, where she and her boyfriend are waiting for a train to travel, one hopes and one imagines, on a journey toward a less authoritarian, less corrupt, and more egalitarian world. It seems to me that Valle-Inclán is experimenting here, through the character of La Sini, with the creation of a new social type, a more emancipated human being, who will gain entrance to a more liberated world. To trace, therefore, women's voices and actions throughout the literary and dramatic art of Valle-Inclán is to acquire a deeper understanding of the emerging, though isolated, stirrings of social protest in the *Comedias bárbaras,* which develop into the full-blown attack on official Spain in the radical vision of the *esperpento.*

Notes

1. See, for example, the following important studies: Melchor Fernández Almagro, "La literatura de hoy. Ramón del Valle-Inclán: Vida y obra," *RHM* 2, no. 4 (1936): 295–301 (Reprinted in *Ramón del Valle-Inclán: El escritor y la crítica,* ed. Ricardo Domenech [Madrid: Ed. Taurus, 1988], 24–33); Roberta Salper de Tortella, "Don Juan Manuel Montenegro: The Fall of a King," eds. A. N. Zahareas, Rodolfo Cardona, and Sumner Greenfield, *Ramón del Valle Inclán: An Appraisal of His Life and Works* (New York: Las Americas Publishing Co., 1968): 317–33; Roberta Salper, *Valle-Inclán y su mundo: Ideología y forma narrativa* (Amsterdam: Rodopi, 1988); Alfredo Matilla Rivas, "La *Comedias Bárbaras:* Una sola obra dramática," ed. Zahareas, *Valle-Inclán: An Appraisal,* 289–316 and *Las "Comedias bárbaras: "Historicismo y expresionismo dramático* (Madrid: Ed. Anaya, 1972); Juan Antonio Hormigón, *Ramón del Valle-Inclán: La política, la cultura, el realismo y el pueblo* (Madrid: Comunicación Serie B, 1972); María del Carmen Porrúa, *La Galicia decimonónica en las "Comedias bárbaras" de Valle-Inclán* (A Coruña: Ediciós do Castro, 1983); and Lourdes Ramos-Kuethe, *Valle-Inclán: Las comedias bárbaras* (Madrid: Ed. Pliegos, 1985).

2. With respect to both the dramatic position and importance of *Aguila de blasón* in the *Comedias bárbaras,* Valle-Inclán provides this most significant commentary in a letter to Rivas Cherif:

> Las tres comedias, en su disposición actual, no constituyen sino una sola trilogía, proporcionadas la primera y la tercera a modo de prólogo y epílogo, en tres jornadas cada una, a señalar la mayor extensión dramática del que diríamos centro de gravedad de la obra, culminante en las cinco jornadas de *Aguila de blasón.*" Quoted by A. Matilla Rivas (1968, 315, n. 15).

> [The three plays, in their present arrangement, constitute but a single trilogy, proportioned, the first and the third like a prologue and an epilogue, to point out the greatest dramatic extension of the one we might call the center of gravity of the work, culminating in the five acts of *Aguila de blasón.*]

3. Indeed, numerous members of the Montenegro household, both victims and observers, contribute, with their commentary, to the mystique of his Don Juan powers. Sabelita describes the effect of his dominion over her. "Soy una esclava y no puedo tener voluntad," ["I am a slave and I can not have a will of my own"] (II. vii. 56); Doña María observes of her husband, "Y nunca tuvo como ahora esa fuerza para cegar a las mujeres, para hacerse dueño de las almas" ["And he never had like now that power to blind women, to become master of their souls"] (III. iv. 82); Cara de Plata seeks to reassure a frightened Sabelita that he does not blame her for what has happened to drive them apart because he knows the power of evil in his father. "A pesar de tantas cosas, no he olvidado aquel tiempo. . . . Y no te culpo, porque conozco el diablo" ["In spite of so many things, I have not forgotten that time. . . . And I don't blame you, because I know who the devil is"] (III. v. 89–90).

4. Ramos-Keuthe, *Valle-Inclán: Las comedias bárbaras*, 91.

5. *Aguila de blasón* (Madrid: Espasa-Calpe, 1976), 4th ed., II, iii, 38. All references to this work are to this edition.

6. By rebelliousness, I mean specifically her resolve to free herself from the conditions of servitude and sinfulness imposed upon her by the despotic Don Juan Manuel.

7. For an insightful study on the significance and function of Micaela la Roja, both as an "ancient voice of rural popular culture" (202) and as a female "able to challenge the patriarchal order" (208), see Salper, "Las dos Micaelas: Un arquetipo de mujer," in *Valle-Inclán y su mundo,* 192–208.

8. Though there is much more to be said on the subject of Carlism as it appears briefly in *Aguila de blasón,* we can at least take note of the last mention and image of Cara de Plata, riding off to war sitting backward on a cow! (V. vi. 149–50). This farcical backward march into history surely conveys a sense of the Cause as both hopeless and absurd.

9. We note the rage of La Roja, who earlier, as we have seen, had tried to warn her master about the scheming Miller and his wife. She turns on Liberata and spits at her with venomous fury. "¡Can rabioso!" ["Mad dog!"] (V. vi. 151). Never have we seen her so angry. Never has she taken such liberties in challenging and reproaching the behavior of her master.

10. Ramos-Kuethe, *Valle-Inclán: Las comedias bárbaras,* 91–92.

11. There are insightful comments of this scene in both Manuel Bermejo Marcos, *Valle-Inclán: Introducción a su obra* (Salamanca: Ed. Anaya, 1971), 121–22; and Sumner Greenfield, *Anatomía de un teatro problemático* (Madrid: Ed. Fundamentos, 1972), 82–83.

12. I am in agreement with Bermejo Marcos (120–21, 125) who finds it difficult to understand how certain critics continue to insist on the heroic character of Don Juan Manuel Montenegro and look on the *Comedias bárbaras* as a "true elegy to the rural nobility." This sense of the *Comedias* as a nostalgic evocation of an idealized feudal past is vigorously presented by José Antonio Maravall, "La imagen de la sociedad arcaica en Valle-Inclán," *Revista de Occidente* 44–45 (1966); 255–56. The "unequivocally heroic" nature of the plays has more recently been restated by John Lyon, *The Theater of Valle-Inclán* (Cambridge: Cambridge University Press, 1983), 48.

13. Carmen Porrúa (*La Galicia decimonónica,* 132–41) is the only critic I have been able to find who devotes significant attention and commentary to Sabelita.

14. On the inner conflict of Doña María and of her spiritual struggle to over-

come her pride and forgive Sabelita, Greenfield (*Anatomía de un teatro problemático,* 80–81) provides insightful commentary.

15. The request is made of Sabelita because it is midnight and she happens to be, at that crucial time, the only passerby at the entrance to the bridge. For the complicated conditions that must be met in order to undo the witchcraft, see III. vi. 91–92.

16. These are the first words of the sacred formula to break the evil spell, pronounced in a low voice by the grandfather and repeated by Sabelita: "Y te bautizo con agua santa del Jordán, como al Señor Jesucristo bautizó el Señor San Juan" ["I baptize you with holy water from the Jordan, as the Lord St. John baptized the Lord Jesus Christ"] (III. vi. 95).

17. Though two passersby speculate, with uncertainty but correctly as it turns out, on her identity as she flees down the street at night (III, v, 88), it is only in *Cara de plata* [*Silver Face*] where we really learn that she is the niece of the Abad de Lantañón and his sister Doña Jeromita.

18. And they respond in a kindhearted way. They care for her and insist that she live with them, at least temporarily, until she can find more permanent shelter. In their company, Sabelita adapts herself to their way of life and her peasant clothing ("atavíos de aldeana") and wooden shoes ("madreñas") seem to have transformed her into another person (V. iii. 139).

From Words to Divinity?: Questions of Language and Gender in *Divinas palabras*

CAROL MAIER

Why *Divinas palabras* [*Divine Words*]?[1] In the first place, a long-time fascination with Mari-Gaila, the tragicomedy's female pro-tagonist, and a more recent interest in exploring with respect to gender the tension I sensed between her well-spoken "coplas" ["verses and songs"] and the mute words of her "ojos parleros" ["talkative eyes"].[2] There were also the eyes of Ana Belén, strug-gling it seemed, as I looked at them in a photograph from a recent film version of the play, with the complexity of Valle-Inclán's char-acter.[3] How difficult it is to "translate" this work to the present day, I thought, recalling an observation by Dru Dougherty about the virtually inaccessible position Valle-Inclán has come to occupy since his canonization as a "classic."[4] Dougherty of course in-tended a certain irony, and it is one Valle-Inclán would likely have shared, given his own (re)definition of the word "clásico" ["clas-sic"].[5] In fact, as Valle-Inclán employed "clásico," the term has connotations both anticanonical and participatory. Literature's true classics, he suggested through the poet-narrator of *La lám-para maravillosa,* are those kept alive by their readers, who assign them constantly changing meanings.[6]

This use of "clásico" mocked the conventional connotations of a harmony Valle-Inclán found static, and it evoked a disquieting mixture. Poured into a work from the past, "new" emotions enable a reader to experience beauty as both "alegría pagana y terror cristiano" ["pagan joy and Christian terror"], a clash of time, a shaking of "la cadena de siglos" ["the chain of centuries"] (MM, VI–VII).[7] Or, it occurred to me as I thought about the dislodging and juxtaposition implied in Valle-Inclán's image of the chain, to experience beauty as Severo Sarduy's shaking of a signifier so as to make visible its both "support" and the inevitable absence, the cover-up occasioned by all signs.[8]

That final association also reminded me that Valle-Inclán's own
title for *Divinas palabras* should have led me far sooner toward
precisely the same questions of "meaning" posed recently by theoretical essays such as those in Sarduy's *Escrito sobre un cuerpo*
[*Written on a Body*][9]: given Valle-Inclán's many comments on language, and the example of *La lámpara maravillosa* in particular,
the juxtaposition of "divinas" and "palabras" hints at a play on
words. For words, as Valle-Inclán's poet-narrator indicates in *La
lámpara maravillosa,* are by their nature earth-bound; they are
even formed of the earth's "baja substancia" ["base substance"]
(MM, V). Words can become divine, he explains, but their divinity
is occurrence rather than attribute; it implies an unsettling miracle
akin to the fusion of old and new that makes a work "classic."
Consequently, a reading of *Divinas palabras* that seeks to engage
the divinity in its words cannot accept the title as a descriptive
explanation of the play's events or "action." Quite the contrary,
that title manifests only the most enigmmatic of "keys": the
reader's[10] point of departure must include an acknowledgment of
the oxymoron—a dynamic, miraculous (im)balance between an-
tipodes—where the play literally takes place.[11]

Once I had begun to consider Mari-Gaila and the contradiction
in her character in terms of language, it was clear to me that she
could best be approached by studying her as a creature of words—
both those Valle-Inclán uses in the stage directions to describe her
appearance and temperament, and those she speaks herself. I had
always assumed, as Myra Jehlin has argued recently, that unless
gender "figures explicitly in a story or poem, it will seldom read
for itself."[12] The fact is, however, that in *Divinas palabras* language
and gender are linked so inextricably that indeed it seems Valle-
Inclán was anticipating the questions psychologists, sociologists,
and linguistics were just beginning to ask systematically throughout
Europe, and with which he no doubt had only limited acquain-
tance.[13]

No doubt the most conventional scholarly method of developing
that linkage between language and gender would have been to un-
fold it as a thesis, a point of departure, citing as evidence the
readings that legitimize it in their respective ways. In the essay
that follows, however, I have taken a somewhat different tack; I
want not only to acknowledge the work of other scholars on which
I draw, but also to document my own inquiry in an effort to identify
the consideration of gender and language prompted by *Divinas
palabras* itself, albeit in somewhat different terms. I assess first,
then, Mari-Gaila's role with respect to the play, and the aesthetics

of "creation-as-destruction" from which it arises. In the second section, I pursue that aesthetics further in three ways: by reviewing *Divinas palabras* and commenting on its relation to *La lámpara maravillosa;* by reviewing some of the texts creatively "destroyed" in the text of *Divinas palabras*; by studying Mari-Gaila as the play's most developed example of creation-as-destruction and investigating that example in terms of gender considerations.

To work this way is to risk a certain tentativeness. At the same time, however, I believe it is also to allow for a fuller discussion of Mari-Gaila as both word and woman—on each count, a phenomenon at once profoundly articulate and disconcertingly ambivalent.

Divinas palabras is divided into three acts, all of which occur in rural Galicia at an unspecified time implicitly contemporary with its composition (1919). The three principal characters are, arguably, Pedro Gailo, a sacristan, his wife Mari-Gaila, and Séptimo Miau, an itinerant puppeteer who becomes Mari-Gaila's lover. Events are set in motion by the death of Pedro's sister, Juana la Reina. The mother of a hydrocephalic, epileptic dwarf (Laureano), Juana has earned her living by making the rounds of taverns and fairs exhibiting her "attraction" in a cart. (Laureano himself can be considered a character only with qualification, although his role is so essential that at least one critic has proposed that he is the play's protagonist.)[14] When Juana dies, care of the child is divided between the Gailos and Marica del Reino, another of Pedro's sisters. On the days that the cart and Laureano ("the idiot") fall to her and Pedro, Mari-Gaila takes them on the same circuit followed previously by Juana la Reina. This new life effects a rapid change in her, and she enters enthusiastically into the banter and carousing of the people she encounters. She pays increasingly less attention to Laureano, and one evening, when she abandons him to make love with Séptimo Miau, he dies in a tavern where some of Mari-Gaila's companions have given him one drink after another. Mari-Gaila returns home with the cart, in a highly erotic dreamlike scene, carried through the air on the rump of a demonic goat. Pedro too sins that night; although he resists Marica's insistent urging that he bring Mari-Gaila forcibly into line, he attempts to seduce his daughter, Simoniña. When Mari-Gaila returns, she and Pedro force the girl to take the cart with Laureano's body to the home of Marica, instructing her to leave without knocking. Marica awakens the next morning, finds the cart outside her door, and discovers Laureano's body half-devoured by pigs.

As she hurls accusations at Pedro and Mari-Gaila, Marica finds herself dealing with a couple divided (by Mari-Gaila's scorn for her husband and by Pedro's own feelings of guilt) and united (in their determination to bury the child). Plans proceed for the burial and Simoniña is stationed outside the church with the cart and Laureano's body to collect money to pay for the funeral. Laureano is soon forgotten, however, when Séptimo Miau reappears to banter with Simoniña and Pedro and to continue his relationship with Mari-Gaila. At the last meeting he has with her, the couple is discovered in a field by some of the villagers. The villagers taunt and threaten Mari-Gaila until she consents to dance naked on a hay cart they direct toward the church. When Pedro learns that the cart is approaching, he climbs the bell tower for a view of the surrounding countryside and then throws himself to the ground. For an instant it seems that he has been killed, but he has not, for, like his rival Séptimo Miau, he seems to have a cat's uncanny ability to escape death.[15] Walking to the courtyard of the church to receive his wife, Pedro meets up with the angry villagers who are about to stone her. He attempts to pacify them with the words of John 8:7 ["Let him who is without sin among you be the first to throw a stone at her"], but the jeers continue. It is only when Pedro repeats the same words in Latin that the crowd begins to break up. As the villagers leave, Pedro Gailo takes Mari-Gaila by the hand and leads her into the church.

In those final moments, a decisive and disconcerting interaction between words and events is strikingly evident. What may not be so evident, however, is how well Valle-Inclán has prepared for that interaction throughout the play. In the opening scene, for example, which in several ways prefigures—perhaps even as a *mise-en-abyme*—the entire work, Pedro Gailo is engaged in a verbal battle with Séptimo Miau.[16] From the outset, the sacristan and his words are associated with old age, decay, and death. His vision is poor and his language incoherent; he talks to himself, and his phrases are "deshilvanadas" ["disconnected"]. Later in the play, Mari-Gaila will refer to him as "latino" ["Latin"] and speak disparagingly of his "textos" and "latines" ["texts" and "Latinisms"]. He is pathetic but ridiculous, and the authority of his official words is clearly bankrupt. A poor match for Séptimo Miau's banter, the warnings he shouts at the puppeteer are hardly capable of shooing him from the churchyard as the play opens, just as in act 2 they will be ineffectual against the demons that tempt him with Simoniña (scene 4) or will provide the girl with only the weakest of "escorts" as she sets out with the cart toward the house of Marica (scene 9). Rather than wielding language as one might expect given his position, Pedro is somewhat "embrujado" ["bewitched"] (II.iv), by the words of others. He is cowed by the "lenguas malas y malhumoradas" ["evil and evil-natured tongues"] in the village, and is thus doubly at the mercy of the empty, deceitful words that are pervasive and influential in his life despite their lack of vitality.

As Pedro's blood relatives are introduced (Juana and Laureano in the first scene and Marica in the fourth), it becomes clear that his exhausted language inscribes a family condition, which, as I will discuss at more length, is also a national affliction (the family name is "Reino" [Kingdom]). Juana la Reina (the Queen), who dies in the second scene and speaks little, holds her sides and moans in pain "a lo largo de sus palabras" ["throughout her words"]. Marica will speak a great deal on several occasions, but she will speak poorly. In her first appearance, for example, she enters shrieking, and the unimaginative "frases rituales" ["ritual phrases"] of her "planto" ["lament"] contrast unfavorably with the eloquence Mari-Gaila displays when she learns that Juana has died. Moreover, Marica's is the most pointed of the "malas lenguas" ["evil tongues"] that urge Pedro Gailo to avenge his honor. Laureano, Pedro's nephew, does not speak at all, and he barely understands the words spoken to him (I.v). His lack of language is significant, however, an indication perhaps that he is less than human. This is suggested by the many references to his "boca belfa" ["thick-lipped mouth"], his stupid grimace, and large head, the fact that the few words he knows are obscenities, and the way in which his howls mix with the singing of toads.[17]

In the first scene, in fact, Laureano contrasts sharply with Coimbra, Séptimo Miau's fortune-telling dog whose capacity for language far surpasses his. What is more, Coimbra is associated with a highly animated and well-spoken master. In their first encounter, Séptimo Miau clearly outtalks Pedro Gailo, who recognizes the shrewdness of his tongue. Mari-Gaila too admires Séptimo Miau's voice, and even before she meets him in person, she responds to a tune he has brought from the end of the world (III. ii). This is not to suggest that Séptimo Miau is any less linked to evil tongues or even to death than Pedro Gailo. On the contrary, in his relentless energy, his frightening ability to "see" more than he wants to— which suggests the "strong vision" associated with "mal de ojo" ["the evil eye"],[18] and his continual transformations there are repeated allusions to his demonic nature. Most telling in this regard are his description of himself as the Devil's "compadre" ["buddy"] and Mari-Gaila's identification of him as her "negro" ["dark or

black one"], especially in the scene where that "negro" is also the
Trasgo Cabrío who carries her home by way of a witches' sabbath.

As for Mari-Gaila, her characterization as a word well spoken
could hardly be more evident. Not only is she praised repeatedly
for the sharpness of her "pico" ["beak"] and the quickness of her
Castilian, her body and her use of language are presented as integral elements; she is "blanca y rubia, risueña de ojos, *armónica
en los ritmos del cuerpo y de la voz*" (emphasis added) ["white
and blond, with smiling eyes and *harmonous rhythms of body and
voice*"]. When Mari-Gaila enters in scene 3, Juana has just died,
and although events will soon prove that her lament is perhaps
even more hypocritical than Marica's, her delivery is far superior,
as judged both by the women listening to her and in Valle-Inclán's
stage directions. There her body is once again a function of language. As she speaks, she is standing at a crest in the road, and
heads turn toward her as, arms opened, "en ritmos trágicos y anti-
guos . . . resucita una antigua belleza histriónica . . . y abre *la
curva cadenciosa de los brazos, con las curvas sensuales de la
voz*" ["in tragic and ancient rhythms . . . she revives an ancient
histrionic beauty . . . and *opens the cadenced curve of her arms,
the sensual curves of her voice*"] (emphasis added).

Séptimo Miau is not present in this scene, but before long he
too will have good words for those same vocal curves; just as
Mari-Gaila was taken by his songs before they met, she introduces
herself to him with a song—not speaking but singing—, "buscando
que la mire el farandul" ["hoping the rogue will look at her"] (III.
iii). She is a woman sure of her body and her voice, aware of the
interaction between them, and fully capable of speaking through
that interaction. This talent, at once verbal and physical, is borne
out by the events of the play, in the comments of the other characters, in the control Mari-Gaila assumes of Laureano and the cart,
and in her ability to push her relationship with Séptimo Miau to
the limit even as she remains separate from him, refusing to make
a pact with either the Trasgo Cabrío or with Séptimo Miau himself.
(As Simoniña says, "Mi madre . . . no quiere encartes" ["My
mother never follows suit"] [III. iii]). When, in the last scene, the
villagers trap and threaten her, Mari-Gaila says few words, but she
speaks with her body and with no sign of repentance. Her flesh
trembles as she mounts the hay cart—she is in danger of being
stoned to death, and she is already bleeding from one wound—,
but she is described as "adusta" ["stern"] and "resuelta" ["reso-
lute"]. Her body itself, its nakedness, is still "rítmica," "antigua,"
and "blanca" ["rhythmic," "ancient," and "white"]. Even as she

approaches the church, this composure remains constant; when she jumps from the hay cart, she covers her sex, but that cart is one of a "triunfo venusto" ["a beautiful triumph"], and its Venus fused-with-Ceres will be "armónica" ["harmonious"] as well as "desnuda" ["naked"] in the final words of the play.

Among those final words, whether Pedro Gailo's Latin, the Castilian of the villagers, or that of the stage directions, Mari-Gaila herself is undoubtedly the most striking. This owes in large part to her nakedness, but her physical appearance is only one element of the complex occurrence that ends the work. In that occurrence, that instant when Pedro Gailo's words become "divine" and are suddenly able to affect the villagers in a way that never could before, Mari-Gaila's role is decisive. She is the one character who both consistently speaks well and is capable of enjoying her body fully, without getting trapped in the dark "flip" of eroticism—the incestuous insinuations of Pedro Gailo, for example, or the obsessive egotism of Séptimo Miau (who makes it clear in the final act that he has been attracted to Mari-Gaila because of the cart and because of the profit he hoped she would bring to him).

Mari-Gaila is thus able to bridge the contradictions of these two antipodal men, and without giving into the demonic impulse that binds them, without transcending or denying either sexual desire or spirituality. Her individual experience as a verb capable of participating in opposing forces[19] and of acknowledging such verbalization (even if only intuitively) is described in the final stage directions when Laureano's head appears to her as a vision at once sublime and grotesque. It is also indicated earlier, however, when she participates—as body-verb—in the words of Pedro Gailo, adding to them her humanity, her vitality, her presence (or, better, her presentness), and enabling him to reach the villagers. Without her, despite the changes suggested in him by his fall, and despite the effect his forgiveness undoubtedly has on *her*,[20] Pedro's Latin words would most likely be as ineffectual as ever against the crowd's "verbo popular y judaico" ["popular, Judaic word"]—the stage directions, for example, point to his eyes "bizcando" ["squinting"] as usual over the open missal. With Mari-Gaila, Pedro's Latin, once the brunt of her ridicule, is miraculously effective, as if his words had gathered a spark of life between Pedro's utterance of them and his walk with her across the courtyard of the church. (Indeed, the words Pedro speaks in Latin and the occurrence of the miracle as reported in the stage directions are separated by a sentence indicating that Pedro gives Mari-Gaila the

candle he has extinguished over her hands and leads her over the
"losas sepulcrales" ["tombstones"].)

Thanks to Mari-Gaila, then, Pedro's Latin is altered. When the
two of them meet at the hay cart, his Castilian has already been
transformed through his determination to receive his wife in front
of the same church where they were married, an act of forgiveness
that precipitates his "fall" from sin and the loss of the horns that
mark him as a cuckold and also suggest his ties—now severed—
with Séptimo Miau.[21] He will not use that language again in the
play, and what replaces it is his newly ancient Latin, a language
reminiscent of the "ingenuo Latin" ["ingenuous Latin"] associated
with the second of La lámpara maravillosa's three aesthetic modes
or "roses," and with a thirteenth century filled with "alquimistas
y teólogos" ["alchemists and theologians"] (ET, III). Such a Latin
conveys not the official, Roman strictures of Catholicism (nor the
imitation of those strictures that, according to the poet-narrator of
La lámpara maravillosa, took root in Spain [MM, VI]), but a more
ancient language, one that is truly "classical," thanks to the vitality
granted by its ability to evoke simultaneously "pagan joy and Christian terror."[22] This is suggested by the "aroma de vida eterna"
["fragrance of eternal life"] sensed by the villagers as Pedro and
Mari-Gaila walk among them—a [man of the] Church and his bride.

Mari-Gaila herself is silent here (her final words having been
spoken in the previous scene, before she mounted the hay cart),
but it is clearly her "rhythm," her sense of eternity (as opposed,
e.g., to that of Séptimo Miau) that infuses the "blanca sentencia"
["white," or "blank," sentence"] of Pedro's words. She is the character who has been marked as blanca—not only in her skin, but
also in her actions, since that adjective is used to describe even
the road she travels the night of her ride with the Trasgo Cabrío—
her "negro." She is blanca, as in not negro (black) and demonic
but also as in "blank", empty of any recognizable Castilian "mes-
sage." A word stripped, like Mari-Gaila herself as she stands facing
the audience, bare but in full possession of her body. Distant but
moved as Laureano's head appears to her, she sees return to life
a being she has effectively put to death, and she sees that being
as a juxtaposition of contradictory aspects. Both grotesque and
lovely, it echoes her own image as she too holds death in a rhythm
of life, ultimately responsible for a killing of the moribund that
has made possible a radical, profoundly collective—albeit highly
ironic—renaissance.[23]

I use that last word, renaissance, somewhat cautiously, but I
also use it enthusiastically because it accurately evokes the occur-

rence of Valle-Inclán's "classicism" that *Divinas palabras* provides. In so doing it also recalls the work's "support," both because it names the creation-as-destruction exemplified by *Divinas palabras,* and because the word *renaissance* itself exemplifies a creation-as-destruction on the part of Valle-Inclán. According to his redefinition, as developed in the paradigm of creation-as-destruction found in *La lámpara maravillosa,* the renaissance should not be considered an historical period so much as a "metaphysical concept" (ET, VII). As such, it is identified with the dynamic conjunction (of "classicism") that, although inscribed by Valle-Inclán in thirteenth-century Italy, can arise at any moment of coupling. With respect to Spanish history, Castilian language and literature, and the poetics of *La lámpara maravillosa, renaissance* could be described as an "idiotic" term, since Spain's Golden Age brought the end of a "relatively rich and varied" literature and the imposition of an inappropriate translation of the word *classic*.[24] Given the tenacity of that imposition, even if its grip is one of a dying hand, a recovery of Spain's "renaissance" can only be achieved through the destruction of its deformation—always bearing in mind that a single word will be used in both instances. Which is to say, that the decaying, degenerated word and its redefined counterpart will differ in direct relation to the poet's ability to do away with existing connotations (which are rigid and dogmatic) and infuse new ones that reflect a truly "classical" spirit and therefore open unexpected perspectives.[25]

That a redefinition of (Castilian) language and a conceptualization of verbal creation-as-destruction are the support of *Divinas palabras* seems abuntantly clear once the play is read or, as Sarduy would say, "shaken" in accordance with the concerns its title suggests, and I believe it is important to push that "discovery" further for several reasons. All of those reasons have to do with the "divinity" of Valle-Inclán's words. A thorough study of any one of them would require more space than I have at present. As I noted at the onset, however, here I want to mention three and rough out what I consider the principal factors or issues involved with each. The relationship between *Divinas palabras* and *La lámpara maravillosa* and Valle-Inclán's "creative destruction" of other literary texts will be discussed rather briefly; I offer a somewhat more in-depth discussion of the third reason, which concerns most specifically the role of Mari-Gaila and issues of gender.

(1) In the first place, I would suggest that to read *Divinas palabras* as an exploration of words and of an aesthetics that is creative

in direct relation to—potentially owing to—a radical affirmation of ambivalence is to find in the work a coherence that has previously eluded Valle-Inclán's critics. This is essential, because despite some excellent studies about *Divinas palabras* (which explain the symbolism of its characters, its ties to the *esperpentos,* and its possible meaning or historical basis), there has been no real agreement about what appears to be its impenetrable "enigma."[26] Whereas for some critics it is strictly a burlesque (John Crispin),[27] or an exercise in unmitigated "demolición" ["demolition"] (José G. Escribano),[28] for others it must be read straightforwardly (Josette Blanquat, Gretchen Gregoria Holbert, and Gustave Umpierre) or historically (Manual Bermejo Marcos).[29]

To read *Divinas palabras* as a "play on words" and their irreverent redefinition is to learn from each of these studies. It is also, however, to glimpse what might, following the poet-narrator of *La lámpara maravillosa,* be called the play's "gesto único" ["individual or unique gesture"] from a different perspective and to insert that gesture as it were into the ongoing series of spiritual exercises and their representation begun with Valle-Inclán's earliest stories. This is a perspective suggested by Blanquat, Holbert, and Umpierre, although none of them has followed it to its limits. Their readings, all of which rely heavily on *La lámpara maravillosa,* are ultimately more a question of noting similarities of images and phrases than defining a resemblance between the actual conceptualization of the two works: Blanquat by speculating that "Exégesis trina," the central chapter of *La lámpara maravillosa,* may have been directly influential in the composition of *Divinas palabras;* Holbert by stressing "redemption through language" as a common theme; and Umpierre by studying sources and the use of allusion.

By building on the studies of Blanquat and Umpierre and by following the suggestions of a reading of *Divinas palabras* as a representation of the recovery of a "classical" Castilian word,[30] I would propose that the play stands in a much closer relation to Valle-Inclán's poetics and in particular to *La lámpara maravillosa* than has heretofore been acknowledged. Not only the fragments from *La lámpara maravillosa* that are woven into *Divinas palabras* but also the context, the *way* in which they reappear indicate a metaphoric bond between the two works.[31] Here again, I am indebted to Sarduy's *Escrito sobre un cuerpo* for an expression that I find useful for discussing Valle-Inclán's work as one that literally occurs—as in "takes place"—in words; and the expression is "squaring metaphor."[32] Although Sarduy works with Góngora and José Lezama Lima, the term is helpful for Valle-Inclán as well (despite his expressed impatience with Góngora),[33] for what I find operative in *Divinas palabras* is a metaphorization of *La lámpara maravillosa*.

In that earlier work (1916), a collection of parabolic meditations about writing, Valle-Inclán discusses poetics but he also exemplifies them. Converting into metaphor his own work as a writer, he creates a poet-narrator who in turn makes of himself a *cifra* [image], an example at once familiar and hermetic. In *Divinas palabras* that activity is returned to incident, but to an incident that metaphorizes *La lámpara maravillosa*. The drama staged there is played out in different words and embodied in different characters that are "other" but also familiar, so much so that it is hard to understand how Valle-Inclán's "clues" to their familiarity have gone unrecognized (I am thinking here, for example, of Valle-Inclán's own "cameo-appearance" in the form of the one-armed soldier who joins wholeheartedly in the degradation and death of the idiot, and of the resemblance between Mari-Gaila and the poet-narrator of *La lámpara maravillosa* that will be discussed below).[34]

As metaphor, then, *Divinas palabras* completes *La lámpara maravillosa* because it offers an explanation of sorts, a further staging of the poet's work. At the same time, however, thanks to its highly disconcerting juxtapositions of dissonant elements, the play also remains perplexing in a way one might refer to as incomplete. In fact, thinking about *Divinas palabras* as a "signifier" while I reread, I kept coming back to a visualization of it as a signifier missing its signified, or—and this seems more appropriate for the reading I have been been developing here—as a metaphor in progress, as the elaboration of the first term that, although itself the completion of one metaphor, pulses or reaches toward the formation of another. Which is to say that, although the situation or incidents of the two works would hardly be more "dissimilar," *Divinas palabras* conveys *La lámpara maravillosa*'s provocative gesture, its attempt to initiate a redefinition as well as to describe one, its motion of subversion, of vision as veiled knowledge (QE, IV), of affirmation as discontentment.

Dis-content-ment. I have broken that last word up because doing so permits a glimpse of yet a further implication of *Divinas palabras* as metaphor, and that is the stripping of contents, of creatively destroying words by purifying them (QE, V), of writing "blank sentences," allowing them to stand bare as Mari-Gaila at the end of *Divinas palabras*. It is letting the task of historicizing fall to the reader with the conviction that when words become truly "divine" (QE, V), their reach will extend in all three temporal directions, where they can reflect, refract, and be "placed"—or, even better, replaced—,[35] as Valle-Inclán himself (re)placed *Divinas palabras* on the stage in 1933, his commentary on contemporary events in Republican Spain.[36]

(2) Although *Divinas palabras* can be read coherently as a *discontent-ment* of Castilian, it is necessary to recognize that the "divinity" of Valle-Inclán's words owes as well to a highly specific relation to precisely the language and literature whose creative death they want to accomplish. This is to say that even as the words of *Divinas palabras* are emptied of incident so as to make possible multiple coincidence, they are also resonant with allusions to the words of other works. These words may be rejected, but at the same time a bond is evoked. Which suggests that for Valle-Inclán divinity, even "blankness" is not so much absolute absence as it is tension or questioning: the introduction of a discontentment that upsets the hold of language, not only problematizing it from within, but also reflecting on the activity of problematizing itself.

This is not an easy aspect of a literary text to approach, much less explicate, but I believe that in *Divinas palabras* it can be studied through an exploration of the wealth of allusions in both the events or "plot" of the play and in Valle-Inclán's words—whether those words are spoken by his characters or found in the stage directions. The purpose here is not to identify those allusions—although the task includes identification—but to identify the implications of "composing" a work to a large degree from what might be called the decomposition of other works. Gustavo Pérez Firmat, discussing this phenomenon with relation to the *esperpento* and to that particularly Cuban humor known as *choteo,* has dubbed it *festive mimesis.* The term allows him to explore Valle-Inclán's writing as a dazzling, irreverent bodily function and to see the *esperpento* as a "motley," formed according to a "carnival principle" of "excess" and "complication." It is a definition that a study of the "motley" in *Divinas palabras* would bear out, although the textual transformations in *Divinas palabras,* as in *La lámpara maravillosa* and several other works (e.g., *Cuento de abril* [April story] or *El embrujado* [A man bewitched]), indicate a conscious effort of transformation that far exceeds Gustavo Pérez Firmat's "pounding and patching" of a particular model (32).[37] In this transformation, even when it is possible to locate one "model"—and I believe that is seldom if ever the case for Valle-Inclán's work—the return to sources is one that operates more within the scope of an entire literature or language than as a tension or parody between two works, authors, or passages.[38]

In *Divinas palabras,* for example, critics have noted ties to paintings by Botticelli (Blanquat),[39] Hieronymous Bosch (Blanquat and David Ling),[40] and Julio Romero de Torres (Maier),[41] and a reworking of such diverse sources as the *Celestina* (Phyllis Zatlin Boring),[42] Cervantes' *Don Quijote,* (Gustavo Umpierre and Carlos Jerez-Farrán),[43] the plays and *autos* of Calderón de la Barca (Umpierre),[44] Martínez Sierra's *La adúltera penitente* (Alfred Rodríguez),[45] Unamuno's *La tía Tula* (Escribano),[46] Emilia Pardo Bazán's "Tetrarca en la aldea" (Emilio González López),[47] and Maeterlinck's *Marie-Magdaleine* (Umpierre),[48] as well as the life of Bernard of Clairvaux (Umpierre and Blanquat).[49] Although each of those possible allusions merits consideration for the commentary occasioned by its appearance and disappearance in Valle-Inclán's play,[50] what the coincidence of *all* the possible allusions suggests is a fragmentation of the corpus we would now call the Castilian "canon," since works are literally dismembered, used in an audacious, random way that respects no center, that forces Castilian to admit the voices of other literatures and languages, both from other countries and from within Spain itself.[51] This final admission is particularly important, for it suggests that in *Divinas palabras* there is something of the effort made so explicit in *Cuento de abril* to alter Castilian's very "nature" by influencing its syntax, vocabulary, and tone. In *Divinas palabras,* of course, the infusion involves not only essentially linguistic and aesthetic allusions, but also a Galician world so tangible that scholars can argue about precise locations on its map, one that in numerous ways belies "official" Castilian Spain.[52]

That this preoccupation with Castilian has implications for the "divinity" of Valle-Inclán's words should be clear, since it indicates that even as those words undergo the thorough stripping of "ideología" ["ideology"] described by the poet-narrator of *La lámpara maravillosa* (MM, II),[53] they convey a particular place and a specific moment. What is more, and this is perhaps an even sharper indication of their "divinity," they also provoke reflection about the difficulty of achieving a word that, like Mari-Gaila or the fleshy *cifra* of *La lámpara maravillosa,* is marked by but not limited to the earth and the particular people from which it arose. In *Divinas palabras* such a marking—or, rather "meta-marking"—is achieved by the random comments of some of the characters, which suggest concrete references,[54] but do not tie the play unequivocally to a specific historical situation. It is also achieved by the appearance of two minor characters who, because of their roles in other works by Valle-Inclán and their hints of autobiographical references to

Valle-Inclán himself, evoke the poet's struggle to attain a "miraculous" location for language.[55]

One of those characters is the soldier who, like the poet-narrator of *La lámpara maravillosa* (AG, I), "[T]iene cercenado un brazo" ["has had one of his arms amputated"], and who participates actively in the death of Laureano, the word of "los Reino" ["the Kingdom family"] the night he dies in Ludovina's tavern (II.vii). The other is "el Conde Polaco" ["the Polish Count"] who never truly becomes a character in *Divinas palabras* since he is only glimpsed in the distance, handcuffed between a pair of Civil Guards.[56] That glimpse of him, however, and the way in which "el Conde" is sought earlier in the play and confused by Mari-Gaila with Séptimo Miau suggest that he is something of a leitmotiv. As such he is more than an isolated phenomenon, since he also figures rather enigmatically in quite a few of Valle-Inclán's works, where—despite a changing identity—he is invariably a foreigner sensitive to national character and its manifestations in language. If, in Valle-Inclán's later work *(Luces de Bohemia)*,[57] "el Conde" becomes "deformed," in earlier pieces hie role is quite different. In *La lámpara maravillosa*, for example, he is presented as "un polaco místico y visionario" ["a mystic, visionary Pole"] who adds to the poet's explanation of "el milagro musical" ["the musical miracle"] the observation that all languages carry an indelible trace of their own distinct origins. The Pole's appearance in *La lámpara maravillosa* is brief, but it precedes several more extensive chapters about the "contaminación ["pollution"] (MM, V) of Castilian language and literature, and immediately follows several chapters that celebrate the "miracle" of language as a clever triumph over the "line(s)" offered by words. He brings into play the two conflicting intuitions that both guide and threaten to shatter the poet of *La lámpara maravillosa* (QE, V), a struggle of national, even universal proportions, that is also evoked subtly and woven between the lines and lives of the characters in *Divinas palabras*.

(3) Mari-Gaila never meets "el Conde Polaco," but it is no coincidence that a discussion of his role in *Divinas palabras* can lead directly to a consideration of her as the play's richest manifestation of Valle-Inclán's preoccupation with creation-as-destruction. Although unknowingly, Mari-Gaila herself even alludes to a possible affinity between them when she confides to Rosa la Tatula that she has suspected "el Conde" of being Séptimo Miau. Such a convergence of identities proves to be impossible, for when "el Conde" is arrested (III. ii), he turns out to be the pilgrim Mari-Gaila and her companions met earlier (II. ii). Mari-Gaila's thought is telling,

however, for several reasons. In the first place, as David Ling has noted, it explains, at least to some extent, her fascination with Séptino Miau, who—she assumes at first—is not merely the picaresque rogue with whom the audience becomes familiar long before she does, but something of a "celebrity" whose "interest in her flatters her vanity and adds an extra dimension to the affair."[58] More importantly, since her assumption is not totally unfounded (there is, after all, something extraordinary about Séptimo Miau), it points to the similarities that do exist between the two men. Not only has "el Conde," like Séptimo Miau, reportedly made his rounds of the fairs "con una mujer de vida" ["with a woman who enjoys life"] (II. ii), he too has an itinerant life and a repeatedly changing identity. In other words, although Séptimo Miau is a demonic, "dark" figure, he is a "pilgrim" also, an "outsider," and the desire Mari-Gaila feels for him is not unrelated to the "gozosa ternura" ["joyful tenderness"] she feels for the pilgrim. In fact, it is not difficult to read those two responses as only apparently contradictory: given "el Conde's" appearance in *La lámpara maravillosa* as one of the mentors of the pilgrim poet-narrator, Séptimo Miau bears close resemblance to the shadow or "flip" of that narrator, haunting him repeatedly as a pull toward lust and self-absorption.[59]

Although Mari-Gaila herself does not reflect on this—on no occasion in the play is she shown to be a self-reflective character— her attraction to "el Conde" and the fact that she senses a link between him and Séptimo Miau recalls her own status as an "unstable" character who both changes dramatically in the course of the work, and becomes an outcast or fugitive with respect to the villagers. That her fate is not to be a thoroughly happy one is clear when Séptimo Miau reads her fortune ("Venus y Ceres. . . . Tu destino es el de la mujer hermosa") ["Venus and Ceres. . . . Your fortune is that of a beautiful woman"] (II. iii). The fortune links Venus with lust (*licencias* [licentiousness]) rather than with love, proclaiming that Mari-Gaila's "moment" (her "trono," or "throne") is spring, season of the Eleusinian mysteries, not fall, when the play takes place.[60] Mari-Gaila's insistence on the negative implications of her fortune ("Mi suerte es desgracia" ["My fate is calamity"], indicates that she is fully aware of this displacement and its implications for her "story." It is at this moment, as her fortune is spelled out, when she seems closest to "speaking for herself," as if she were about to articulate the precarious existence of a woman who speaks well and speaks out.[61]

Mari-Gaila's comment about her fate is a telling one, because it points to an aspect of her character of which critics have taken little note. On the contrary, what has been stressed, whether as reprehensible or triumphant, is her sensuality and her vitality.[62] That she is described as adulterous, lascivious, and greedy (with respect to Laureano) is acknowledged, but to a large degree she has been read nevertheless as an affirmation, consistent—as Umpierre explains—with the newly egalitarian view of women prevalent in European society since the end of the nineteenth century.[63] This is best seen perhaps in the discussions of the incident with the hay cart, its evocation of Hieronymous Bosch's *Hay Wagon*,[64] and the "faunalia" it represents. "The final image is one of "a pagan goddess surrounded by her retinue of satyrs," Lyon remarks, for example.[65] Or, as I wrote above, "She is the one character . . . capable of enjoying her body fully," the one who is able to avoid the "dark 'flip' of eroticism."

Given Mari-Gaila's overwhelming vitality and her appeal to "audiences" both within the play and in the theater, it would be foolish to contest Leda Schiavo's assertion that everyone falls in love with her, "desde el narrador de las acotaciones" ["beginning with the narrator of the stage directions"].[66] At the same time, however, in order to understand Mari-Gaila fully it is important to observe and to emphasize (1) that she, like Séptimo Miau, "el Conde," and the pilgrim becomes an outcast, a wanderer; and (2) that her situation as one who has crossed a significant boundary or limit arises not only from her association with those men. Quite the reverse, it arises from her own, apparently deliberate decisions, in particular from her participation in the scene with the hay cart. In that participation and in her offer to dance naked if the men refrain from touching her, she joins the mob and its carousing but she also separates herself from the people around her. "Conformarse con esto!" ["Make do with this!"], she tells them, forbidding the men any physical contact but inviting them to look as she rips off her shift and raises her "blanca desnudez" ["white nakedness"] before their eyes.

The transitive verb ("raise" [*levantar*]) is important in that last sentence because it is Mari-Gaila herself who takes the last step toward nakedness. She has been pushed, of course, to this extreme decision, but the final move is hers. As she makes that move, she both speaks her final words in the play" ("Conformarse con esto!") ["Make do with this!"], and for the second time comes close to speaking "for herself." During the rest of the scene with the hay cart and during the final scene, she will dominate the stage, but she will be silent. "Adusta y resuelta" ["severe and determined"], she acts as subject by giving herself as object. Her flesh will become word, but that transformation will be at the price of her tongue, throughout the play her sharpest, "best" feature. Simultaneously raised up and cut down, then, she will also be simultaneously human and hybrid, a woman subject to the crowd but also a subject with respect to it.

Joining the mob gazing at Mari-Gaila, a reader or spectator of *Divinas palabras* will no doubt find that the similarity between *The Hay Wagon* and Valle-Inclán's scene only partially explains the complexity of Mari-Gaila as both subject and object. The discussions by Blanquat and Umpierre are helpful because their attention to Mari-Gaila's fortune as Venus and Ceres (its evocation of a pre-Christian tradition and echo of the pre-Castilian world recalled in the descriptions of Mari-Gaila herself) contrasts with or even contradicts another of Valle-Inclán's descriptions, that of her excellent Castilian. To recognize this contradiction is instructive, because it suggests the extent to which Valle-Inclán has inscribed in Mari-Gaila the tensions of his own Castilian, the one he has used to create her. In this way, as a character she literally embodies the effort to embody in Castilian the vitality of the pre-Castilian *romances* [ballads] praised by the poet-narrator in *La lámpara maravillosa* (MM, V–VI). She also evokes in a striking way "the grain goddess," in particular her manifestation as the Celtic "goddess in the wagon" whose mutilation and eventual transformation to Catholic saint has been documented recently.[67]

Valle-Inclán's contribution to the exploration of the syncretism undergone by the goddess in the wagon is of unusual interest from at least two perspectives. In the first place, it not only seems to anticipate (indirectly) the work used by contemporary scholars like Pamela Berger and Marina Warner, who have worked with few— if any—Spanish sources, but it also draws (directly) on Galician sources that Valle-Inclán knew intimately. In the case of Mari-Gaila, a familiarity with Galician religious festivals suggests that a very likely model for Mari-Gaila and the final incident would be the festival of Nuestra Señora de Franqueira [Our Lady of Franqueira]. A village in the diocese of Tuy, La Franqueira is located in the mountainous interior of Pontevedra, the province in which Valle-Inclán was born. It is the site of a famous church and shrine where for centuries pilgrims have worshipped an image of the Virgin revealed miraculously to an old shepherdess. Because the event occurred at a spot on the border between two villages and because the terrain made construction difficult, there was a dispute about where to locate a hermitage to house the image. In order to effect a resolution, the image was placed in a cart pulled by oxen from the opposing towns. The oxen were blindfolded and spurred to wander in circles until they "agreed" on the best route for leaving the mountainous site where they were confined. At the point of their exit, a hermitage was built.[68]

Although the incident with the disputed image and the cart is enough to indicate a resemblance with *Divinas palabras*, the "romería" ["fair"] held in La Franqueira each 8 September increases that resemblance considerably (when the scene with the hay cart begins in *Divinas palabras*, harvest is in progress).[69] On the day of the fair, the image of the Virgin is taken from its throne and carried through the streets on a cart pulled by blindfolded oxen. Since so many of the pilgrims want the honor of leading the cart and spurring the oxen, that honor is auctioned off to the highest bidder. With respect to *Divinas palabras*, of course, that description evokes "el carro, con sus bueyes dorados, y al frente el rojo gigante que los conduce" ["the cart with its golden oxen, and the red giant in front, directing them"]. At the same time, and perhaps even more importantly for an understanding of Mari-Gaila, it also evokes a peculiar twist added by Valle-Inclán, as through the use of Nuestra Señora de Franqueira, he plants a fusion of the occupants of the (hay) cart: the idiot and Mari-Gaila.

That fusion both intensifies and polemicizes the syncretism of the wagon goddess, providing a second perspective on Valle-Inclán's use of a traditional figure. This becomes clear if, as Blanquat and Umpierre advise,[70] the legend of Bernard of Clairvaux is borne in mind during the final scene.[71] As Blanquat and Umpierre point out, Pedro's use of Latin recalls the "musical miracle" achieved by Saint Bernard, whose tone of voice was so moving that he raised an army of recruits, despite the fact that none of them was able to understand anything he said (MM,II). Given the very same links between *Divinas palabras* and *La lámpara maravillosa*, however, it also recalls another element of the chapter of "El milagro musical" ["The Musical Miracle"] in which Saint Bernard appears. That element, which Blanquat and Umpierre do not discuss, is the explicit equation of Bernard's miracle with the miracle of the Assumption. "El milagro realizaba el misterio de la Asunción" ["The miracle was achieving the miracle of the Assumption"].

An example of the fusion of Mary and Christ in the "attainment of that divine likeness in which man was created and from which he has fallen through concupiscence and sin,"[72] Bernard's miracle in *La lámpara maravillosa* both challenges and evokes the Assumption. The figures of Bernard and the Virgin call to mind Bernard's devotion and his ability to communicate despite the "foreignness" of unfamiliar words, but at the same time the associations of Bernard within *La lámpara maravillosa* itself serve to undermine or "unmake" the associations of traditional Catholic and Christian symbolism. When read in the context of other "miraculous" figures, Bernard is thus a counterpart not only of Saint Francis of Assisi but also of the heterodox, alchemic poet Christ who figures at the very center of "Exégesis trina" ["Three-part Exegesis"], the center book of *La lámpara maravillosa*. In *Divinas palabras*, Valle-Inclán plays with the image of the Virgin as much as he plays with that of Saint Bernard in *La lámpara maravillosa*, except that he makes her "Assumption" even more literal: by exploiting to the utmost the fusion of Mary and Christ implicit in the "milagro musical," he has Mari-Gaila present herself as an offering, assuming, simultaneously, the traditional connotations of Jesus and the Virgin and the characteristics of the pagan goddess that were stripped from her when she became the bride of Christ. Literally re-covered with those characteristics at the end of *Divinas palabras*, the nakedness restored to her blurts out a complex, wildly disconcerting utterance, the coincidence of diametrically opposing gestures.

In order to focus the final scene more clearly in terms of language, it is important to look even more closely at Mari-Gaila's complexity, in particular at the progression in the previous paragraph from a resemblance between Pedro Gailo and Saint Bernard, to a fusion between the Saint and Mari-Gaila and the implication that Pedro's miracle is one of the Assumption, which, as noted earlier, could not have been realized without Mari-Gaila's intervention. This is to say, of course, that Mari-Gaila is truly the central figure in the final scene. Not only does she dominate with her physical presence, that presence is both Christ-like on several counts and, through her association with Pedro Gailo (as a Saint Bernard reminiscent of the Virgin Mary), evocative of the Church to which she is espoused. Moreover, Mari-Gaila is also fused with Christ as His mother as well as His person. It is to her, and apparently only to her, that the idiot figure appears, transformed "como una cabeza de ángel" ["like the head of an angel"].[73] It is hard not to think here of John the Baptist and his prefiguration of Christ, or of the various beheadings suggested throughout *Divinas palabras*,[74] or of the Janus-like head at the center of *La lámpara maravillosa* (ET, V), which looks with sin or love in all three temporal directions. It is also hard not to remark on Mari-Gaila's own hint that she has become pregnant and that consequently the head she sees in the final scene announces a future birth.[75]

If that is the case,[76] it is important to note that a complex "holy family" stands at the end of *Divinas palabras* and that it refracts provocatively the family of Séptimo Miau, Poca Pena, and their infant son in the play's opening scene. The most striking difference here, of course, if the figure of Mari-Gaila. In that first family, Poca Pena is so inessential to Séptimo Miau that she will soon disappear completely. Mari-Gaila is, however, central to such an extent that she not only embodies the entire family, she reaches, like a figure in one of Velázquez's canvases, beyond the frame of the play itself, becoming fused with the poet-narrator of *La lámpara maravillosa* and, through him, with the other poet characters in Valle-Inclán's works that the poet-narrator suggests. This association is reinforced by her attraction to characters like "el Conde" and the one-armed soldier and by phrases in the stage directions that suggest that her "empty," "white" path are the same paths walked in *La lámpara maravillosa* by a hybrid, alchemic Christ, or by his disciples who followed the androgynous path of the classical redefined in *La lámpara maravillosa*'s second aesthetic "rose."

That suggestion is striking, perhaps even more striking that it seems at first glance. Although Mari-Gaila as an androgynous figure is a topic that deserves study,[77] even more provocative is the suggestion that she is androgynous because of her association with the poet-narrator in *La lámpara maravillosa*. That association indicates that, as a figure, she holds both masculine and feminine characteristics, that she is an incarnation of the poet every bit as much as the narrator of *La lámpara maravillosa,* or Max Estrella, or Don Friolera. She stands, then, on the hay cart, for and as the poet, an extravagant, well-spoken figure scorned but proud, who has walked on broken glass and chewed nails in a way not unlike Max Estrella in *Luces de Bohemia*.[78] As a poet figure, she is even more provocative than Max, however, because through her association with the narrator of *La lámpara maravillosa* and his deliberate female masking, she suggests a male poet who disguises himself as a woman whom he veils so a to write as a "pregnant" man and thus experience and represent verbal creation as an act of both engendering life and giving birth. (QE, V)[79]

Although it may seem like an overly unorthodox ending, I want to close with two observations, both of which are directly linked to Mari-Gaila as a male word-gendered female. The first is that Valle-Inclán's representations (and, given the strong autobiographical hints in *La lámpara maravillosa,* representations that I believe it is fair to call self-representations, as long as "self" is used to indicate self as Poet rather than—or at least far more than— poet) suggest a continual concern with issues now discussed as questions of gender. Carlos Jerez-Farrán has written recently that although Mari-Gaila's world or role would hardly be acceptable to today's woman, Mari-Gaila nevertheless represents an effort on Valle-Inclán's part to offer "la defensa radical de una nueva moralidad sexual femenina, el desenmascaramiento de la hipocresía moral cristiana y la destrucción del mito sobre la mujer creado por la mojigatería sexual que tanto la Iglesia como la burguesía habían creado a lo largo de los siglos" ["the radical defense of a new feminine sexual morality, the unmasking of Christian moral hypocrisy and the destruction of the myth about women created by the sexual prudishness created for centuries by the Church as well as bourgeois society"].[80]

Although I will not take issue entirely with that position, I will argue that the strong associations between Mari-Gaila and the poet's word as represented in *La lámpara maravillosa* indicate that much of what is to be learned from Mari-Gaila and *Divinas palabras* about women and their position is to be learned indirectly. In all of Valle-Inclán's work, the work of verbal creation, especially that of a (non-Castilian) writer writing in a second, "dominant" (Castilian) language, is presented as a tremendous struggle with far-reaching ethical and moral implications. That this struggle and the continual painful rejection it so often occasions would be so embodied (either covertly, as in *La lámpara maravillosa,* or explicitly, as in *Divinas palabras*) suggests to me that Valle-Inclán's estimation of the role in which his society cast women (and I refer here to role, to gender, and not to individual women) was every bit as low as some of his comments indicate. Were this not the case, a woman would not have served so well for the drama of the word enacted in *Divinas palabras,* where Valle-Inclán was able to bring Mari-Gaila almost to subjectivity precisely through his intense identification with her as object. This is to say that I find her most dead as a woman exactly at the instant when she is most alive and scintillating as a representation of (male) poetic subjectivity—a contradiction found also in the work of other turn-of-the-century writers, Baudelaire, for instance, who, as Walter Benjamin noted, used the figure of the whore to represent for male readers "the unavoidable necessity of prostitution for the poet."[81]

The question to be asked, then, with respect to a character like Mari-Gaila or some of the other female characters who achieve a similar dimension in Valle-Inclán's work,[82] is how can they be best translated by or for a contemporary reader who is as apt to be female as male in her (or his) response? Why study those characters and trace their creation if they provide yet another example of "carnal knowledge" but offer none of the "carnal knowing" whose absence Margaret R. Miles has discussed so poignantly as characteristic of religious art of the Christian West?[83] Why return to Mari-Gaila when, ultimately, her magnificent body is in fact a metaphor for the male poet and she herself is not permitted to give voice to (and perhaps not even to recognize) the epiphany she embodies. Think, for example, of the final scene, when her once talkative eyes are silent as they see the transformation of Laureano, when—despite the continual quips once spoken by her mouth—there is no clear indication that Mari-Gaila could begin to articulate her experience. A complex word, she represents the most heterodox of verbal marriages, but in the final scene her eyes are devoid of words, just as they are half-closed as she enters the *garita* [sentry box] with Séptimo Miau (II, v) or rides through the air on the back of the Trasgo Cabrío (II, viii).[84] At such moments she is daring enough to be licentious, but she is also weak and "feminine," the "excess"—to use Gayatri Chakravorty Spivak's image—of her clitoris cut out;[85] she faints as the goat carries her through the air; she holds back even as she lets Séptimo Miau embrace her; and, despite a shudder when Séptimo Miau bites her mouth, she enjoys his brutality, "fallecida y feliz" ["unconscious and content"].

As a tentative answer to those questions, I would offer my second observation, which owes to a hunch, which there is of course no way to confirm,[86] that the title of *Divinas palabras* refers to a passage from Miguel de Molinos's *Guía espiritual* [Spiritual guide]. In that passage, Molinos reproduces and praises the words of God reportedly spoken to Sor Catalina Paluci when she questioned the wisdom of obeying a "nonobservant" spiritual advisor and was told to attend to the instructions and rather than worry about the imperfection of the speaker who transmitted them. "¡Oh divinas palabras" ["Oh divine words!"], he says, "dignas de estamparse en los corazones de aquellas almas que desean adelantarse en la perfección" ["worthy of being stamped on the hearts of those souls who wish to advance toward perfection"].[87]

Or, to use the words I would dare to say Valle-Inclán might speak through Mari-Gaila to a contemporary reader, "Conformarse con esto!" ["Make do with this!"] These are words, language, body, and this is all you get: *cifras* that will work miracles or fall flat, depending on a precarious relation of voice and ear. Or, to use my words, Valle-Inclán's female characters like Mari-Gaila have much to teach about the use of language and its perils for one determined to write "against the grain" of prevailing social discourse. Through them he was apparently determined to explore the "feminization" of a (male) writer given to recording voices that offended the conventional ear,[88] to dramatize the risks involved in countering a national literary tradition—by challenging the Calderonian honor code, for example, with an adulterous wife who is not stoned to death but likened to a figure of redemption."[89]

If, as I believe to be the case, such femininzation is highly paradoxical, with respect to women, I would return to the gaze of Ana Belén with which I began. As I conclude this essay, it seems evident that for Belén assuming the role of Mari-Gaila also meant assuming the assumptions of Valle-Inclán inscribed in her character. Thus in her eyes, the recognition that for Valle-Inclán one of the greatest perils associated with the use of language was the extent to which even the most accomplished writer is inevitably used by it and the ideology with which it is bound inextricably. Thus, the paradox that despite his own marginal position as a writer and despite his fascination with the idea of androgyny, Valle-Inclán was not able to conceive of female characters who were truly literate and therefore not able to explore fully in words the limits of his own imagination. His women could stand for him, and they could provide a space for him to stand, but within that space he permitted *them* to stand only insofar as they were subsumed as individuals—only insofar as the initial Assumption was the donning of a female guise by the poet himself.

To keep that poet alive, to attempt to make of him a true "classic," is to acknowledge but then to interrogate his (dis)guises. The glimpse of subjectivity that Valle-Inclán's female characters offer must be explored so as to expose those characters as objects, as metaphors waiting to be squared by the creative, dissenting *discontent-ment* they provoke.

Notes

1. This essay developed from a talk presented at Marquette University in the spring of 1989. I would like to thank Anne Pasero for the invitation to speak about Valle-Inclán, and her colleagues and students for their warm reception and thought-provoking responses.

2. I, iv and II, iii, respectively. I have used primarily the following two editions of *Divinas palabras:* (Madrid: Tipografía Yagües, 1920) and 3rd ed. (Madrid: Espasa-Calpe, 1966). Since there is no definitive edition of the play and the first

edition is not readily available, future references will be made in parentheses in the text, indicating act and scene. All translations from the play are my own. A complete English translation by Edwin Williams was published in Michael Benedikt and George E. Wellwarth, *Modern Spanish Theatre: An Anthology of Plays* (New York: Dutton, 1968), 1–78.

3. Manuel Longares, "Valle-Inclán en Venecia," review of José Luis García Sánchez's film of *Divinas palabras, Cambio 16*, 7 September 1978; 85.

4. Personal correspondence, 23 February 1988.

5. I refer here to the definition embedded in *La lámpara maravillosa*. In this context, it is interesting to note that Valle-Inclán had already been judged a "classic" in 1903, in G. Martínez Sierra's review of Melchor Fernández Almagro's *Sombras de vida*, for which Valle-Inclán supplied the prologue (*Helios* 1, no. 1 [1903]: 500). Given Valle-Inclán's continual allusions and rewritings in *La lámpara maravillosa*, it would not be surprising if, among other allusions, his use of "clásico" referred to that pronouncement.

6. "El milagro musical," chap. 7. Given the lack of a definitive edition and the inaccessibility of the two editions published during Valle-Inclán's lifetime, future references to *La lámpara maravillosa* will be made in parentheses in the text, using the following abbreviations: AG ("El anillo de Giges"); MM ("El milagro musical"); ET ("Exégesis trina"); QE ("Quietismo estético"); and PS ("Piedra del sabio"). I have used 2d ed., *La lámpara maravillosa* (Madrid: Artes de la Ilustración, 1922).

7. All translations of *La lámpara maravillosa* are my own. A complete English translation has been published by Robert Lima: *The Lamp of Marvels: Aesthetic Meditations* (West Stockbridge, Mass.: Lindisfarne Press, 1986).

8. Severo Sarduy, *Escrito sobre un cuerpo* (Buenos Aires: Editorial Sudamericana, 1969), 30.

9. *Written on a Body*, trans. Carol Maier (New York: Lumen Books, 1989).

10. I use the word *reading* deliberately here, since the present discussion is primarily a reading—although I will turn to reading-viewing at the end of the essay. The simultaneous distinction and interaction of the two terms is generally not acknowledged sufficiently when critics write about Valle-Inclán's theater, and it merits a study in itself.

11. To my knowledge, this has not yet been a starting point for reading *Divinas palabras*. María Eugenia March comes closest to doing that in *Forma e idea de los "esperpentos" de Valle-Inclán* (Chapel Hill, N.C.: Estudios de Hispanófila 10, 1969), 64, when she recognizes "la *palabra*, considerada como sonido, desprovista de significado conceptual" [the word, considered sound, stripped of conceptual meaning] as "el *leit-motif* más importante de la obra" [the most important *leitmotiv* in the work] (emphasis in the original).

12. Myra Jehlin, "Gender," *Critical Terms for Literary Study*, eds. Frank Lentricchia and Thomas McLaughlin (Chicago: University of Chicago Press, 1990), 273.

13. A study of Valle-Inclán's development as a writer vis-à-vis contemporary intellectual history is yet to be written, and much of the work that exists, discusses his thinking either in relation to earlier phenomena such as theosophism, or in terms of Hispanic literature and society (the Generation of '98 and "modernismo"). At present, the best-documented source for an understanding of his awareness of contemporary national and international currents and events is Dru Dougherty's collection of interviews and comments (*Un Valle-Inclán olvidado* [Madrid: Espiral Fundamentos, 1982]).

14. Gretchen Gregoria Holbert, "Who Is Laureaniño? An Analysis of the Protagonist of *Divinas palabras*" (Master's thesis, University of Nevada, Reno, 1984). Although he does not call Laureano the protagonist, Gustavo Umpierre also refers to him as "el personaje más singular" (*"Divinas palabras": Alusión y alegoría* [Chapel Hill, N.C.: Estudios de Hispanófila 18, 1971]), 17.

15. José G. Escribano too notes this resemblance, although without exploring it in "Estudio Sobre *Divinas palabras*" (*Cuadernos Hispanoamericanos* 273 [1973]: 560). As will be suggested, the resemblance between the two men is that of a dark, sinful nature, linked with their individual ties to lust and death.

16. Escribano, *Cuadernos Hispanoamericanos,* 556; Josette Blanquat, "Symbolisme et "esperpento" dans *Divinas palabras,*" in *Mélanges à la mémoire de Jean Sarrailh,* vol. 1 (Paris: Centre de Reherches de l'Institut d'Études Hispaniques, 1966), 148.

17. "Un sapo anónimo que canta en la noche" [An anonymous toad that sings in the night] is listed as one of the characters in the play.

18. For a discussion of "mal de ojo" with respect to Galicia, see Jesús Rodríguez López, *Supersticiones de Galicia y preocupaciones vulgares* (Lugo: Ediciones Celta, 1971), 197–204.

19. Mari-Gaila is married to Pedro Gailo but, as Venus, she shares the "star" of Séptimo Miau-Lucero (See Umpierre, *"Divinas palabras,"* 16, for a discussion of the relation between Lucifer and Venus-Astarte).

20. It is after Pedro's reception of her (the extinguishing of a candle over the hands she has crossed in front of her sex and the striking of her hands with his missal), and his accompaniment of her into the church, that Mari-Gaila steps over death and sees the transformed head of Laureano.

21. It is important that, although Marica suggests several lines above that Pedro might lose his "astas" ["horns"], Valle-Inclán made that loss explicit for publication in 1920, adding Quintín Pintado's line (final installment [no. 26] of *Divinas palabras,* published in *El Sol* (Madrid), 14 July 1919.

22. Leda Schiavo also notes this use of a "decadent" Latin in *Divinas palabras,* in her edition of the play (Barcelona: Círculo de Lectores, 1990), 27.

23. Her companions give the idiot his last drink, but Mari-Gaila abandoned him. She was also the first to offer him liquor and to encourage him to perform tricks (I, v).

24. Or, as Tine Barrass has written more recently, "It was the general complaint of Spanish authors in the early sixteenth century that the fact that the Castilian language was relatively undeveloped was due to the lack of 'modern classics' of the stature of Dante, Boccaccio, and Petrarch" ("The Function of Translated Literature within a National Literature: The Example of Sixteenth-Century Spain," 183).

25. See Dru Dougherty, *Valle-Inclán y la Segunda República* (Valencia: Pre-Textos, 1986), for a discussion of Valle-Inclán's concept of medieval Spain in the context of the Second Republic.

26. See John Lyon's *The Theatre of Valle-Inclán* (London: Cambridge University Press, 1983), 92, for a concise summary of this perceived aporia on the part of Valle-Inclán's critics.

27. John Crispin, "The Ironic Manichaean Battle in *Divinas palabras,*" *ALEC* 7, no. 2 (1982): 189–200.

28. Escribano, "Estudio sobre *Divinas palabras,*" 556.

29. Blanquat, "Symbolisme et 'esperpento'"; Holbert, "Who Is Laureaniño?"

Umpierre, *"Divinas palabras"*; Manuel Bermejo Marcos, *Valle-Inclán: Introducción a su obra* (Salamanca: Anaya, 1971).

30. Holbert's work ("Who Is Laureaniño?") is provocative in this regard because of her explanation of Laureano as the protagonist of *Divinas palabras*. It would be hard to "build" on that work, however, because I find her assumption unconvincing. Despite the eloquence with which she describes Laureano as a Christ figure, I am not persuaded that he is in fact the "Christ" at the play's "center." I would certainly agree that Laureano is an "'esperpentic' image of Christ the Savior" (40), but I would qualify my agreement by pointing to his displacement from the "center" of the play's argument, by stressing Mari-Gaila's Christ-like trajectory, and by emphasizing the highy equivocal nature of any redemption that might arise from the language in *Divinas palabras*.

31. A bond, I might add, that does not prove to be the "illustration" John Lyon fears when he discusses the danger of interpreting *Divinas palabras* in terms of *La lámpara maravillosa* (*The Theatre of Valle-Inclán*, 94).

32. Sarduy, "Sobre Góngora: La metáfora al cuadrado" (*Escrito sobre un cuerpo*), 55–61; "Góngora: Squaring Metaphor" (*Written on a Body*), 45–48.

33. Letter from Valle-Inclán to Giménez Caballero, 15 February 1972. Reprinted in José Esteban, *Valle-Inclán visto por . . .* (Madrid: Editorial Gráficas Espejo, 1973), 343.

34. In this "self-portrait" Valle-Inclán performs a role similar to that of the poet-adventurer who narrates the opening chapter of *La lámpara maravillosa* (AG, I) and who later tells of digging a grave in which to bury "esta hueca y pomposa prosa castiza" [this hollow, pompous Castilian prose] (MM, VI).

35. Although I will develop this suggestion elsewhere, I believe it is important to note at least in passing the close resemblance between the metaphorization discussed here and what Valle-Inclán apparently thought of as "allegory" (PS, IV), in a way not unlike that Carlos J. Alonso and the critics he cites have discussed recently with respect to Rómulo Gallego's *Doña Bárbara* ("'Otra sería mi historia': Allegorical Exhaustion in *Doña Bárbara*," *MLN* 104, no. 2 [1989]: 418–38).

36. About that staging, see Dougherty, *Valle-Inclán y la Segunda República*, 128–31.

37. Gustavo Pérez Firmat, "Circulation," in *Literature and Liminality: Festive Readings in the Hispanic Tradition* (Durham, N.C.: Duke University Press, 1986), 32–49. José Zorrilla's *Don Juan Tenorio* is cited and discussed by Pérez Firmat as a single model for *Galas*. It is interesting to note that Valle-Inclán seems close here to Sarduy's *choteo-doblaje* in "Dispersión (Falsas notas/Homenaje a Lezama)," in *Escrito sobre un cuerpo*, 61–89—a possibility that Pérez Firmat has either not recognized or chosen to ignore as an element of his own "choteo."

38. As I was preparing the final version of this essay, I had the opportunity to read Stephen M. Hart's recent article, "A Tale of Two Genres: Puppet Show and Calderonian Honor Play in *Los cuernos de don Friolera* and *Amor de don Perplimplín*," in which he demonstrates how Valle-Inclán's "rewriting" undermines the way the "Law of the land and the Law of literature have colluded in an exclusive gesture which banishes the discourse of the Quotidian" (*Golden Age Spanish Literature: Studies in Honour of John Varey by His Colleagues and Pupils*, eds. Charles Davis and Alan Deyermond [London: Westfield College, 1991]), 107. Hart's work argued in terms of gender and the Lacanian Name of the Father, confirms the ambitiousness I have long believed motivated Valle-Inclán's parodies (and which I discussed, e.g., in "Valle-Inclán Reads Calderón

de la Barca: Aspects of Parody and Homage in *Los cuernos de don Friolera*" (paper delivered at the Congreso Internacional en Honor a don Pedro Calderón de la Barca, Lincoln, Neb., 17 October 1981).

39. Blanquat, "Symbolisme et 'esperpento'," 145.

40. Ibid., 147–49; David Ling, "Greed, Lust, and Death in Valle-Inclán's *Divinas palabras*," *Modern Language Review* 67 (1972): 336.

41. See n. 78.

42. Phyllis Zatlin Boring, "More on Parody in Valle-Inclán," *Romance Notes* 15, no. 2 (1974).

43. Umpierre, *"Divinas palabras": Alusión y alegoría*, 22–24; Carlos Jerez-Farrán, "Séptimo Miau y Ginés de Pasamonte: Un caso de duplicidad biográfica cervantina en *Divinas palabras* de Valle-Inclán," *Revista Hispánica Moderna*, Nueva Epoca 61, no. 2 (1988): 91–104.

44. Umpierre, *"Divinas palabras": Alusión y alegoría*, 21.

45. Alfred Rodríguez, "Un posible modelo paródico de *Divinas palabras*," *Explicación de Textos Literarios* 14, no. 2 (1985–86): 83–87.

46. Escribano, "Estudio sobre *Divinas palabras*," 560–62.

47. Emilio González López, "Valle-Inclán y la Pardo Bazán: *Divinas palabras* y "El tetrarca en la aldea," *Grial* 20 (1968): 212–16.

48. Umpierre, *"Divinas palabras:* Alusión y alegoría," 24–27.

49. Ibid., 44; Blanquat, "Symbolisme et 'esperpento'," 160.

50. The suggestion Rodríguez makes of a link between *Divinas palabras* and *La adúltera penitente,* for example, makes one think of other possible "reverberations" of Martínez Sierra's work in Valle-Inclán's play. To cite just one possible echo, in which Martínez Sierra refers to World War I, that would be worth pursuing: "Ahora mismo, en esta desolada tragedia sin sentido que, lanzado pueblos contra pueblos, como inmensos rebaños irresponsables, amenaza acabar con la vida de Europa, los hombres arrastrados por bellas palabras embusteras que disfrazan muy mal los impulsos hediondos de rastería, rapacidad, tiranía y plutocracía, se matan, se mutilan, se destruyen desesperadamente. . . . Todas las conquistas del entendimiento sobre la materia se han puesto al servicie de la muerte; todas las artes de la paz se han trocado en negros artificios para la guerra. . . . Tú mujer, ¿qué haces entretanto, y que debes hacer?" [Now, in this grievous, meaningless tragedy, in which nations are pitted against nations like immense irresponsible flocks, and the life of Europe is threatened, dragged along by beautiful, deceitful words that disguise poorly rotten motives of theft, greed, tyranny, and plutocracy, men kill, mutilate, and destroy each other in desperation. . . . All the victories that understanding has won over matter have been placed at the service of death; all the arts of peace have turned into the black artifice of war. . . . You, woman, what are you doing through all this, and what should you do?] (*Feminismo, feminidad, españolismo* (Madrid: Renacimiento, 1917), 50–51.

51. Or, as Castelao explained so eloquently, Valle-Inclán wrote little in Galician, but "su romance maravilloso es el resultado de traducir literalmente del gallego al castellano" [his wonderful language is the result of translating literally from Galician to Castilian], *Galicia y Valle-Inclán* (1939; reprint, Lugo: Ediciones Celta, 1971), 36. I am grateful to Leda Schiavo's "Valle-Inclán, modelo para armar" for reminding me of this passage (*Quimera* 72 [1988], 28).

52. Compare, for example, William J. Smither's comments about the location of *Divinas palabras* (*El mundo gallego de Valle-Inclán: Estudio de toponimia e indicaciones localizantes en las obras gallegas* [A Coruña: Ediciós do Castro,

1984], 53–56) with those of José Caamaño Bournacell (*Por las rutas turísticas de Valle-Inclán* [Madrid: Gráficas Valencia, 1971], 100.

53. Valle-Inclán's use of "ideología" here deserves a study in itself. It is important to note, however, that, in addition to underlining the irony of this passage in *La lámpara maravillosa* (which contradicts what it says) and echoing other statements by Valle-Inclán about the "content" of words (e.g., *modernismo*), *ideología* as used here could be said to "anticipate" its use as "the indispensible practice—including the 'systems of representation' that are its products and supports—through which individuals of different class, race, and sex are worked into a particular 'lived relation' to a social-historical project" (James H. Kavanagh, in *Critical Terms for Literary Study,* 319.

54. The lemon seller's comments about Carolina de Otero, for example (II. iii).

55. Several other characters, like the *peregrino,* also evoke Valle-Inclán's preoccupation with poetics, but in a more general way.

56. He is not listed in the cast of characters.

57. See Jacques Fressard, "De Ernesto Bark à Basilio Soulinake: Retour et métamorphose d'un personnage de *Valle-Inclán,*" *Iris* (Université Paul Valéry, Montpellier) 2 (1985): 41–52.

58. Ling, "Greed, Lust, and Death," 333.

59. Lyon also notes this resemblance between "Séptimo's fortune-telling ideas" and "the idea of Satan in *La lámpara maravillosa* (93), and Umpierre stresses Séptimo Miau's Luciferian nature throughout his study.

60. Umpierre also comments on this passage, although he does not acknowledge either the ambivalence of Venus or the possibility that the qualities associated with her may be manifested ambivalently in Mari-Gaila. "Frutos y licencias" [Fruits and licentiousness] are, for him "dos principios que revelan las principales funciones de la Mujer, como madre y como amante" ["two principles that reveal Woman's primary roles as mother and lover"].

For a discussion of Venus as a turn-of-the-century figure, see Noël M. Valis, "The Female Figure and Writing in *Fin del siglo* Spain," *Romance Quarterly* 36, no. 3 (1989), who, citing Eric Neumann, observes that "Venus as an archetype has always been seen as an ambivalent figure of fertility and destructiveness. . . . For many, Venus was simply a euphemism for prostitute" (374). See also Neumann's comments about the Terrible Mother ("The Negative Elementary Character") and about Ceres, Demeter, Kore, and Persephone, *The Great Mother,* trans. Ralph Manheim [1955; reprint (Princeton: Princeton University Press, 1972)].

Traditional commentary on both Venus and Ceres reinforces this ambivalence with respect to Mari-Gaila. Ceres, for example, is usually discussed in conjunction with Persephone and their close bonding as mother and daughter. Mari-Gaila also has a daughter, but they are hardly similar ("La madre, blanca y rubia, risueña de ojos, . . . la hija, abobada, lechosa, redonda con algo de luna, de vaca y de pan" ["the mother, white and blond, her eyes smiling, . . . the daughter, stupid-looking, milky, plump, reminiscent of the moon, cows, and bread"] (I. iii). Woman bond only in the most negative way in *Divinas palabras,* as "hijas de la serpiente" ["daughters of the serpent"] (II, i).

61. Although his comments refer principally to Renaissance English, Richard Stallybrass's discussion of Renaissance surveillance of women comes to mind here ("Patriarchal Territories: The Body Enclosed," in *Rewriting the Renaissance: The Discourses of Sexual Difference in Early Modern Europe,* eds. Margaret W. Ferguson, Maureen Quilligan, and Nancy J. Vickers [Chicago: University of Chicago Press: 1986]), in particular his observations about the "connection

between speaking and wantonness" (126), which meant that "the signs of the 'harlot' are her linguistic 'fullness' and her frequenting of public space" (127). See also 128.

62. Carlos Jerez-Farrán praises her in "Mari-Gaila y la espiritualización de la materia: Una revaloración de *Divinas palabras* de Valle-Inclán," *Neophilologus* 76 (1992): 392–408. Sumner Greenfield (*Valle-Inclán: Anatomía de un teatro problemático* [Madrid: Fundamentos, 1972], 157); and Anthony N. Zahareas (ed. *Teatro selecto de Valle-Inclán* [New York: Las Américas, 1969], 57) refer to her as an adultress—Zahareas even declares that "es adúltera de verdad" [she is a real adultress].

63. Umpierre, *"Divinas palabras": alusión y alegoría,* 17.

64. Blanquat, "Symbolisme et 'esperpento,'" 146.

65. Lyon, *Theatre of Valle-Inclán,* 94.

66. Leda Schiavo, Introducción, *Divinas palabras,* 29.

67. See, for example, Pamela Berger, *The Goddess Obscured: Transformations of the Grain Protectress from Goddess to Saint* (Boston: Beacon Press, 1985), esp. 31ff.; and Marina Warner, *Alone of All Her Sex: The Myth and the Cult of the Virgin Mary* (New York: Knopf, 1976), 87, 143. Despite the dissimilarity between Mari-Gaila and Simoniña just noted, there is perhaps something of Persephone in Simoniña. She is not carried off by Hades, but she does have to ward off her own father, who would carry her to "hell."

68. For my information about La Franqueira, I am indebted to conversations with Xosé Conde Corbal and Amalia Magán and to P. Martín Brugarola, "La romería de Nuestra Señora de Franqueira," *Revista de Dialectología y Tradiciones Populares* 14 (1958): 507–14.

69. "Serenín de Bretal, que como un patriarca hace la siega del trigo con los hijos y nietos, . . ." [Serenín de Bretal, who is harvesting wheat with his sons and grandsons like a patriarch, . . . (III. iv)].

70. Umpierre, *"Divinas palabras": alusión y alegoría,* 44; and Blanquat, "Symbolisme et 'esperpento,'" 160–61.

71. Not only with respect to his pronouncement of the "divine words" or *La lámpara maravillosa*'s "musical miracle," but also his leap from the tower when he sees Mari-Gaila approaching on the hay cart. ("As a young man, when assailed by sexual desire at the sight of beautiful women, he [Saint Bernard] threw himself into a half-frozen pond." [J. C. J. Metford, *Dictionary of Christian Lore and Legend* (London: Thames and Hudson, 1983), 48].

72. Warner, *Alone of All Her Sex,* 129.

73. Antonio Buero Vallejo also stresses that only Mari-Gaila and the author see the transformed head of Laureano, "De rodillas, en pie, en el aire," *Tres maestros ante el público* [1966; reprint (Madrid: Alianza, 1973)], 43.

74. The description in II, vii, for example, of Laureano as he died, his enormous head rolling as if it had been severed ("cortada").

75. "¡Si por vuestra culpa malparo, a la cárcel os llevo!" ["If I miscarry because of you, I'll take you all to jail!"] (III. iv). This line was not in the original version of *Divinas palabras* published in *El Sol* in 1919.

76. Blanquat, for one, says it is not: "Symbolisme et 'esperpento,'" 162.

77. A point of departure for future work will be "Mari-Gaila, un personaje andrógino de Valle-Inclán," a paper read by Adelaida López de Martínez at the MLA convention, Chicago, 28 December, 1990. I also want to note here an essay by Jean Andrews that I read well after this study was completed ("Saints and Strumpets: Female Stereotypes in Valle-Inclán," in *Feminist Readings on Spanish*

and Latin-American Literature, eds. L. P. Condé and S. M. Hart [Lewiston, N.Y.: The Edwin Mellen Press, 1991], 27–35). Andrews also discusses Valle-Inclán's androgynous rose with respect to feminist aesthetics, in particular Hélène Cixous's "écriture féminine," and she suggests that the freedom enjoyed by Mari-Gaila may place her in Cixous's "realm of the gift" rather than the "phallocentric realm of the proper," in which Valle-Inclán's earlier work would be situated (34).

78. The reference is to scene 11 in *Luces de Bohemia,* first published in 1920. I owe the translation of "mascando ortigas" to Anthony N. Zahareas and Gerald Gillespie, trans., *Bohemian Lights* (Austin: University of Texas Press, 1976), 180.

79. I have referred to this dual representation in "*La lámpara maravillosa* de Valle-Inclán y la invención continua como una estética constante," in *Actas del VIII Congreso de la Asociación Internacional de Hispanistas,* ed. A. David Kossoff, Jose Amor y Vázquez, Ruth H. Kossoff, and Geoffrey W. Ribbans, vol. 2 (Madrid: Ediciones Istmo, 1986), 242. For a discussion of Valle-Inclán's female masking in *La lámpara maravillosa* and the ambivalent redemption offered through a naked female reminiscent of the "triads" found in several paintings by Valle-Inclán's friend Julio Romero de Torres, see my article, "De cifras, desciframiento, y una lectura literal de *La lámpara maravillosa,*" in *Suma Valleinclaniana: Homenaje a Emma Susana Speratti-Piñero,* ed. John P. Gabriele (Madrid: Anthropos, 1992), 233–49.

Hart's comment that the play's female protagonist and the text itself commit a similar "infidelity in respect to the Author text" is very provocative in this context ("A Tale of Two Genres," 108).

80. Jerez-Farrán, "Mari-Gaila y la espiritualización de la material," 393. I am grateful to Prof. Jerez-Farrán for allowing me to read this essay before its publication.

81. Walter Benjamin, "Central Park," trans. Lloyd Spencer, *New German Critique,* 34 (1985), 53 (sec. 41). See also secs. 21 and 23. I am grateful to Christine Buci-Glucksman's "Catastrophic Utopia: The Feminine as Allegory of the Modern" for acquainting me with "Central Park" (*The Making of the Modern Body: Sexuality and Society in the Nineteenth Century,* eds. Catherine Gallagher and Thomas Laqueur (Berkeley: University of California Press, 1987): 220–29. Rita Felski makes the gender of the reader even more explicit in this instance ("The Counterdiscourse of the Feminine in Three Texts by Wilde, Huysmans, and Sacher-Masoch," *PMLA* 106, no. 5 (1991): 1094–1105.

82. Sabelita in *Aguila de blasón* (1907), for example, or Sini in *La hija del capitán* (1927).

83. Margaret R. Miles, *Carnal Knowing: Female Nakedness and Religious Meaning in the Christian West* (1989; reprint, New York: Vintage, 1991).

84. It is interesting to note here that Biruté Ciplijauskaité has commented that Valle-Inclán's early female protagonists "son más ricas en silencios que en palabras" [have been endowed with more silences than words] and has discussed the difference that separates them from the characters today's female readers find satisfying. Essay in this volume.

85. Gayatri Chakravorty Spivak, "Displacement and the Discourse of Women," in *Displacement, Derrida and After,* ed. Mark Krupnick (Bloomington: Indiana University Press, 1983), 191.

86. It is possible to say with certainty, however, that Valle-Inclán could have been familiar with the *Guía,* through the edition that Rafael Urbano published in Barcelona in 1906, or through Urbano's publication of selections of it in *Sophia* the preceding year.

87. Miguel de Molinos, *Guía espiritual: Defensa de la contemplación,* ed. José Angel Valente (Barcelona: Barral Editores, 1974), 159.

88. See Iris Zavala's *La musa funambulesca. Poetica de la carnavalización en Valle-Inclán* (Madrid: Orígenes, 1990), for the best discussion to date of voice and intent in Valle-Inclán's work.

89. In addition to Hart's comments on this countering with respect to *Los cuernos de don Friolera* ("A Tale of Two Genres"), see Frank P. Casa's remarks on the staging of *Divinas palabras* in celebration of the twenty-fifth anniversary of Valle-Inclán's death (1971), when "it was considered necessary to employ a famous writer, Gonzalo Torrente Ballester, to remove the more equivocal words and situations" ("The Assimilation of Ramón del Valle-Inclán's Dramas into Contemporary Spanish Theater," in *The Contemporary Spanish Theater: A Collection of Critical Essays,* eds. Martha T. Halsey and Phyllis Zatlin (Lanhan, Md.: University Press of America, 1989), 168.

With This Ring: Woman as "Revolutionary Inseparable" in Goya's *Caprichos* and Valle-Inclán's *Tirano Banderas*

C. CHRISTOPHER SOUFAS, JR.

Since male authors and artists tend to revalidate patriarchal preju-dices in their representations rather than to acknowledge or ques-tion them,[1] it is significant to encounter in the hierarchical Hispanic milieus portrayed in Goya's *Caprichos* [*The Caprices*] and Valle-Inclán's *Tirano Banderas* [*The Tyrant, A Novel of Warm Lands*] that critiques of cultural conflicts are exposed in terms of infelici-tous gender dynamics.[2] Although separated by more than a cen-tury, both works offer a vision of culture as a sexual dialectic reflective of an instability inherent in inflexible ideologico-cultural systems incapable of positive change and thus susceptible to sub-version.[3] Goya and Valle-Inclán juxtapose a more irrational mode of representation (a characteristic also frequently associated with female stereotypes) to an empirically based aesthetic—neoclassi-cism in Goya's case, realism in Valle-Inclán's—in order to manufac-ture what may be called an unhappy artistic "marriage." The authority and values of the dominant patriarchal order are under-mined by a subversive counterpoint, an inseparable feminine sphere of influence that weds the ideological dilemmas of these societies to a vision of the way men and women deal with each other.

The unhappy wedding motif is central to *Los caprichos* and re-flective of the even deeper ambivalence of Goya the artist and person in the elaboration of this series of eighty engravings. The two self-portraits (nos. 1 and 43) clearly suggest a dual focus. Plate 43, the renowned "el sueño de la razón produce monstruos" ["The Sleep/Dream of Reason Produces Monsters"], features, at his drawing desk and surrounded by creatures capable of seeing in the darkness, an unconscious Goya no longer a disciple of Reason and its light-bound, empiricist values and thus on the verge of a new and independent imaginative sensibility.[4] Plate 1 ("Francisco Goya y Lucientes, pintor") portrays a much different Goya, a respectable middle-class citizen, aging, overweight, and somewhat weary, perhaps a consequence of the personal experiences associated with the profession he proclaims in the caption, *pintor*—painter of the patriarchs of Spanish high society—and not the less prestigious avocation of engraver. Beginning with what appears to be a condemnation of contemporary societal vices, the images cede after plate 43 to a long series of irrational evocations of an underworld of witches and monsters.

Of central importance in *Los caprichos* is how best to read the series of visual-verbal episodes that represent the artist's vision of contemporary culture. A temporally numerically elaborated sequence of signification (1–80) is appropriate only if the participation of the conscious will is to be considered an integral factor in the production of meaning, something noticeably absent from *Los caprichos* and often exacerbated by the ambivalence of the captions, thus further enhancing the idea that these images are the monstrous products of dreams and not imitations of directly observed reality. To understand these images more fully requires that the viewer also learn to read, as the foolish old aristocrat in "Esto si que es leer" ["This Is Really Reading," no. 29], with eyes closed to the book in front of him and thus also to empirical reality that, like the creatures in number 43 who see in the darkness, is yet open to the "sueño de la razón" in which the artist's consciousness plays no part. That such a sleep and dream of reason leads the reader-viewer in two contradictory directions suggests that the reading process itself should proceed in a like manner. If one possible reading sequence proceeds as one would read a traditional book from the first image, that of Goya awake, an alternative is provided by reading in the opposite direction, from the second self-portrait, the sleeping artist (no. 43), to the beginning and back again, that is, from numbers 42–2 and from 80–44.[5]

Reading in traditional fashion with the eyes open, one can indeed interpret *Los caprichos* as an exposé of the irrational vices of society. Reading with the eyes closed (i.e., with the eyes of the imagination), one can make an equally strong case for *Los caprichos* as an investigation of Goya's personal obsessions during this time in his life. Even a superficial glance at the caprichos reveals that only a few are devoted to specifically political problems. What they really expose are the vicissitudes of male-female relationships and the consequences of excessive sexual passion. Since the only two figures clearly drawn from nature in *Los ca-*

prichos are Goya himself and the Duchess of Alba, invoked in numbers 19 and 61, it is likely that a great many of the images originate as the involuntary memories of a love affair between an aging Goya and a much younger woman.[6] As an examination of Goya's attitude toward his own recent past, the emphasis in *Los caprichos* is on gender issues, the ways men and women treat each other. Any universalist inference that Goya's goal is to strengthen the patriarchal system via the advocacy of rationalist reforms is possible only by reading *Los caprichos* as a traditional book.[7] Such a reading denies the possibility that they instead originate in the tormented functioning of an actual psyche, the thinking subject Francisco de Goya, beset, obsessed, yet also stimulated artistically by the less than rational memory of the past, the personification of which is the Duchess of Alba. Leaving aside the satiric politicoartistic allegories of numbers 37–42, *Los caprichos* is comprised of two long sequences of 35 (nos. 2–36) and 37 (nos. 44–80), respectively, each with an image of the Duchess of Alba at the approximate mathematical center, numbers 19 and 61. The fact that these numerals are upside-down mirror images of each other, that their sum is equal to the number of engravings in the series, and that in both of her representations Alba is strongly associated with violent, cataclysmic change and flight, suggests the idea of a counteraxis and countermovement and that a force alien to a conscious intention to produce societal satires (the bourgeois Goya of no. 1) is also at work here.[8]

The order in which these images are read makes all the difference—for example, a sequence from 2 to 36 or from 36 to 2—for they either culminate in the defeat, or in the consolidation, of female power. As prostitutes, women are most susceptible to having "bad nights," as depicted in number 36, "Mala noche" ["Bad Night"]. If married, men become their victims, as in number 2, "El sí pronuncian y la mano alargan al primero que llega" ["They Say Yes and Give Their Hands to the First Passer-By"], which depicts a masked woman who has conveniently married an old man and who openly displays her inconstancy even at the moment of her wedding vows. All relationships in society seem in fact to operate on a victim-victimizer paradigm. The female practitioners of witchcraft whose rituals are dedicated to the usurpation of male power, an essential ingredient of which is the teeth of hanged men (no. 12, "A caza de dientes" ["Hunting Teeth"]), fall victim to an equally superstitious patriarchal institution, the Inquisition (nos. 23 and 24). Overt references to the relationship of these scenes to the overall functioning of society are infrequent but explicit, as in number 13, "Están calientes" ["They Are Hot"], where toothless monks overcompensate for the absence of sex in their lives by the consumption of hot food, and in number 33 where an aristocratic dentist, in a fashion similar to the witch in number 12, plucks teeth from live subjects who apparently volunteer for such humiliation. One's place in society and the power of institutions seem to depend upon how well sexual desires can be channeled into other activities. Differences among men, women, and institutions are traceable in the degree to which sexual passion is or is not allowed to have a role. In number 30, "Porque esconderlas?" ["Why Hide Them?"], for example, the explicit suggestion is that the wrinkled old man's accumulation of wealth has been gained at the expense of sexual experiences for which he is now, in decrepitude, tempted to spend his fortune.

At the heart of these scenes of public posturing of lovers and the seamy underworld of Madrid prostitutes is Goya's allegory of his own victimization at the hands of the Duchess of Alba in number 19, "Todos caerán" ["All Will Fall"]. She is pictured here as a Goddess Fortuna-bird of prey that has lured any number of men-birds—of the same substance and thus no better than she—to their ruin.[9] The head of the bird-man closest to her is clearly that of Goya. More important than his victimization, however, is that Goya acknowledges his own behavior as the basis for making the more universal claim that all will fall. Indeed, all the male and female protagonists of these engravings could well be stand-ins for Goya and the Duchess of Alba. López Rey[10] and others have correctly observed the likeness of the poses of a number of the women in *Los caprichos* to sketches made of the Duchess of Alba in the *Sanlucar Notebooks,* especially the exposed calf of the prostitute in number 17, "Bien tirada está," which has been variously translated as "It Is Well-Tied," in reference to the stocking she is pulling up, or, in ironic reference to the frequency with which she performs her services, as "She Has Been Well-Tried." Yet as a personal reference to a remembrance of a similar pose by the Duchess, the caption can also be translated, "It Is Well-Implanted," in reference to the obsessive images that her memory has supplied Goya's imagination.

These self-referential moments enhance the idea that Goya's images do not represent a direct observation of reality. Rather, they are dominated by an obsessive memory that, in conjunction with the imagination, functions to produce images grounded only in the interchange between these two internal faculties. Reading with the eyes "closed," from the "mala noche" of the prostitute in number

36 to number 2 ("El sí dicen y la mano alargan al primero que llega"), one also finds the story of the Duchess of Alba and Goya. The first "passer-by" to meet the inconstant young woman-Duchess was Goya himself, in number 1, "Francisco Goya y Lucientes, pintor," a composite rich old man and "young" lover whose caprichos are the testimony of his failure in love and his equal failure to free himself of an imaginative obsession. Goya's use of his mother's name may thus also be a subtle acknowledgment of his present inability to sign his name as in the earlier celebrated portrait of the Duchess of Alba in which he portrays her wearing a ring that bears the name "Goya" on a finger that points to the words "Sólo Goya" written in the sand beside her feet. His present inability to be "only Goya" signals a reversal of fortune and the equal recognition that there are powerful counterforces working within his soul. He and his artistic vision are personally subject to a countercurrent explicitly associated with female power from which he cannot extricate himself. The themes of dependency and bondage are more explicit in the numerous plates chronicling the activities of a matriarchal society of witches but especially in the image of frustrated immobility in number 75, "¿No hay quien nos desate?" ["Is There No One to Untie Us?"], which depicts a man and a woman bound together at the waist.

The untenable relationship in which these engravings are inspired has also produced an aberrant mental condition dominated by the persistent memory of one woman. As a journey ever more deeply into the darkness of the human soul rather than as a progression toward the light of a new day and the triumph of the rational faculties (the traditional reading offered by most art historians), these images evince a progressively greater degree of autonomy from empirical reality. At the heart of this pilgrimage-voyage of witches and goblins is number 61, "Volaverunt," which depicts the bewitching Dutches of Alba flying over a trio of Fate-like witches who support her. These Fates also appear in number 44, "Hilan delgado" ["They Weave Finely"], to suggest that the thread that binds these images together is thinner perhaps than even that woven by the grotesque version of the classical Fates represented here. As the cluster of unborn babies suspended in midair by these weavers emphasizes, human autonomy does not exist at any time. The theater of the human mind is a puppet theater, the only difference between life and theater being the visibility or invisibility of the threads that bind it together and thus give it the illusion of rationality and coherent meaning.

In the final analysis, Goya is critiquing a fundamental patriarchal tenet, the notion of the rational thinking subject, as he also harkens back to the medieval notion of the Great Chain of Being. *Los caprichos* is, in a sense, a perverse version of a Great Chain of Being that leads not to the Rational Father of the Enlightenment, but back to a single obsessive consciousness whose production of images is unified only by the contradictory truth that names its own open-ended essence. "El sueño de la razón produce monstruos." The caprichos originate and exist in the space between the two self-portraits which in turn frame the time of the sleep and dream of reason: the time between the closing of the eyes to the images of empirical experience and the opening of the eyes of the imagination. Goya's vision of the forces at work simultaneously in society and his tormented soul are instructive with regard to a reading of *Tirano Banderas* that more than a century later confronts a similar set of aesthetic-ideological givens. In *Los caprichos* Goya weds his vision of an impotent patriarchal order to an active, destabilizing counterforce identified with feminine power that subversively undermines rational intentions and affirmations. Instead of exposing society's faults, however, Goya exposes himself and the negative revelation that men and women do not simply fall asleep to Reason, they self-destructively embrace Unreason. The tormenting image of the witch-temptress Duchess of Alba that obsesses Goya's imagination exerts power, therefore, as an inseparable part of the social-psychic milieu in which it resides and which, paradoxically, it is also helping to destroy.

In *Tirano Banderas* Valle-Inclán represents a cycle of revolution, the decisive impetus for the consumation of which is the unwitting subversion of one woman, Doña Lupita (also unwittingly assisted at a later point by another Lupita, later called "la Romántica"), who sets in motion unforeseen happenings that ultimately bring destruction upon the Banderas regime and herself. Her long-standing relationship with Banderas epitomizes the structural "weddedness" that prevails among the constituents of Tierra Caliente and that has weakened and destabilized the succession of political regimes that have attempted unsuccessfully to govern it. If Goya's vision of society is shaped by an obsessive memory from which he cannot disassociate his rational faculties, Valle-Inclán's is ordered around the forgetfulness and displacement from the mainstream of history of a culture that as a consequence has trivialized itself to the point of immobility. As in *Los caprichos,* the primary conflict in *Tirano Banderas,* at both the ideological and personal levels, is between the forces of "reason," or "science," ironically associated with the Coronelito de la Gándara, and the less than rational prac-

tices such as the special powers of "adivination" ascribed to Lupita
la Romántica and, more significantly, the private denunciations in
which Doña Lupita engages that typify the unpredictable workings
of the Banderas machine.[11] The Coronelito de la Gándara correctly
stresses to the revolutionary leaders to whom he defects that he
is not simply a soldier but rather "un científico" ["a scientist"][12]
and, invoking the high empiricist rhetoric of the nineteenth and
early twentieth centuries, asserts that "[l]a guerra es una técnica
científica" ["war is a scientific technique"] (11). It is principally
by means of this repressive "science" that the Banderas regime
has functioned at all. Indeed, in reaction to a suggestion by the
Cuerpo Diplomático that the sale of alcohol be suspended to the natives, the Dictator is quick to recognize how untenable his rule
would become if the masses were allowed to come to their rational and sober senses. "[S]i tal hiciese, sobrevendría un motín de
la plebe" ["If I were to do that, there would be an uprising by the
masses"] (253).

Ironically, it is Doña Lupita's beverage establishment and Gándara's breaking of "cuatro copas" ["four glasses"] (241) there while
drunk, that start an unlikely chain of events which ultimately leads
to Banderas's undoing. Indeed, the order to arrest Gándara on
trivial charges at Doña Lupita's insistence seems to defy all rationality. It immediately forces Gándara into the camp of the revolutionaries where he quickly becomes prominent and in a position
to advance himself. Indeed, Banderas understands that the cause
of his overthrow will not result from a failure in social or economic
policy, but as the direct consequence of his acceding to the demands of a woman whose only official complaint was that Gándara
had broken a few glasses for which he would not pay.

> Por mero la cachiza de cuatro copas, un puro trastorno habéis vos
> traído a la República. . . . Doña Lupita, por menos de un boliviano me
> lo habéis puesto en la bola revolucionaria! Doña Lupita, la deuda de
> justicia que vos me habéis reclamado ha sido una madeja de circunstan-
> cias fatales: Es causa primordial en la actuación rebelde del Coronel
> de la Gándara (241).

> For the sake of four glasses, you have brought pure confusion to the
> Republic. . . . Doña Lupita, for less than a *boliviano* you've put him
> in the revolutionary camp! Doña Lupita, the debt of justice that you
> have demanded from me has been a web of fatal circumstances: it is
> the primordial cause for the rebellion of Coronel de la Gándara.

Indeed, the ex-compadre Gándara, who before the decisive battle of the revolution rushes onto the field "sobre un buen caballo" ["on a good horse"] (270), may well emerge in the collective imagination of Tierra Caliente as one who "encauce las fuerzas vitales del país" ["guides the vital forces of the country"] (21) to become the next strongman of Tierra Caliente. Thus, as Gándara defeats his political "father" and betrayer, and his female denouncer, he also assures the reestablishment of the patriarchal values that invariably accompany such "hombres providenciales" ["providential men"] (21). As experience proves in the case of Banderas, they are only laying the groundwork for the very type of subversion that proves fatal to the fallen patriarch. The novel's greatest irony, that the balance of power shifts to the rebels because of one woman's trivial complaint, underscores the triviality of most of the novel's content which in turn exposes the precariousness and fragility of a society that can never free itself from the "madeja de circunstancias fatales" ensuing as the consequence of an inconsequential "causa primordial." The allusion, via Banderas, to a philosophical first-cause tradition, therefore, only enhances the pathetic absurdity of what is nevertheless a correct explanation of the "cause" that has produced such catastrophic "effects."[13]

Gándara's drunken behavior is clearly a pretext and not the motive for Banderas to order his arrest. The real reason is the longevity of his special relationship with Doña Lupita, for over fifty years a camp follower and trusted informer, and the distrust he surely harbors toward his opportunistic *compadre*: "estamos en deuda con la vieja rabona del 7o. Ligero. Para rendirle justicia debidamente, se precisa chicotear a un jefe del Ejército" ["we are in the debt of the old camp follower from the 7th. Quickly. To render her due justice, it is necessary to get rid of a leader of the Army"] (741). Although Gándara is often without funds, had he perceived that his life and career depended on it, he could certainly have made a quick restitution to Doña Lupita before the fact, if by no other means than by taking the extraordinary step of pawning his expensive ring which, as Quintín Pereda reveals at one point, Gándara had done on a previous occasion.

Gándara's costly ring and the cheap one resembling it that adorn Lupita la Romántica's fingers allude to another "wedded" relationship that develops between them and that, thanks to La Romántica's newly revealed powers as a "medium of the present," allows her to warn Gándara of his fall from grace and impending arrest as the consequence of the wrath of the other more well-connected Lupita. La Romántica's "power" as a medium to save Gándara ultimately proves, unwittingly, to be more powerful as regards the ultimate course of political events in Tierra Caliente. When Banderas learns of Gándera's escape thanks to the second Lupita, he immediately understands the seriousness of the threat to his continued rule.[14] It is at this point that he begins to make conciliatory overtures to the idealistic yet ineffectual opposition leader Roque Cepeda in the hope of securing a cease-fire. With the "scientist" Gándara in a position to assist the rebel offensive, however, the forces of revolution acquire an irreversible momentum. One subverted patriarchal structure crumbles as a new one emerges, made possible by female agents whose influence has expressed itself privately in unconsciousness and blindness yet whose effects are inevitably public and destructively powerful. As a consequence of these unrelated acts, Doña Lupita will become one of the first victims of the bloody revolutionary retribution while her younger counterpart will more than likely occupy a role identical to the old Lupita in the new regime in which Gándara will be even more prominent, if not the actual leader.[15]

Like *Los caprichos*, *Tirano Banderas* is focused not only on society and politics but also on the twisted history of an infelicitous gender dynamic. The plot, in fact, turns almost solely upon the complications ensuing from Doña Lupita's denouncement of Gándara. The "weddedness" of the principal characters, however, is further underscored in the unhappy fates which befall minor characters in the central, and longest, section of the novel who become the subsequent owners of Gándara's ring.[16] More than a powerful symbol, the ring becomes a participatory agent in the unhappy and destructive "unity" that binds together the citizens of Tierra Caliente. As Gándara is expelled from Banderas's inner circle, he rids himself of the ring by giving it to others who attempt to profit from it. The ring, however, only brings destruction, as witnessed in the grotesque episodes involving Zacarías el Cruzado's wife Laurita, their son, and the greedy *gachupín* [Spanish immigrant] Quintín Pereda upon whom Zacarías later exacts vengeance. Although it is worth a great deal, it proves impossible to profit from the ring or convert it into usable currency. It thus re-creates on a smaller scale the same problems facing the Banderas regime and Tierra Caliente, its economic unviability and lack of autonomy.[17] A society so inextricably intertwined in its own false assumptions precludes free exchanges of any sort and ensures the type of unhappy "weddings" that lead to the dead end with Gándara's ring seems to demand.

The reality of Tierra Caliente is indeed its immobility, a "biomagnetic" field of interlocking, parasitic human interdependencies that, ironically, provides the groundwork for its seemingly endless "revolutions." In sharp contrast with the persistent image of Goya's tormenting beloved which he cannot erase from his consciousness, Doña Lupita's power expresses itself in the unconsciousness and blindness of those who discover after the fact, as does Banderas, that they have become wedded to a course of action from which there is no retreat. The tyrant, whose most characteristic physical posture is "la expresión inmóvil" ["the immobile expression"] (81), soon understands that all his choices are untenable. Choosing the services of Lupita or Gándara over the other, means denying himself a vital tool to remain in power since he needs both the military "science" of Gándara and the network of secret informants upon which his repressive state apparatus also depends. This dilemma underscores the precariousness of Banderas's power and the fact that, although the form of government he has instituted strongly affirms a seemingly hegemonistic patriarchal tradition, such a system has never been free from a dependence upon destabilizing counterforces associated with matriarchy and feminine power.

Banderas's headquarters is located on the site of a "desmantelado convento de donde una lejana revolución había expulsado a los frailes" ["razed monastery where a distant revolution had expelled the friars"] (15), a reminder of the earlier theocratic order displaced by a series of governments culminating in the regime presided over by an utterly cynical Indian who in his speeches nevertheless often appeals to an even earlier time, "la originaria organización comunal del indígena" ["the originary communal organization of the indigenous natives"] (211), a primordial time before the division into haves and have-nots when the communal values of matriarchy dominated and the patriarchal society, now so "fregada por el individualismo español" ["mopped over by Spanish individualism"] (211), had yet to manifest itself.

Again, the notion of a maternal "first cause" undermines the legal and ethical basis for Banderas's rule by associating this model of societal organization with the "natural" and with "firstness." Oblivious to the dangerous implications of such rhetorical invocations, Banderas is also blind to the sexual conduits into which his repression has channeled the collective desire to determine the national destiny. The macrocosmic political wedding of fundamental incompatibles, "un entelequía con tres cabezas: el criollo, el indio y el negro" ["an entelechy with three heads: the creole, the Indian and the Negro"] (26), finds its fullest expression in a succession of failed regimes that continues to exchange one head for another. The true shape of reality in Tierra Caliente is not evolution among the societal institutions, but rather a constant reformulation of the same givens, continual "revolution"—that is virtually indistinguishable from cultural immobility—at the most trivial and ineffectual level imaginable. In Tierra Caliente, "revolution" simply means a violent, and ironic, turn of events and nothing more. As underscored in Banderas's killing of his daughter to spare her the cruel reprisals of the victors, there will never be a political or personal legacy for the powerful in Tierra Caliente.[18] There is no continuity and no clear understanding of what will succeed a regime so hated and feared, only another set of masks with which to displace one cycle of "revolution" and to identify the next.

Also as in *Los caprichos,* the dividing line in *Tirano Banderas* between politics and sexual power, reason (or empirical science) and irrationality, is virtually indistinguishable. A parody of empirical science called "biomagnetism" is often ascribed rational agency in matters both romantic and ideological.[19] Existing in fields around human bodies rather than metallic objects, this force ultimately provides a "scientific" formula and explanation for revolution. As Gándara and Doña Lupita, who come into brief physical contact with each other, repel "biomagnetically," Gándara is, ironically, moved in the direction of his "opposite pole" which, thanks to Lupita's incitement, becomes Banderas. With regard to the irrational forces at work in this society, "rational" explanations seem to underlie them, as, for example, the meanings associated with the word *bruja.*[20] The word is often used in its conventional sense to refer, as in *Los caprichos,* to the traditional irrational agents of feminine power, Lupita's "spell-casting" power over her male enemy, and, because of her honored position in Banderas's circle, the patriarchal order itself. As also used in the novel, however, *bruja* additionally refers to the more compelling, and rational, reason why both Gándara and Banderas come under one or the other Lupitas's influence: they do not have enough monetary resources of their own and thus come to depend upon these women to help them maintain their positions.

As epitomized in Doña Lupita, Banderas relies on a network of informants to bring him information which he can in turn use in order to obtain money and other things he needs to maintain power. In the novel, the latest victim is the transvestite Spanish Ambassador to whom Banderas, with intercepted letters from his lover Currito, turns in desperation in order to pressure him to have the "Madre Patria" save the "father" of his country. The Dictator must thus depend upon a series of multileveled "intereses contrarios" ["contrary interests"] (73) that turn against his own self-interest upon a feminine counteraxis in a contrary and fatal direction. Valle-Inclán, therefore, does not so much expose the evils of Latin American culture or politics but rather its perverse dedication to a contradiction, the patriarchal values of the "Madre Patria." "Estas Repúblicas, para no desviarse de la ruta civilizadora, volverán los ojos a la Madre Patria. Allí refulgen los históricos destinos de veinte naciones!" ["These Republics, in order not to deviate from the direction of civilization, will turn their eyes to the Mother Country. There shine the historical destinies of twenty nations!"] (53). Banderas falls primarily because the patriarchal model he embraces is as untenable as the countermyth he also invokes of an originary, matriarchal Indian culture. The "wedding" of cultures has been forced, an imposition of antagonistic wills that, as in an unhappy marriage from which there is no escape or divorce, binds everyone in a stifling immobility.[21]

Valle-Inclán's ideological understanding of Hispanic culture in *Tirano Banderas,* however, is also indistinguishable from his aesthetic purpose.[22] As with characters who function as dense, puppetlike masks rather than as autonomous human subjects—their immobility enhanced by the vocabulary used to represent them, thus enacting a similar immobilizing effect upon the reader attempting to penetrate the text's verbal denseness—the patriarchal structure to which they dedicate themselves exists only as a surface phenomenon. The true basis for culture expresses itself as an interminable sexual power struggle that as its by-product generates ideological and artistic positions, and oppositions: a work of art ostensibly about politics whose panoramic vision of the forces responsible for the Hispanic predicament is traceable from the pathetic "first cause" for the consumation of the revolution in Tierra Caliente, the inconsequential complaint of an old woman, to the seemingly endless chain of "motherly" values in which such an insignificant act acquires destructive power.

The fact that women and the displaced matriarchal order that their activities help to reveal make strong cases as the true protagonists of both *Los caprichos* and *Tiranos Banderas* also underscores the hybrid status of these works. Both works rely on their readers' intimate association with a dominant empirical tradition embodying strongly patriarchal values in order to graft to it a contrary point of view associated with female values and the destructive power women exert in a male-dominated society. Both works thus evince a paradoxical double "first cause," that is, a wedding, a causal chain that leads in contradictory directions to a Fatherland

and a "Madre Patria" that are grotesque reformulations of each other. In both works, what appears to be an immediate, spontaneous, sensual, and directly observed reality proves ultimately to be either a remembrance (in *Los caprichos*) or a reformulation (in *Tirano Banderas*), not an original and unique event but merely an imaginary repetition. If a persistent memory dominates Goya's imagination in *Los caprichos* to the extent that it can never fully situate itself in empirical reality, the immediate present in *Tirano Banderas* communicates the same effect for the opposite reason: it becomes merely a re-creation of a past experience completely forgotten by principals condemned to repeat its violent revolutionary cycles.

The domains of the masculine and the feminine exist in a broad continuum that encompasses all of human values and their human embodiments in an unholy, unhappy wedding of contraries united only by their monstrous unviability and mutual dependence. Such a continuum, however, also includes the authorial medium in which these weddings are ultimately staged. If Goya's psychic puppet show is the self-conscious product of a tormented imagination beset by the burden of oppressive experiences, the actors in Valle-Inclán's imaginative vision, bereft of an experiential or historical consciousness, are also guided by an external will or force that has given them life because it has understood with clarity both their untenable superficiality and their immense density.[23] Truth and freedom do not belong to any of these "characters," only to the authorial force that places them in a context in which their truth will become apparent as a consequence of the fundamental understanding that to "mirar por la cultura es hacer patria" ["to observe through the medium of culture is to build a nation"] (79). Valle-Inclán's *patria*, like the metaphysical medium of Goya's representations, is the human consciousness itself that simultaneously binds him to his vision as it also allows him to penetrate to the marrow of its contradictory underpinnings. Like the double starting point of *Los caprichos*, Valle-Inclán offers his reader a similar double option: to accept his vision passively as a self-referential end in itself and thus for the reader to reenact the tragedy of Tierra Caliente in his own tepid imagination, or to understand this land as a means, a structure upon which to build a more complete picture. Valle-Inclán invites his reader to adopt the cynicism of Banderas, to recognize that only from a vantage point of alienation and distance from the events transpiring in Tierra Caliente can one begin to comprehend their terrible truth. He offers the reader a "sucesión de imágenes violentas y tumultuosas" ["succession of violent and tumultuous images"] (35), a sordid discourse similar to the illicit love letters which the Dictator's underground network uncovers, yet from which the reader may also attempt to generate something of greater value. As the Coronelito de la Gándara himself states immediately preceding the decisive battle of the revolution, "El presente, todavía no es la Historia, y tiene caminos más realistas" ["The present is still not History and it offers more realistic roads"] (12). For the reader as well as for Valle-Inclán, that present is the imagination itself. Wedding oneself consciously to it in this land of pure present and forgotten pasts is also the only means available to become a true agent of "revolution" in the culture-aesthetic-ideology that is Tierra Caliente.

Notes

1. In spite of a certain revisionism, as feminist theory seeks to integrate itself with other critical schools, recent feminist writing continues to make this assumption a significant theme of gender-oriented writing. See especially Rita Felski, *Beyond Feminist Aesthetics: Feminist Literature and Social Change* (Cambridge: Harvard University Press, 1989); Carolyn G. Heilbrun, *Hamlet's Mother and Other Women* (New York: Columbia University Press, 1990); Karen V. Hansen and Ilene J. Philipson, eds. *Women, Class and the Feminist Imagination: A Socialist-Feminist Reader* (Philadelphia: Temple University Press, 1990); Linda J. Nicholson, *Feminism/Post-Modernism* (London: Routelege, 1990); and Camile Paglia, *Sexual Personae: Art and Decadence from Nefertiti to Emily Dickinson* (New Haven: Yale University Press, 1990).

2. Indeed, Noël M. Valis, "The Novel as Feminine Entrapment: Valle-Inclán's *Sonata de otoño*," essay in this volume, contends that writing for Valle-Inclán is something of a sexual "power play" (369). See also Catherine Nickel, "Valle-Inclán's 'La Generala': Woman as Birdbrain," essay in this volume; Claire Paolini, "Valle-Inclán's Modernistic Women: The Devout Virgin and the Devout Adultress," *Hispanófila* 30 (1986): 27–40; and Biruté Ciplijauskaite, "The Role of Language in the Creation of Valle-Inclán's Female Characters," essay in this volume.

3. The acknowledgment of male and female components in the signatures of these artists—"Ramón y María del Valle-Inclán" and, in the caption to the initial self-portrait of *Los caprichos*, "Francisco Goya y Lucientes, pintor," which uncharacteristically includes the maternal last name—is suggestive of kindred sensibilities, in different historical moments, struggling to overthrow an exhausted aesthetic tradition dominated by hegemonistic patriarchal values. Indeed, the aesthetic and spiritual kinship between Valle-Inclán and Goya has long been recognized. See Rodolfo Cardona and Anthony N. Zahareas, *Visión del esperpento. Teoría y práctica en los esperpentos de Valle-Inclán* (Madrid: Castalia, 1970); Emma Susana Speratti-Piñero, *De'Sonata de otoño' al esperpento. Aspectos del arte de Valle-Inclán* (London: Tamesis, 1968); and Peter K. Klein, "'El esperpentismo lo ha inventado Goya': Valle-Inclán und die Goya-Rezeption seiner Zeit," in *Ramón del Valle-Inclán (1866–1936)*, ed. Harald Wentzlaff-Eggebert (Tubingen: Niemeyer, 1988): 19–61.

4. For a more in-depth discussion of the critical tradition regarding this seminal image and the epistemological overturning it represents, see C. Christopher Soufas, "'Esto si que es leer': Learning to Read Goya's *Los Caprichos*," *Word and Image* 2 (1986): 311–30. Two positions continue to argue over the ambiguity of the word "sueño," which can mean either "dream" or "sleep" and which has led to two contradictory affirmations. Goya is upholding Enlightenment values in this series, or, he is rejecting them. Among recent studies, John Dowling, "The Crisis of the Spanish Enlightenment: *Capricho 43*; and Goya's Second Portrait of Jovellanos," *Eighteenth-Century Studies* 18 (1985): 332, n. 2 affirms the traditionalist position, while Ronald Paulson, *Representations of Revolution* (New Haven: Yale University Press, 1983): 333–34, upholds the romantic Goya. See also Paul Ilie, "Goya's Teratology and the Critique of Reason," *Eighteenth-Century Studies* 18 (1985): 35–56.

5. I refer the reader to Soufas, "Learning to Read Goya's *Los caprichos*," 312–20 for a more detailed exposition of the epistemological consequences for such a reading. For a more recent discussion on the significance of plate 43, see José B. Monleón, *A Spectre Is Haunting Europe: A Sociohistorical Approach to the Fantastic* (Princeton: Princeton University Press, 1989): 40–42.

6. Although every significant discussion of *Los caprichos* has emphasized the decisive influence of the Duchess of Alba in Goya's life during the time of the production of *Los caprichos*, few have attempted to account for her impact on its production. José López-Rey, *Goya's 'Caprichos': Reason, Beauty, and Caricature*, 2 vols. (Princeton: Princeton University Press, 1953) like many others, devotes many pages of his study to the couple yet ignores the possible shaping influence of the affair.

7. In the preliminary stages of production, Goya featured what was eventually to become plate 43 at the beginning of a series tentatively entitled "Ydioma Universal," the reference being to universal language schemes that posited deeper understanding usually by means of ideographic writing. *Los caprichos* subverts the possibility of universal understanding by offering a double starting point. See also James Knowlson, *Universal Language Schemes in England and France* (Toronto: Toronto University Press, 1975); and M. M. Slaughter, *Universal Languages and Scientific Taxonomy in the Seventeenth Century* (Cambridge: Cambridge University Press, 1982).

8. A notable exception to the critical reticence to explore the personal aspects of this work is Paulson, *Representations of Revolution,* 324 who feels there are only two real protagonists, the repeated images of "Godoy-Goya" and the Duchess. "If Godoy-Goya is the male protagonist, Alba is the female, in the constant play back and forth of exploiter and exploited. Like her analogues, Alba betrays and threatens Goya, and she is perhaps as much as anything else the reason that the *Caprichos* take the form they do."

9. As Edith Helman, *Trasmundo de Goya* (Madrid: Revista de Occidente, 1963) and others have documented, Goya suppressed from the series an engraving entitled "Sueño de la mentira y de la ynconstancia" ["Dream of Lying and Inconstancy"] that, among other things, pictures a two-headed Duchess holding hands with two men who look very much like Goya. This doubling may well be Goya's conscious acknowledgment of the painful coincidence of art and life in his production.

10. *Goya's 'Caprichos': Reason, Beauty, and Caricature,* 2 vols. Princeton: Princeton University Press, 1953, 5–11.

11. Although the boundaries between "reason" ("science") and "unreason" in

the novel are not clear, the Coronelito de la Gándara must be considered something of a military strategist, especially in comparison to the disorganization of the revolutionaries and their terroristic strategies which include burning a convent and raping nuns (6). I thus disagree with the views of Speratti-Piñero, *Aspectos del arte de Valle-Inclán*, 81–84, who discounts Gándara's leadership potential; Verity Smith, *Tirano Banderas* (London: Grant and Cutler, 1971), 43–56, who does not consider the Coronel among the novel's major characters; and Dante Liano, "El problema del héroe en *Tirano Bandera*," *Quaderni Ibero-Americani* 57–58 (1984–85): 47, who sees nothing admirable in him but does recognize that "lo que le importa es el poder" ["what does matter to him is power"]. I should also like to mention important studies with a different critical perspective from my own regarding this novel by Susan Kirkpatrick, "*Tirano Banderas* y la estructura de la historia," *Nueva Revista de Filología Hispánica* 24 (1975): 449–68; and also, "*Tirano Banderas* and *El señor preisdente:* Two Tyrants and Two Visions," in *Actes du VII Congrés de l'A. I. L. C.*, eds. Milan Dimic and J. Ferraté (Stuttgart: Bieber, 1979): 229–33; and Mary K. Addis, "Synthetic Visions: The Spanish American Dictator Novel as Genre," in *Cultural Studies: Crossing Boundaries*, Critical Studies Book Series, Guest editor Roberta L. Salper (Amsterdam: Rodopi, 1991), 189–219.

12. All quotations from the novel are taken from the edition by Alonso Zamora Vicente (Madrid: Clásicos Castellanos, 1978). Subsequent quotations will be taken from this edition and cited in the text.

13. The "first-cause" parody serves to underscore the great distance between the motives for the events taking place in the imaginary Tierra Caliente, and the empirical order (and also the domain of the reader attempting to make sense of the text). This enhances the metafictional quality of the novel while further serving to link it to a Spanish avant-garde tradition and Goya. In Goya's announcement of the sale of his engravings, he claims that they are not products of mimesis but of an imagination "acolarada con el desenfreno de las pasiones" ["heated with the licentiousness of the passions," reprinted in Helman, *Trasmundo de Goya*]. In similar fashion, Valle-Inclán understands that he is working with a closed set of characters engendered in his own "hothouse." Both artists, therefore, are very much aware of the power and the limitations of the imagination and that the true metaphysical "first cause" ultimately resides in their physical persons. See also Ricardo Gullón, "Técnicas en *Tirano Banderas*," in *Ramón del Valle-Inclán. An Appraisal of His Life and Works*, ed. Anthony H. Zahareas (New York: Las Américas, 1968), 723–30.

14. The fact that later, at the most critical moment of the revolution, Banderas brings Lupita la Romántica to his headquarters for a demonstration of her alleged power as "medium of the present," illustrates the significance he has associated with the two acts by the two Lupitas that together have "engendered" the emergence of possibly the next strongman of Tierra Caliente.

15. Although there have been allusions to the irony of both Doña Lupita's and Lupita la Romántica's participation in events which culminate in revolution, only Virginia Milner Garlitz, "Teosofismo en *Tirano Banderas*," *Journal of Spanish Studies: Twentieth Century* 2 (1974): 21–29; and Gonzalo Díaz-Migoyo, *Guía de Tirano Banderas* (Madrid: Fundamentos, 1984), 97–103 and "*Tirano Banderas* o la simultaneidad textual," *Revista Hispánica Moderna* 41 (1988): 61–65, have understood the interrelatedness of their efforts as part of an irrational chain of cause and effect. Less useful but also in line with these temporal/structural studies are contributions by Robert C. Spires, "*Tirano Banderas*," in *Transparent*

Simulacra (Columbia: University of Missouri Press, 1988): 90–107; and Peggy Lynne Tucker, *Time and History in Valle-Inclán's Historical Novel and Tirano Banderas* (Valencia: Albatros, 1980). Only a gender-oriented reading, however, underscores their centrality in the structure of both the novel and the larger society.

16. Victor Ouimette, "El centro patético en *Tirano Banderas,*" *Letras de Deusto* 19 (1989): 233–49, has a much different reading of events which transpire in the fourth section, especially regarding the character Zacarías el Cruzado. He suggests, however, that "[l]o que puede parecer de una trivialidad excesiva es en realidad decisivo en la novela" ["what may seem to be an excessive triviality is in reality decisive in the novel"] (241). My gender-based reading stresses a different set of trivialities as the decisive motivation for events represented in the novel. Additionally, the ring motif is a frequent occurrence in Valle-Inclán's writing, appearing in, among others, *La lámpara maravillosa, Cuento de abril, Sonata de primavera,* and *La cabeza del dragón.*

17. The ring also suggests that the future will very much resemble the present since its identifiable characteristics make it something of a faceless coin that nevertheless refers back to Gándara. If this is a portent of how the economy will function under Gándara, then Tierra Caliente is in for continued bad times.

18. Not a small irony, especially in the present context, is the fact that Banderas acts as both father and mother to his incapacitated daughter, again reaffirming his wedded immobility.

19. See Garlitz, "Teosofismo en *Tirano Banderas,*" 21–25.

20. See the glossary in Emma Susana Speratti-Piñero, *Aspectos del arte de Valle-Inclán* (Madrid: Espasa-Culpe, 1978), 205–34 and also notes in *Tirano Banderas,* ed. Zamora Vicente.

21. It is precisely at the point of conscious gender invocation that the categories lose their specificity. Without a clear sense of gender divisions, therefore, there can be no real movement in society. Valle-Inclán's characters wear a multiple burden that is cultural, political, aesthetic, and sexual. All they can be is characters in a scenario in which they participate yet of which they have no real consciousness or comprehension, a condition which nevertheless re-creates the state of the Hispanic consciousness.

22. For the most part, the numerous studies dedicated to Valle-Inclán's aesthetics such as those by Antonio Risco, *La estética de Valle-Inclán* (Madrid: Gredos, 1966) and *El demiurgo y su mundo* (Madrid: Gredos, 1977); Guillermo Díaz Plaja, *Las estéticas de Valle-Inclán* (Madrid: Gredos, 1972); Melchor Fernández Almagro, *Vida y literatura de Valle-Inclán* (Madrid: Taurus, 1966); and Alonso Zamora Vicente. *La realidad esperpéntica* (Madrid: Gredos, 1969) have unfortunately separated aesthetics from other important considerations, such as history and ideology. More recent studies by Leda Schiavo, *Historia y novela en Valle-Inclán* (Madrid: Castalia, 1980) and especially by Roberta L. Salper, *Valle-Inclán y su mundo: Ideología y forma narrativa* (Amsterdam: Rodopi, 1988) signal a more productive mode in discussing the relationship between formal and ideological dimensions in Valle-Inclán's work.

23. This is not the case for the reader who is free to supply what these characters lack and thus to achieve the consciousness and understanding of which they are incapable. This also effectively re-creates the phenomenon of the writing of the novel.

Marina Mayoral's *Cándida otra vez:* Invitation to a Retroactive Reading of *Soñata de otoño*

ROBERTA JOHNSON

At the end of her article, "The Novel as Feminine Entrapment: Valle-Inclán's *Sonata de otono*," Noël Valis challenges the reader to imagine *Sonata de otoño* [*Sonata of Autumn*] written by a woman.[1] Marina Mayoral anticipated the challenge in her first novel, *Cándida otra vez* [Cándida, once more (1979)], a novella of about the same length as *Sonata de otoño* which replicates many of the details of Valle-Inclán's 1902 masterpiece.[2] As in many cases of intertextuality, the subsequent text distorts, inverts, or parodies elements of the original, creating a work whose meaning acquires depth and nuance in the reader's knowledge of the two texts. But, if *Cándida otra vez* gains additional resonance when set alongside *Sonata de otoño,* the reverse also occurs; the relationship between the texts is specular. A work containing intertextual references can suggest new readings of, and insights into, its intertexts. *Doña Perfecta* and *Pepita Jiménez, Niebla* [*Mist*] and *El amigo manso* [*Our Friend Manso*] are earlier examples of such intertextual dynamics.[3] Within the "system of literature," *Doña Perfecta* forms part of the literary context of *Pepita Jiménez* and highlights its exalted idealism, just as *Niebla* underscores the metaphysical theme and novelistic innovation of *El amigo manso.*

I borrow Michael Riffaterre's term "retroactive reading" to name this phenomenon, although he is referring to the experience of revising one's views of earlier material in the same text as one reads subsequent passages of that text.[4] I extend his concept of "retroactive reading" in consonance with his comments on intertextuality made in the same article. If intertextuality is "the corpus of texts the reader may legitimately connect with the one before his eyes, that is, the texts brought to mind by what he is reading,"[5] a subsequently published text can serve as well as an anterior one. The changes to which Mayoral subjects Valle-Inclán's model foreground the gender and class consciousness that are more oblique and tangencial to the story told by the Marqués de Brandomín.[6] In a retroactive reading of *Sonata de otoño,* filtered through a text that modernizes some of its seemingly outmoded values of gender and class, one becomes more aware of Valle-Inclán's own antitraditionalist approach to such issues, of his latent parody of nineteenth-century literary treatments of women, and of his critique of the Galician social hierarchy.

Cándida otra vez, like *Sonata de otoño,* is narrated in the first person by a Galician male, who responds to the summons of an aristocratic Galician woman in trouble. Cándida writes Pedro that a university student, who is doing research in the family library of her home (and with whom she is having an affair), has begun publishing libelous material about her powerful aristocratic family, and she fears for his safety. By the time Pedro reaches Galicia, the student has died in a suspicious automobile accident, while driving Cándida's car. Pedro attempts to sort out the truth of the story, which includes evidence that the student was Cándida's illigitimate half-brother, but ultimately he gives up, after a night of lovemaking with Cándida. Both *Sonata de otoño* and *Cándida otra vez* are constructed on a romance plot framework in which a "princess in distress" is attended by a "galant knight," and each novel begins with the "galant swain"—the Marqués de Bradomín or Pedro— reading a letter from the "princess" who supplicatingly requests his presence and moral support. The man and woman in each case were childhood friends, and there has existed a sexual attraction between them (although Mayoral's couple have not previously had an affair). Upon receiving the summons, each man promptly sets out on a journey to the woman's side, and during a brief stop en route, memories of his childhood years with the woman occupy his autobiographical thoughts. Each novel ends with the sexual union of the man and woman in the woman's old artistocratic Galician family home.

However, in Mayoral's version of the liaison narrated from a masculine perspective, the protagonists are of different social classes (whereas the Marqués and Concha are both aristocrats). Cándida Monterroso y Cela is from an old aristocratic Galician family, but her galant swain Pedro is of humble origins (his father was an overseer on the Monterroso family estates, and he is now a labor lawyer in Madrid). Pedro's view of Cándida is consistently colored by his inferior social rank, which forms the center of the novel's class consciousness. Mayoral also includes feminist inversions of some of Valle-Inclán's arrangements. Rather than the sickly, consumptive, pseudo romantic woman figure embodied in Concha, Cándida is a modern woman—physically strong and a trained professional (she is a practicing doctor). Both women do share the classic romance trait of unusual physical beauty that focuses on extraordinary hair, although Cándida's is blond and Concha's black. In *Cándida otra vez* it is the man who is ill; Pedro has just suffered a heart attack and is away from Madrid recuperating when he receives Cándida's letter requesting his presence in Galicia. It is Cándida who undresses Pedro, but in a clinical manner as she wants to listen to his heartbeat with her stethoscope (in contrast to the Marqués's elaborate religious-*modernista* dressing and undressing of Concha). And it is Cándida who seduces Pedro in her "palace," while the Marqués is the sexual aggressor at the Palacio de Brandeso.

In both novels, the masculine narrative voice is the key to both unilateral and intertextual readings. As a homodiegetic (autobiographical) voice, the male narrator/protagonist has a limited and self-interested approach to the story he tells. The self-interestedness has its degrees, however, and is much more pronounced in the Marqués de Bradomín, whose entire narration is interlarded with indications of his self-consiousness.[7] The more innocent and ingenuous nature of Pedro's voice heightens our awareness of the subversive nature of the Marqués's elaborate narrative confection, especially in relation to issues of gender and class. Pedro's innocence stems in part from Mayoral's complication of *Cándida otra vez*'s genre models, which interweaves elements of the detective novel into the basic romance plot that undergirds *Sonata de otoño*. Pedro is thrown into the role of novice gumshoe when he receives Cándida's letter about the student's potential peril. When he arrives in Galicia, he picks up numerous leads to the truth underlying the student's death, but unlike the Marqués, whose ego and creative imagination cast in pseudo-romantic/*modernista* style dominate most of *Sonata de otoño*'s narration,[8] Pedro is never completely in control of the events he narrates, and he fails to solve the mystery of the student's death.

Mayoral's inversion of the masculinist, pseudoscientific detective genre in which a man solves a crime through keen observation and logical deduction,[9] reminds us that Valle-Inclán subverts the romantic genre in which a central figure's self (again usually male) usurps the center of the work. The Marqués's romantic version of his past is exaggerated to the point of caricature; his egoism, as well as the significant amount of time that has elapsed since the events narrated, make him, as Robert Spires has pointed out (without using this specific term), an unreliable narrator. Even though Pedro as narrator has the same opportunity as the Marqués de Bradomín to aggrandize his role, he does not choose to do so; in fact, he is rather self-deprecating, especially when he suggests that Cándida subverted any moral indignation he might have felt by seducing him and flattering his male ego. Also, Pedro's inferior social status vis-à-vis Cándida gives him a more limited view of the desired female object (he does not actually see Cándida until late in the novel, and he enters her domestic space only at the end). Pedro's power over Cándida is reduced by his social status and by his limited perspective on her story. The Marqués, on the other hand, as a male of the same class as his female object, exercises absolute power over her, and his presence dominates her living space throughout the narration. His social position leverages his ridiculous posture as a declining Don Juan, who is attempting to recapture a "glorious" past that features the conquest of a woman on her deathbed.

Mayoral also reduces the "time lapse" element of her protagonist's narration. Even though the events narrated do occur at some previous time vis-à-vis the character's present, it appears to be a more immediate past than that of the Marqués de Bradomín, who emphasizes the long hiatus intervening between what transpired during a few days at the Palacio de Brandeso and his present situation as an elderly man.[10] The passing of time has given him some perspective on the motives of his earlier self, enriching the layers of parody. The reader is hardly persuaded that he is a reformed sinner, as the elderly Marqués would seem to intend by his few belated, but unrepentant, insights into his own egotistic behavior.

> ¡Había muerto aquella flor de ensueño a quien todas mis palabras le parecían bellas! ¡Aquella flor de ensueño a quien todos mis gestos le parecían soberanos! . . . ¿Volvería a encontrar otra pálida princesa, de tristes ojos encantados, que me admirase siempre magnífico? Ante esta duda lloré. ¡Lloré como un Dios antiguo al extinguirse su culto![11]

> [That dream flower to whom all my words had seemed beautiful had died. That dream flower to whom all my gestures seemed sovereign! . . . Would I ever again find another pale princess with sad, enchanted eyes, who would admire me as ever magnificent? I wept at the thought. I cried like an ancient God whose cult has been extinguished.]

The Marqués's final thoughts are much more damning than Pedro's last meditation, which also indicates a certain level of self-awareness and parody, but he includes a universal observation on the static Galician social hierarchy that contrasts sharply with the Marqués's narcissism.

—No, yo no soy un Monterroso de Cela. . . sólo un fiel servidor que a veces reclama su soldada. . . . El cielo era gris plomo y hacía frío. Miré una vez más el sólido caserón y bajé despacio hasta el Obradoiro. Las calles estaban desiertas, sin coches, sin gente. Podía ser una mañana cualquiera de hace cien años, doscientos. . . A mediodía llamé a Herda.—Asunto concluido. Esperame esta noche. . . por favor.[12]

[—No, I am not a Monterroso de Cela. . . only a faithful servant who sometimes demands his wages. . . . It was cold and the sky was lead-gray. I looked once more at the large solid old house and slowly went down to the Obradoiro. The streets were deserted; there were no cars, no people. It could have been any morning a hundred or two hundred years ago. . . . At midday I called Herda.—The job's done. Wait for me tonight. . . please.]

At first glance, *Sonata de otoño* appears to continue the nineteenth-century literary tradition which often portrayed a weak woman controlled by a completely masculine world. Concha, the adulteress, is punished by dying a slow consumptive death, her agony filled with religion-inspired remorse for her sins. Jane Clifford in Gail Godwin's *The Odd Woman* has aptly termed this phenomenon the "Emma Bovary syndrome": "literature's graveyard positively choked with women who . . . 'get in trouble' (commit adultery, have sex without marriage; *think* of committing adultery, or having sex without marriage) and thus, according to the literary convention of the time, must die."[13] But Marina Mayoral's inversion of masculinist elements in Valle-Inclán's novel, reminds us that Valle-Inclán is also inverting and subverting the nineteenth-century literary tradition by placing it in the voice of a highly self-conscious and linguistically stylized Don Juan. *Cándida otra vez* begins with a long letter from Cándida to Pedro, just as the overture to the *Sonata* refers to a letter from Concha to the Marqués de Bradomín, except that the Marqués recalls only a small fragment of the feminine epistle, while Pedro quotes the entire letter (almost a fifth of the novel).

The Marqués's ego is all too evident in his treatment of Concha's prose; after reciting one line "'¡Mi amor adorado, estoy muriéndome y sólo deseo verte!'" (31) ["'My adored love, I am dying, and my only wish is to see you'"], he interrupts her voice to return to his own meditations. "¡Ay! Aquella carta de la pobre Concha

se me extravió hace mucho tiempo. Era llena de afán y de tristeza,
perfumada de violetas y de un antiguo amor. Sin concluir de leerla,
la besé" (31) ["Ay! I misplaced poor Concha's letter long ago. It
was full of desire and sadness, perfumed with violets and a former
love. Without finishing the letter, I kissed it"]. His assessment of
her style reminds us that his own narration is likewise couched in
a language full of desire and sadness, perfumed with violets and
old love. In fact, the Marqués's purple prose stands pervasively in
the way of Concha achieving the tragic dimensions of an Emma
Bovary. Rather than a novel of female entrapment, *Sonata de
otoño* traps the male, or rather, he traps himself in his own language.

In both *Cándida otra vez* and *Sonata de otoño,* several secondary characters act as counterweights to the male protagonist's vision of himself, of his society, and of the central female character.
The heightened sexist and classist nature of these alternative perspectives in *Cándida otra vez* invites a rereading of *Sonata de
otoño.* Such a rereading reveals that in several cases the alternative
perpsective is, as in *Cándida otra vez,* made available through the
intervention of a character from the lower classes. In *Cándida otra
vez* the illegitimate stepbrother, although he has no direct voice
and is known to be dead about halfway through the narration, is
central to the novel's critique of the Galician social hierarchy. The
unproved suspicion that he was murdered by a Monterroso family
member, possibly even by Cándida herself, is an unveiled commentary on a ruling class ready to extinguish anyone, even a family
member, who threatens its political hegemony (one of Cándida's
relatives who is slandered in the student's publications is running
for political office).

Florisel in *Sonata de otoño* plays a role similar to that of Cándida's illegitimate stepbrother as a marker of class distinctions in
hierarchical Galician society. Like the stepbrother, Florisel's relationship to the powerful ruling family is unnatural (and though
more veiled than in *Cándida otra vez,* a possible sexual liaison
between Florisel and Concha is alluded to). Concha has transformed this eldest son of one of her tenant farmers into a page
who helps her maintain the illusory medieval world she has created
at the Palacio de Brandeso. This anachronistic fabricated page
"con su vestido de estameño, sus ojos tímidos, su fabla vistigótica y
sus guedejas trasquiladas sobre la frente, con tonsura casi monacal,
parecía el hijo de un antiguo siervo de la gleba" (51) ["looked like
a medieval serf with his serge outfit, his timid eyes, his Visigothic
speech and his long locks shorn over his forehead, a sort of monk-

line tonsure"]. His chief duty is to teach blackbirds to sing, casting an ironic light on his answer to the Marqués, who asks the boy what his parents do: "pues no hacen nada. Cavan la tierra" (51) ["well, they don't do anything. They till the soil"]. Concha has removed this young peasant from his "natural" social position as a tiller of the soil in a real medieval social hierarchy that persists in modern Galicia and inserted him into an artificially constructed medieval world based on literary romance models that have no referent in the real world. In the literary version of the medieval world, life outside of playing princess and page in a beautiful palace, that is, "tilling the soil," has no place. Candelaria, a more authentic rendition of the servant's role—preparing meals, doing handwork, and tending her mistress—, serves as a contrast to Florisel's highly artificial situation.

Pedro presents Cándida as a cold, calculating woman, who would be entirely capable of committing the murder in which she is implicated, but another viewpoint is interpolated through the voice of an indigent patient at Cándida's clinic. This very chatty woman informs Pedro of Cándida's generosity with the poor. She is the only doctor who never refuses to take a patient even if she has to work extra hours, she remembers everyone's name and situation, and is genuinely concerned about the welfare of all her patients. It is also the voice of a lower-class character that overrides the Marqués's vision of an infantile, self-centered Concha to reveal that she, like Cándida, has a charitable side. The miller tells the Marqués that he pays "un foro antiguo a la señora del Palacio, un foro de dos ovejas, siete ferrados de trigo y siete de centeno" (36) ["an ancient tribute to the lady of the palace, a levy of two sheep, seven barrels of wheat, and seven of rye"], but last year Concha exempted him from the tribute because of the drought. He notes that Concha "[e]ra una señora que se compadecía del pobre aldeano" (11) ["was a lady who felt compassion for the poor villager"]. When the Marqués includes someone else's viewpoint, Concha appears less childlike and removed from reality; she is a landowner-businesswoman who is capable of making fair judgments.

The portrait that each of the two protagonist/narrators draws of himself contrasts with that of another character who is a more authentic version of what the character himself would like us to believe him to be—the Marqués, a chivalrous man; Pedro, an altruist. Javier shares Pedro's inferior social class, the profession of labor lawyer, leftist politics, and a lifelong fascination with Cándida Monterroso, but Javier has always been a committed political activist (having been jailed and tortured) as compared to Pedro's more cautious approach to his political beliefs. Javier actually did date Cándida during their university years, while Pedro only longed to do so. And Javier's wife Marta believes he is currently engaged in an affair with Cándida, while Pedro is only granted a one-night stand.

Don Juan Manuel similarly serves to further highlight the Marqués de Bradomin's posturing. Like the Marqués, Don Juan Manuel is aristocratic and perpetuates a medieval version of man-hood, but, in contrast to the contemplative, more sedentary Mar-qués, he is an active knight, who has served in the Guardia Noble de la Real Persona and is described by Florisel as a "gran caba-llero" (53) ["great cavalier"]. His appearances in the novel are all associated with daring horsemanship, and he recovers from a seri-ous riding accident in a miraculously short time. By contrast, the Marqués's exploits take place in the bedroom of a dying woman, and he is the antithesis of the Christian knight in his insistence upon sexual relations with a woman who wishes to remain sinless on the eve of her death. Don Juan Manuel represents the authentic chivalric knight that is parodied in the figure of the Marqués de Bradomín.[14]

Incest is important to the social commentary in each of the nov-els, although its impact is more latent in *Sonata de otoño*. In each case death attends upon one of the incestuous partners, but in a way more obviously linked to social class in *Cándida otra vez*, as the aristocratic Cándida is implicated in the demise of her illigiti-mate halfbrother-*cum*-lover. Her tenuous moral position is further undermined by her appealing for help to Pedro who was at a dis-tance, when Javier (also a lawyer) was close by. Perhaps she wanted a lawyer who might not arrive in time and who also possessed a letter proving that she had attempted to protect the boy. Unlike Concha, Cándida feels no remorse for her transgressions (sexual relations with a stepbrother, the stepbrother's death, sexual rela-tions with Javier, husband of her best friend and cousin). Incest as a critique of social class is more metonymic in *Sonata de otoño*. Since Concha's death does not involve a criminal act on either her part or that of her partner, the commentary derives solely from the aristocratic social class of the incestuous couple. The Marqués has quite a history of incestuous relations, having initiated his amo-rous conquests with an aunt at eleven years of age and then suc-cumbing to the charms of Concha's sister (also his cousin) minutes after Concha's death. Cándida too has a history of incest as her husband, from whom she is divorced, was her cousin, linking her intertextually to the Marqués as well as to Concha (I have already noted that she usurps the Marqués's role as seducer). But the death of the incestuous partner in *Cándida otra vez,* rather than condemning the living partner to eternal nostalgia, as in the case of the Marqués, sets Cándida free for other possible crimes or incestuous relationships.

Cándida's final moral transgression is to buy Pedro's silence with her own body. And so Mayoral's novel closes, like *Sonata de otoño,* with the sexual union of the "princess in distress" and the "galant swain" who comes to her aid. Again Mayoral's revision of the original story has gender and class associations not so readily apparent in Valle-Inclán's novel. The physical union of Cándida and Pedro is a moment of triumph for the woman over a man who suspects her of murder. It is, however, also a triumph for the ruling class, which maintains its hierarchical position through murder and bribery (in this case a form of prostitution). For its part, Valle-Inclán's ending insinuates a critique of gender roles through the egotistic and amoral posturing of the Marqués. Concha, when compared to Cándida or the Marqués, appears to have a much stronger moral character. Concha could be considered a martyr when the final sexual union hastens her death, whereas Cándida is cast in the role of witch or at least bewitcher. The Marqués's narration projects the image of a compassionate and deeply religious (although infantile) Concha, while Pedro's view of Cándida is ultimately ambiguous, even latently damning. And Concha's name is symbolic, while Cándida's is ironic. Concha (Concepción) bears a religious connotation and a suggestion of her nature as sex object of the Marqués, but Cándida is a flagrant misnomer. She attempts to create the impression that she is a candid and open person, who has told Pedro everything about her stepbrother's situation, but Pedro's doubts are not allayed.

In Cándida, Mayoral has created a strong woman, but not an entirely positive one. The crossing of gender and class is complex and sends mixed messages. Cándida, the strong *woman,* is also the principle focus of the class critique; she "does in" two men of a lower class—the halfbrother and Pedro. Valle-Inclán's arrangement of gender and class, by comparison, is more straightforward. Concha is an aristocratic woman who has also manipulated the lower classes (especially Florisel) for her own ends, but as an object of manipulation herself (at the hands of the Marqués de Bradomín, an even more powerful *male* aristocrat), her position is ultimately less ominous. And the Marqués's outmoded sexist and classist demeanor can be viewed in the same ironic light in which his entire pseudoromantic narration is cast (e.g., his commentary upon arriving at the miller's house: "como si aquello fuese nuestro feudo, llamamos autoritarios a la puerta" (34) ["as if it were our fief, we gave an authoritarian knock"]).

Both *Sonata de otoño* and *Cándida otra vez* travel two roads simultaneously, one that points to an incorporation and critique of traditional gender and class roles inscribed in earlier literature, and another that comments on gender and class distinctions in Spanish society, particularly the Galician hierarchy. The mediator in each instance is art. Mayoral's treatment of art's role is once again much more overt; she introduces an artist into the novel as another one of the oblique commentators on Cándida's character. Marta, Cándida's cousin and Javier's wife, is a painter. Her pleasant Galician landscapes find favor with everyone, except her activist husband who believes his wife's art should reflect more political awareness (social realism is the only viable artistic style for him). Ironically enough, as Marta's suspicions of Javier's sexual involvement with Cándida have increased, her painting style has acquired a new edge. In her most recent paintings Pedro notices a sadness and lack of tranquillity, especially in a depiction of Cándida's house, the old Monterroso family estate.

The painting foreshadows Pedro's final meeting and night of love-making with Cándida, setting up the metonymic relationship between Cándida's house (aristocratic, beautiful, and disquieting) and its owner (aristocratic, beautiful, and treacherous): "El tejado de la casona se recortaba contra un cielo rojizo y la luz del atardecer daba un tono más cálido a los viejos muros. Inevitablemente pensé en Marta, pero es una hermosa casa" (87) ["The roof of the large house was profiled against the reddish sky, and the afternoon light gave the old walls a warm tone. Inevitably I thought of Marta, but it is a beautiful house"].[15] Once inside, Pedro experiences a sense of timelessness and anachrony: "En aquella habitación el tiempo parecía no existir. . . . Era una enorme estancia, anacrónica e impresionante" (90) ["In that room time did not seem to exist. . . . It was an enormous room, anachronistic and impressive"]. Similarly, Valle-Inclán uses art and architecture as a metonymic signifier. The Marqués's prose is anachronistic (laden with romantic and *modernista* touches) as is the Palacio de Brandeso, where most of his story takes place: "El Palacio de Brandeso, aunque del siglo décimo octavo, es casi todo de estilo plateresco" (56) ["The Brandeso Palace, although of the eighteenth century, is nearly all done in Plateresque style"]. The same equivalency inheres; the palace (feudal and anachronistic) stands for Concha and the Maqués who are likewise feudal and anachronistic.

But ultimately Valle-Inclán prefers to leave the association between architecture and society an implicit one, while Mayoral makes it explicit. In their final conversation, Pedro and Candida allude openly to Galicia's outmoded social structure. When Cándida refers to Pedro's father as an "hombre honesto y un fiel servidor" (97) ["honest man and faithful servant"], Pedro responds that "[e]l tiempo de los fieles servidores ha pasado" (97) ["the time of faithful servants has passed"], and he continues:

> Tendría que haber vivido en un pueblo pequeño, en una aldea de labradores y marineros, de gentes que trabajan, que viven pendientes del tiempo: hay borrasca y no se puede ir a la mar, llovió por San Juan y se estropeó la cosecha, habrá que ir a pedir un aplazamiento, un préstamo, cruzar una vez más la gran cancela de hierro, atavesar las losas del patio, llegar a la fachada de piedra donde está el escudo de los Monterroso, del señor (100).

> [One would need to have lived in a small village, in a village of farmers or fisherfolk, people who work and whose lives depend on the weather: there is a storm and you can't go to sea, it rained in June and the crop was ruined; we will have to go ask for an extension, a loan, enter once more through the great iron gate, cross the patio stones, arrive at the stone facade bearing the master's Monterroso coat of arms.]

But since he has allowed himself to be seduced (bribed) by Cándida, he ends up calling her "princesa" (101), and himself "un fiel servidor" (100), openly acknowledging that, despite his modern-day political awareness, nothing has really changed. Pedro, like the Marqués de Bradomín, is trapped in that ambiguous time between two eras. In Pedro's post-Civil War Spain, a young man from the working class can become a lawyer, but he has not entirely eluded medieval social formulas. That the Marqués's life, or at least the one about which he reminisces, is out-of-sync with the narrative present is implied in his outdated literary language.[16]

Sonata de otoño goes out of its way to include markers of anachronistic class distinctions, but prefers to allow them to speak for themselves unadorned by overt commentary; the commentary resides in the seemingly gratuitous nature of the references to members of the underclass. The numerous instances in which servants and peasants appear are told as natural adjuncts to the aristocratic life, but they are in fact extraneous to the Marqués's sensual memoir, and their cumulative presence calls attention to implicit social discrepancies. At the miller's home there is a "pobre mujer" ["poor woman"] or "mujeruca" ["peasant woman"] attending a "fuego miserable" ["miserable fire"] in stark contrast to the "servilleta adamascada" ["damask napkin"] and "vasos de plata que nuestras abuelas mandaban labrar con soles del Perú" (35), ["silver goblets that our grandmothers had made from Peruvian coins"] that the steward takes from the saddle bags in preparation for a meal. When the Marqués enters the Palace grounds, he is greeted by "los pagadores de un foral" (38) ["tenant farmers"]. The Marqués and Concha encounter Concha's mother's aged and blind lady's maid during their memorious inspection of the Palace. When the Marqués gets up to find a glass of wine for Don Juan Manuel, the latter admonishes: "—¡No te muevas! ¿Habrá algún criado en el Palacio?" (69) ["Don't get up! Isn't there a servant in the Palace?"], and as the two *caballeros* ride toward the Pazo de Lantañón, they observe "algún rapaz aldeano que dejaba beber pacíficamente a la yunta cansada de sus bueyes" (75) ["a village boy who was letting his tired yoke of oxen drink peacefully"].

Twice on that brief journey peasants stand aside to allow the noblemen to pass: "los pastores que volvían del monte trayendo los rebaños por delante se detenían en las revueltas, y arreaban a un lado sus ovejas para dejarnos paso" (75) ["the shepherds who were returning from the back-country bringing the flocks in front of them, stopped at the bends in the road, and hustled their sheep to one side to let us pass"], and

> Los tres espoliques habían arrendado sus mulas sobre la orilla del camino, para dejarme paso. Cuando vieron el cuerpo de Don Juan Manuel cruzado sobre mi caballo, habláronse en voz baja. No osaron, sin embargo, interrogarme. Debieron presumir que era alguno a quien yo había dado muerte. Juraría que los tres villanos temblabon sobre sus cabalgaduras (76).

> [The three grooms had reined their mules over to the side of the road to let me pass. And when they saw Don Juan Manuel's body crosswise over my horse, they spoke in low tones. They did not dare, however, to question me. They must have assumed that it was someone I had killed. I would swear that the three villagers trembled on their mounts.]

And, as the wounded Don Juan Manuel and the Marqués reenter the grounds of the Palacio de Brandeso:

> Allá lejos, pegados a las tapias del Palacio, cruzaban dos criados hablando en dialecto. El que iba delante llevaba un farol que mecía

acompasado y lento. Tras los vidrios emapañados de rocío, la humosa llama de aceite iluminaba con temblona claridad la tierra mojada, y los zuecos de los dos aldeanos. Hablando en voz baja se detuvieron un momento ante la escalinata, y al reconocernos, adelantaron con el farol en alto para poder alumbrarnos, desde lejos, el camino. Eran los dos zagales del ganado que iban repartiendo por los pesebres la ración nocturna de húmeda y olorosa yerba. Acercáronse, y con torpe y asustadizo respeto bajaron del caballo a Don Juan Manuel. El farol alumbraba colocado sobre el balaustral de la escalinata. El hidalgo subió apoyándose en los hombros de los criados. (77–78).

[There in the distance, staying close to the palace walls, the servants were passing, speaking in dialect. The one in front carried a lantern that swung slowly and rhythmically. Behind the glass clouded with dew, the misty gas flame illuminated the wet earth and the peasant's clogs with tremulous clarity. Speaking in a low voice, they stopped for a moment at the stairway, and upon recognizing us they came forward, holding the lantern high so as to light our way from a distance. They were the two stock tenders who were placing the nightly ration of damp, fragrant grass in the mangers. They went over to Don Juan Manuel, and with a clumsy frightened respect lowered him from the horse. The lantern, set now on the railing of the stairs shed its light. The nobleman went up, leaning on the shoulders of the servants].

In each passage, fear and deference, distance and inequality between the two social classes are just as present as in *Cándida otra vez,* but they are manifested in gestures or postures rather than in discursive observations. These passages may be extraneous to the story of the Marqués and Concha, but not to the moral implications of their relationship—condemnation of the decadent and outmoded social hierarchy in which the two casts (master and servant) remain permanently alienated: "Don Miguel Bendaña había sido un caballero déspota y hospitalario, fiel a la tradición hidalga y campesina de todo su linaje. Enhiesto como un lanzón, pasó por el mundo sin sentarse en el festín de los plebeyos" (94) ["Don Miguel Bendaña had been a hospitable and despotic gentleman, faithful to the tradition of the country nobility of his lineage. Erect as a dagger, he passed through the world without ever sitting down at a plebian feast"].

Marina Mayoral has gained more from her illustrious Galician literary forebear than a plot framework on which to build a modernized text; from Valle-Inclán she has learned how to harness intertextuality and literary parody to social commentary.[17] Valle-Inclán masterfully wove romantic and *modernista* clichés into the Marqués's nostalgic reminiscence to cast a parodic shadow over his figure and the gender and class it represents. Mayoral, in turn, subverts Valle-Inclán and the detective genre to comment upon the same unchanging social structures, although she may, in the process, have created a more ambiguous role for the woman, an ambiguity that doubtless reflects the changes that have occurred in the lives of Spanish women since 1902.

Notes

1. Noël Valis, "The novel as female entrapment: Valle's *Sonata de otoño*," essay in this volume.
2. When I pointed out the similarities between *Sonata de otoño* and *Cándida otra vez* to Marina Mayoral in a personal interview with her on 11 April 1991, she claimed to have been unaware of them, but she admitted that the evidence for comparing the two novels was undeniable. Aside from her work as a creative writer, Mayoral is a professor of Spanish literature at the University of Madrid, and, of course, knows the Spanish classics well, especially those by her Galician compatriots. She has wittingly or unwittingly included intertextual references to other works of the Generation of '98 in her novels (see my article, "La narrativa revisionista de Marina Mayoral," *Alaluz* 12 (1990): 57–63. But the novelistic world she creates in her three long novels as well as in *Cándida otra vez* most resembles that of Valle-Inclán in which members of the old Galician aristocracy clash with the changes wrought by modernity.
3. See Vernon A. Chamberlin, "*Doña Perfecta:* Galdós' Reply to *Pepita Jiménez*," *Anales Galdosianos* 15 (1980): 19–21, for an insightful study of Galdós's inversion and parody of the idealistic *Pepita Jiménez* in *Doña Perfecta*. And see H. L. Boudreau, "Rewriting Unamuno Rewriting Galdós" (paper circulated for discussion at the meetings of the Midwestern Modern Language Association held in Kansas City, Missouri, in November 1990), for revealing analyses of three of Unamuno's novels (including *Niebla*) that rely heavily upon Galdosian models. Some rewritings are more conscious than others. Chamberlin provides much circumstantial evidence to indicate that Galdós was probably very mindful of his model, but Unamuno, whose reading was astoundingly voluminous and diverse, often referred to other writing less consciously, a situation more akin to Mayoral's allusions to Valle-Inclán in *Cándida otra vez*.
4. Michael Riffaterre, "Syllepsis," *Critical Inquiry* 6 (1980): 625. "Retroactive reading occurs at every step of normal (from page top to bottom) reading, growing more important as more textual space is covered. Working forward from beginning to end, the reader keeps reviewing and comparing backward, recognizing repetitions, recognizing that some segments of the text are variations upon a semantic sameness and therefore variants upon the same structure(s). Intertextual reading is the perception of similar comparabilities from text to text. . . ."
5. Ibid., 626.
6. Fredric Jameson formulates an "overlapping modes of production" that allows him a way around subordinating either gender to class or vice versa: "[S]exism and the patriarchal are to be grasped as the sedimentation and the virulent survival of forms of alienation specific to the oldest mode of production of human history with its division of labor between men and women, and its division of power between youth and elder" ("On Interpretation: Literature as

a Socially Symbolic Act," in *The Political Unconscious* [Ithaca, N.Y.: Cornell University Press, 1918], 99–100).

7. Robert Spires, *Transparent Simulacra* (Columbia: University of Missouri Press, 1988), 35–47, offers a comprehensive and, I believe, definitive analysis of the Marqués de Bradomín's voice. Spires improves on Daniel E. Gulstad's study of "Parody in Valle Inclán's *Sonata de otoño*," *RHM* 36 (1970–71): 21–31, by introducing the concepts of the posited author and reader and their effect on the real reader. Spires focuses particularly on the various instances of double-voicing or narrative refraction to conclude, as I do here, that the ultimate sense of the narrative is to parody the Marqués. But Spires does not find, as I do, that this parody has important consequences for gender and class. Rather, he concludes that artistic concerns prevail over social ones in the novel. My conclusions coincide more closely with those of Michael Predmore, who interprets the *Sonatas* as a portrayal of "an ancient seignorial way of life that is slowly but inexorably exhausting itself" ("Satire in *Sonata de primavera, HR* 56 [1988], 315). Predmore, however, does not address the issue of gender.

8. Jose Alberich, "Ambigüedad y humorismo en las *Sonatas* de Valle Inclán," *HR* 33(1965): 360–82, was, I believe, the first critic to point out the clichéd nature of the Marqués's speech, noting that his style borders dangerously on "la cursilería de un romanticismo trasnochado" ["the vulgarity of a stale romanticism"] (362). But Alberich does not insist, as I do here, on the primacy of the Marqués's hackneyed language (given his privileged position as the sole source of the narration) in the interpretation of his character and of the novel.

9. Kathleen Gregory, *The Woman Detective: Gender and Genre* (Urbana and Chicago: University of Illinois Press, 1988) has found some female versions of the detective, but excludes Miss Marple, probably the best-known of the type, because she is an amateur rather than a paid professional.

10. Leda Schiavo in the Introduction to her edition of *Sonata de otoño* and *Sonata de invierno* (see n. 11) calls the temporal distance and other self-conscious mechanisms "filters," a handily descriptive term for this phenomenon.

11. Ramón del Valle Inclán, *Sonata de otoño,* ed. Leda Schiavo (Madrid: Espasa Calpe, 1989), 103. All references to this work are from the same edition.

12. Marina Mayoral, *Cándida otra vez* (Madrid: Ámbito Literario, 1979), 100, 102. All references to this work are from the same edition.

13. Gail Godwin, *The Odd Woman* (New York: Knopf, 1974), 302.

14. Roberta L. Salper, *Valle-Inclán y su mundo: Ideología y forma narrativa* (Amsterdam: Rodopi, 1988), 140, points out that the contrast between the two *caballeros* is more evident in *Sonata de invierno:* "Valle crea un personaje (Bradomín), el cual, a su vez, ansia parecerse a Don Juan Manuel, duplicación ésta— más aparente en la *Sonata de invierno* que en cualquier texto anterior . . ." ["Valle creates a character (Bradomín) who, in his turn, longs to resemble Don Juan Manuel, a duplication more apparent here than in any earlier text"].

15. In each novel the narrator emphasizes the seignorial nature of the woman's house as he approaches it for the first time after several years: "Subí presuroso la señorial escalera de anchos peldaños y balaustral de granito toscamente labrado. Antes de llegar a lo altor, la puerta abrióse en silencio, y asomó una criada vieja, que había sido niñera de Concha" [*Sonata* 38, "I hurriedly ascended the wide steps of the grand stair with its roughly carved granite balustrade. Before I arrived at the top of the stairs, the door silently opened, and an old servant, who had been Concha's nanny, peered out"]. "Crucé las grandes puertas y subí las escaleras de cantería con el pasamanos de piedra labrada. El mismo farol que

apenas iluminaba el enorme portal, la misma puerta de caoba con la mirilla redonda y el borlón. Había también un timbre. Preferí tirar de la borla y oír el
sonido lejano de la campanilla. Unos segundos después, el disco de la mirilla giró
y permaneció abierto como si alguien me estudiara cuidadosamente antes de
decidirse a abrir" [*Cándida* 87, "I passed through the great gates and climbed
the stonework stairs. The same light dimly illuminated the great door, the same
mahogony door with the round peephole and the large tassel. There was also a
doorbell. I preferred to pull the tassel and hear the distant sound of the little bell.
A few seconds later, the cover of the peephole rotated and remained open, as if
someone were studying me carefully before deciding to open"].

16. See Jameson, "On Interpretation," in *Political Unconscious,* 17–102, for a
penetrating analysis of the synchronicity of economic systems and its significance
for literary texts.

17. Valis, "Valle-Inclán's *Sonata de otoño:* Refractions of a French Anarchist,"
Comparative Literature Studies 22 (1988): 218–30, is the only study I am aware
of to see Valle-Inclan's use of intertextuality as a weapon for social commentary.

Contributors

MARY K. ADDIS, is Associate Professor of Spanish and Chair of the Program in Comparative Literature at the College of Wooster. She also teaches in the Program in Women's Studies. Her articles on modern Peninsular and Spanish American writers, including Ramón del Valle-Inclán, Luisa Valenzuela, Alejo Carpentier, Gabriel García Márquez, and Antonio Skármeta, have appeared in *Crítica, Romance Languages Annual,* and *Critical Studies.* She is presently at work on a book about the Spanish American "novel of the dictator" and is also engaged in research on the politics of culture in contemporary Nicaragua.

MARYELLEN BIEDER is Professor of Spanish at Indiana University, Bloomington. Her articles on gender issues in Emilia Pardo Bazán, Concepción Gimeno de Flaquer, Mercè Rodoreda, Benito Pérez Galdós, and Valle-Inclán, have appeared in numerous journals. She has contributed essays to *Spanish Women Writers: A Bio-bibliographical Sourcebook, In the Feminine Mode: Essays on Hispanic Women Writers, Cultural and Historical Grounding for Hispanic and Luso-Brazilian Feminist Literary Criticism,* and the forthcoming *Breve historia feminista de la literatura espanola* and *Culture and Gender in 19th-Century Spain.* She is currently working on a study of gender and language in Emilia Pardo Bazán and other nineteenth-century Spanish women writers.

BIRUTÉ CIPLIJAUSKAITÉ, was born in Lithuania, obtained an M.A. in Spanish at the Université de Montréal, and a Ph.D. from Bryn Mawr College. Since 1960 she has been teaching at the University of Wisconsin, where she is also a member of the Institute for Research in the Humanities. Among the eight books she has authored, two address women's issues specifically: *La mujer insatisfecha* (Barcelona, 1984), and *La novela femenina contemporánea (1970–85)* (1988).

CATHERINE DAVIES is Lecturer in Hispanic Studies at Queen Mary and Westfield College (University of London). She taught previously in the University of St. Andrews, Scotland. Her publications include *Rosalía de Castro no seu tempo* (1987) and a critical guide to *Follas Novas* (1990). She has published articles on Galician literature, Rubén Darío, Lorca, and Cuban literature. She is currently editing a book on women's writing in Spain and South America, to be published by Edwin Mellen Press, and a special issue of *Forum for Modern Language Studies* on contemporary female-authored fiction in Europe. Her current research interests are Spanish women writers and the literature of postrevolutionary Cuba and the Spanish Caribbean.

ROBERTA JOHNSON, Professor of Spanish and Department Chairperson at the University of Kansas, has published books on Carmen Laforet and Gabriel Miró and articles on twentieth-century Spanish fiction in numerous professional journals. Her most recent book is *Crossfire: Philosophy and the Novel in Spain: 1900–1934*. She has been a Fulbright Professor in Spain, a member of the MLA Twentieth-Century Spanish Division Committee and the MLA Delegate Assembly, and she currently serves on the PMLA Advisory Committee. She also sits on the editorial boards of *Hispania, Letras Femeninas,* and *Siglo XX/Twentieth Century.*

CAROL MAIER is Professor of Spanish at Kent State University, where she is affiliated with the Institute for Applied Linguistics. She is the author of numerous articles about Valle-Inclán, in particular about his aesthetics and *La lámpara maravillosa,* about which she is currently preparing a book-length study. Her other publications include *In the Feminine Mode: Essays on Hispanic Women Writers,* which she coedited with Noël Valis; translations of Severo Sarduy's *Written on a Body* and Rosa Chacel's *Memoirs of Leticia Valle;* and several articles about the work of Xosé Conde Corbal, whose print appears on the cover of *Ramón María del Valle-Inclán: Questions of Gender.*

CATHERINE NICKEL is Associate Professor at the University of Nebraska-Lincoln. She is the coeditor of the *Journal of Interdisciplinary Literary Studies/Cuadernos Interdisciplinarios de Estudios Literarios* and has published essays on Valle-Inclán in journals such as *Hispania, Romance Notes, Studies in Short Fiction, Siglo XX,* and *Revista de Estudios Hispánicos.*

MICHAEL P. PREDMORE (Wisconsin Ph.D., 1965), is Professor of Spanish and Chair of Spanish and Portuguese at Stanford University. A recipient of the Fulbright, Guggenheim, ACLS, and NEH fellowships, he has published several books and numerous articles on twentieth-century Spanish literature, among them: *La obra en prosa de Juan Ramón Jiménez* (1966), *La poesía hermética de Juan Ramón Jiménez* (1973), and *Una España joven en la poesía de Antonio Machado* (1981). He is currently working on the *Sonatas* and the *Comedias bárbaras* of Ramón del Valle-Inclán.

ROBERTA L. SALPER (Ph.D., Harvard) is author of *Valle-Inclán y su mundo: Ideología y forma narrativa* (1988), *Female Liberation: History and Current Politics* (1972), and guest editor of *Cultural Studies: Crossing Boundaries* (1991). She has written numerous articles on Caribbean literature and cultures and modern Spanish literature. Currently Head of the Division of Humanities and Social Sciences and Professor of Spanish and Women's Studies at Penn State/Erie, she has also taught at Tel Aviv University and the State University of New York at Old Westbury. From 1970 to 1971, she served as Director of the nation's first Women's Studies program, at San Diego State College.

C. CHRISTOPHER SOUFAS, JR. is Associate Professor of Spanish at Louisiana State University, Baton Rouge and has most recently published *Conflict of Light and Wind: The Spanish "Generation of 1927" and the Ideology of Poetic Form.* He has recently completed a manuscript titled "Directing the Stage: Audience and Authority in the Theatre of Federico García Lorca," and has begun research for a study of Spanish attitudes to mimesis from the Enlightenment to Naturalism.

NOËL VALIS (Ph.D., Bryn Mawr College) is Professor of Spanish at the Johns Hopkins University. She is the author of *The Decadent Vision in Leopoldo Alas; The Novels of Jacinto Octavio Picón; Leopoldo Alas (Clarín): An Annotated Bibliography;* coeditor (with Carol Maier) of *In the Feminine Mode: Essays on Hispanic Women Writers,* and editor of annotated texts by Pereda, Picón, and Carolina Coronado. Her articles have appeared in *MLN, PMLA, Novel, Hispanic Review, Romanic Review, Bulletin of Hispanic Studies,* and other journals. She is currently working on a book titled "Metaphor and Identity in Modern Spain," which focuses on *lo cursi* (an "enriched," polymorphous form of *kitsch*) as a cultural metaphor of middle-class society in modern Spain.

IRIS M. ZAVALA is Professor of Spanish and Literary Theory at Rijksuniversiteit, Utrecht. Her books include *Rubén Darío bajo el signo del cisne* (1989), *La musa funambulesca. Poética de la carnavalización en Valle Inclán* (1990), *Unamuno y el pensamiento dialógico* (1991), *Una poética dialógica. Mijail Bajtin y su círculo y la postmodernidad* (1991), and *Colonialism and Culture: Hispanic Modernisms and the Social Imaginary* (1992). She has also published four books of poetry, two novels, and *El Bolero. Historia de un amor* (1991). She directs book series for John Benjamins, Rodopi (Holland), Alianza Editorial (Madrid), and Anthropos (Barcelona). The Spanish government recently awarded her the Lazo de Dama de la Orden del Mérito Civil for her contribution to Hispanic Studies.

Index